Using Authentic Video in the Language Classroom

Cambridge Handbooks for Language Teachers

This series, now with over 40 titles, offers practical ideas, techniques and activities for the teaching of English and other languages, providing inspiration for both teachers and trainers.

Recent titles in this series:

Using Authentic Video in the Language Classroom

Jane Sherman

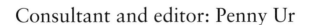

Consultant and editor: Penny Ur

CAMBRIDGE
UNIVERSITY PRESS

CAMBRIDGE UNIVERSITY PRESS
Cambridge, New York, Melbourne, Madrid, Cape Town, Singapore,
São Paulo, Delhi, Dubai, Tokyo

Cambridge University Press
The Edinburgh Building, Cambridge CB2 8RU, UK

www.cambridge.org
Information on this title: www.cambridge.org/9780521799614

First published 2003
4th printing 2009

Printed in the United Kingdom at the University Press, Cambridge

A catalogue record for this publication is available from the British Library

ISBN 978-0-521-79961-4 Paperback

Contents

Contents

Part B
Activities with authentic video

Contents

Thanks and acknowledgements

My thanks to:
Sally McLaren for the description of the opening scene from *Night of the Living Dead* in the activity Favourite scene.

Ughetta Palmieri, Silva Marcoccio and Silvia Frigo for the *Chirp's Gazette* story in the activity News story.

The authors and publishers are grateful to the authors, publishers and others who have given permission for the use of copyright material identified in the text. It has not been possible to identify the sources of all the material used and in such cases the publishers would welcome information from copyright owners.

P48 Excerpt from *What's eating Gilbert Grape* © VCP Paramount; p58 Smoky Bacon Ice Cream sketch from *The Two Ronnies*, © Ronnie Barker; p98 Countdown numbers game, reproduced with permission of Yorkshire Television Limited: p110 Woolworths slogan, reproduced with permission of Woolworths plc; p114 Description of advertisement for Biactol, ©The Procter and Gamble Company, Used by permission; p115 Description of advertisement for Ariel, ©The Procter and Gamble Company, Used by permission; p115 Extract from CIC Video's TV advertisement 'Horse', reproduced by permission of Gordon Graham and Vince Squibb at Lowe and Partners; p138 Extract from *Accidental Hero* by Leonore Fleischer (Penguin, 1993) based on a screenplay by David Webb Peoples, Copyright © Columbia Pictures Inc, 1992; p179 Transcript of dialogue from *Home and Away* reproduced by permission of Channel 5 Broadcasting Limited; p183 Adapted from 'When Helen freezes over' from *Radio Times* 20–26 May 2000; p191 Extracts from letters to the editor from Marie Little, Norma E W Cannon and Ross Laidlaw, from *Radio Times*, 20–26 May 2000; p197 Script extract from BBC documentary 'Predators'; p200 Extract from 'The Day Today', reproduced with permission of Chris Morris and Armando Iannucci; p218 Programme previews from *Radio Times* 20–26 May 2000; p241 Programme billing for rugby league from *Radio Times* 28 April–4 May

Photographs on p135: (TL) © Ed Kashi/CORBIS, photograph of Steve Jobs; (TR) © 2001–2002 Getty Images Inc., photograph of US judge by David Young-Wolff; (BL) © Shakespeare Birthplace Trust, photograph of Claudius at RSC 1997 by Malcolm Davis; (BR) © The Ecumenical Monastic Community of St Benedict, California, photograph of Benedictine monk.

Dedication

To Ann and Sam

Introduction

This book is about learning English using authentic video, that is, all the kinds of programme you normally see at the cinema, on TV or on DVD: feature films, documentaries, commercials, game shows, etc. Video is a wonderful resource for opening up the English-language world and can be used with great pleasure and profit – and very little sweat.

The assumptions are that you enjoy video and television yourself; you have access to some English video material and a video player; you have tried out video for teaching and found it promising; and you would like some ideas about using it more. You may not, however, have strong convictions about the *value* of authentic video. Many feel that it is a fun extra, but generally too difficult for most students. The question of difficulty is indeed crucial and will be discussed later (see pages 118–22). But first let's start with some of the reasons why authentic video is an essential element of learning languages today. I hope these will not only encourage you to use video but also give you ammunition for persuading school managers or budget controllers of the institutional need for video equipment and software.

Why use authentic video?

Accessibility

There are now few countries without access to English-language television programmes and feature films. You can watch the TV news on the Internet, pick up sports programmes on satellite TV, and rent or buy video cassettes and DVDs directly or by post. In many countries, English-language feature films with English subtitles are sold in newsagents. The supply is enormous and the materials are very high quality, relatively cheap and constantly renewed. Audio-visual input is now as accessible as print. It's a resource we can't ignore, and our students certainly won't.

Motivation

Many of you will have experienced the compelling power of video in the classroom, a power that is even enhanced by concentration on short sequences. The eye is caught, and this excites interest in the meaning of the words. Authenticity itself is an inducement – there is a special thrill in being able to understand and enjoy the real thing. In addition, video is today's medium. Print may still be powerful but many people spend more time with audio-visual media; video techniques, discourses and clichés are more familiar to them than the world of books and papers.

Uses in language teaching

What is not so much appreciated is the range of uses of authentic video in language teaching and how it stretches the boundaries of the classroom. What is it *good for*?

- *For its own sake* People want access to the world of English-language media: they want to be able to view the news, get information from advertisements, see a film – in short, to use these language products like normal consumers. This may well be one of your students' major goals in learning English and in all fairness they ought to be able to get a glimpse of their goals. If we are prepared to teach 'reading newspapers' or 'conversation' we should also teach these major audio-visual genres.
- *For comprehension of the spoken language* Video brings us all kinds of voices in all kinds of situations, with full contextual back-up. One obvious advantage for comprehension is the visual dimension, particularly for pragmatic understanding in dialogue; also important is the access to a variety of recognizable genres and the long-term contextual understanding built up as the programme develops.
- *As a language model* Authentic video provides a vast up-to-date linguistic resource of accents, vocabulary, grammar and syntax, and all kinds of discourse, which shows us language in most of its uses and contexts – something neither coursebook nor classroom can do. Authentic video can be a model for specific language items or a general pool for students to pick and choose from. Each genre contributes its own particular discourse structures and lexis; drama video is particularly valuable because it illustrates the kind of inter-active language most foreign-language students seldom encounter.
- *For culture* Video is a window on English-language culture. Apart from giving access to global cultural products like feature films, it also shows how people live and think and behave – local culture with a small 'c' A small amount of showing is worth hours of telling from a

teacher or a coursebook.

- *As a stimulus or input* Video can be used for discussions, for writing assignments, as input for projects or the study of other subjects. The 'film of the book' is particularly useful in the study of literature, and work-based scenarios and training films are useful in special-purpose language teaching.
- *As a moving picture book* Video gives access to things, places, people, events and behaviour, regardless of the language used, and is worth thousands of picture dictionaries and magazines.

You will agree that it is difficult to fulfil this range of functions except by living in an English-speaking country – an opportunity that most learners do not have. Authentic video helps to substitute for this experience; it brings the English-language world to the learner.

What you need

Fortified with these arguments, check your resources.

Setting up

As regards hardware, most well-known makes of video recorder are satisfactory. For individual video machines, highly desirable features are:
- a good freeze-frame, to allow you to catch and hold the picture
- a counter, to help you find your place and tell you where you are
- a long-play as well as a short-play playback facility – some recordings play back at twice the normal speed unless you have the long-play facility
- a slow-motion playback facility

With a DVD player you have all these features as a matter of course. You can move around the film, call up subtitles in several languages, choose the dubbing or subtitling language, freeze pictures immaculately, enlarge details and do slow-motion replays at various speeds.

If you have any control over the purchase of equipment, I would strongly recommend setting up some kind of self-access viewing facility to make video homework and independent work possible, e.g. in a viewing room with video machines and double sets of earphones (for pairwork) for each machine.

For classroom use, what's very important is *availability* – if we are to use the video frequently and for short sequences it must be to hand, ready to use when we need it. Many schools regard the video machine like the old film projector, to be kept in a darkened room or lecture theatre and used only for hour-long films played to classes assembled en masse. If this is your school's policy, it has to go! If there are only a few machines available, get them mounted on trolleys so they can be booked by teachers and transported easily from classroom to classroom. They also need a secure home, with a lock and key.

Positioning in the classroom is the next thing you should look at, and here even the best-equipped schools slip up: it is amazing how easy it is to create unworkable video set-ups if the users are not consulted. Video is an intimate medium, so it should not be far away from the viewers, but the screen must be big enough and high enough for everyone to see easily. Make sure students are grouped so that they can see and hear – the ones at the back can sit on tables if necessary. Resist central operating systems which require remote-control technicians – make sure you have a machine that you and your students can operate easily yourselves. Also make sure the machine is manoeuvrable, not fixed, so you can point it at a group or turn it round; and check that it doesn't face a wide window through which the sun streams.

Preventing disaster

The problem with depending on a machine is that it can go wrong – and often does! Video in the classroom creates heightened expectations, and disasters are that much more embarrassing. So if you are new to video or using alien equipment, take one basic precaution: *try it out in advance.* Check that the equipment works, that your cassette is ready to go at the right point, that you have counter numbers if necessary, that you know how to operate the controls, that the students can see and hear. Above all, know where to plug it in! In class, if the worst comes to the worst (and if your dignity permits), appeal to the students – they generally know more than we do and are delighted to help.

Finally, have a back-up lesson to hand just in case!

Software and copyright

Video material (DVD and videotape) is available commercially in video shops and by mail order. Some TV channels make available both transcripts and recordings of some of their programmes. Some full-length films can be hired from special agencies, though usually at rather high cost. Programmes can also be recorded from local TV and satellite channels or downloaded from the Internet. The copyright regulations about what you can show, how much, and to whom, differ from place to place, and you should check the legal position in your country before using material in class.

Organizing the material

If you are going to have a video library, start a catalogue or database giving the title of the cassette, the type of sequence/programme, a name for it, the programme it comes from, and ideas for using it. Get plastic covers for cassettes (they are cheap) and make sure that the title (the same one) is on both the cover and the cassette. Train staff and students to rewind tapes when they have finished using them and to put DVDs back in their sleeves or boxes. Store films/programmes by genre (e.g. feature films, documentaries) or in alphabetical order; or number them as they come in and compile a printed list in alphabetical order, with the accession numbers. If you have 'the book of the film', keep it in a box together with its matching film.

Give some thought to making individual items and clips easy to find. If you have off-air recordings, allow a separate cassette for each long programme, to make them easy to classify. Cassettes with a mixed bag of contents can go in 'Miscellaneous', but *must* have a list of contents attached securely inside or on the cover, with especially useful items starred. Simple procedures like these save hours of time.

Selecting material

What material should you aim to stock up on? The obvious elements of a video resource base are popular feature films and drama programmes, documentaries on subjects which interest students, and the daily news. Apart from these, adopt a magpie approach: look for anything that's interesting, attractive to the eye and linguistically easy on the ear, or full of things that people say, do or handle in normal life. Don't neglect the things which are often ignored, e.g. commercials, programme trailers. Keep anything which you feel is really high quality – you may not be able to see how to use it right away, but it will find its place in time. If other teachers are also looking for material, swap your findings and ideas. Don't automatically reject difficult language – there are many ways around the problem of comprehension (see pages 118–22). (*Note:* When selecting material for students from different cultures, avoid taboo language and subject matter. Also consider that feature films are not always suitable for all ages. You will find the Board of Censorship age rating [UK: Uc, U, PG, 12A, 12, 15, 18, Restricted 18; US: G, PG, PG-13, R, NC-17] on the cassette case.)

Inspiration is most likely to strike if you enjoy watching video yourself: you will not only remember sequences when you need them, but your senses will be sharpened and you will develop the habit of spotting usable material. So become a couch potato, a dilettante viewer: turn on the box, put your feet up and tell your family you are preparing your lessons!

Ways of using video

Types and uses

There is a wide variety of types of video recording and many ways to use them. For example, we have:

- drama video (films, soaps, sitcoms, etc.)
- documentaries
- TV news and weather
- discussions
- interviews
- TV commercials
- sports programmes
- talk shows
- game shows
- educational films

and we can use them:

- as complete recordings or short extracts
- for their own sake – just exposing students to the recordings and letting them enjoy them
- for the sake of the encounter with the culture
- for listening comprehension
- to provide models of the spoken language
- as input/stimulus for some other activity
- as a moving picture book

Any given sequence can be used in many different ways and for many different purposes. You might like to think about how you personally have already used video (tick the appropriate boxes below) and what remains open to you.

	Whole or clip?	For itself	For culture	For comp-rehension	Language models	As input/ stimulus	For the pictures
Drama video	☐	☐	☐	☐	☐	☐	☐
Documentaries	☐	☐	☐	☐	☐	☐	☐
TV news and weather	☐	☐	☐	☐	☐	☐	☐
Discussions	☐	☐	☐	☐	☐	☐	☐
Interviews	☐	☐	☐	☐	☐	☐	☐
TV commercials	☐	☐	☐	☐	☐	☐	☐
Sports programmes	☐	☐	☐	☐	☐	☐	☐
Talk shows	☐	☐	☐	☐	☐	☐	☐
Game shows	☐	☐	☐	☐	☐	☐	☐
Educational films	☐	☐	☐	☐	☐	☐	☐

The approach in this book

How can we exploit these multiple possibilities for using video?

The 'Friday afternoon' approach is to use an entire video programme straight through as a one-off lesson, with little preparation or follow-up. This has the advantage of extensive exposure and perhaps of novelty. But it is the equivalent of giving students only whole books to read, allowing only a short time to read them and then snatching them away. Using video *only* in this way doesn't integrate video into the normal teaching programme, and does a disservice to both the programme and the resource.

The other extreme is to work the text to death with worksheets on vocabulary, content and structure. This is admirably thorough but doesn't suit most students, since many worksheets (especially detailed ones to be completed while viewing) may ruin enjoyment (and learning too). It also doesn't suit most teachers, who already have other materials, don't have much surplus class time and certainly don't have time for a lot of extra lesson preparation. They will use more video if the path is made smooth but not if it will break their backs.

A third approach to using authentic video (and the one recommended here), is *generic*, *generative* and *gentle*:

- The activities are *generic* in that they emerge naturally from the particular kind of video programme, sequence or shot, and exploit its particular qualities.
- They are *generative* in that they can be used again and again with other similar programmes, sequences or shots.
- They are *gentle* on the student because what they ask for tends to come naturally.

The activities are also *gentle* on the teacher in that they require little or no preparation, and become progressively easier as they reinforce professional skills. They will help you to build up a repertoire of activities that you can pull out, ready for use, whenever you find a piece of useful video, so that you become as relaxed, inventive and capable with video as you are with written texts.

How to use this book

Most classroom activities are inspired by the material and not vice versa: the question is not usually *What shall I use?* but *How do I use this? What is it good for?* Knowing your material is the starting point. You have a soap scene that will appeal, a film that everyone wants to see, a documentary on the right subject, and you try to think of what to do with it. This is where this book can help you: it is organized generically so that you can look up ways of using what you've got. Or you may just want to use more video, perhaps for a particular purpose or level. Here too, this book will help you to find the right activities.

The book is organized in two parts. Part A contains a series of chapters about how to use particular kinds of video material (e.g. feature films, soaps, documentaries, the news). There are also outlines of independent study projects. All the suggested activities are given in **bold** type in the text and are described in detail in the alphabetical bank of activities in Part B. They are also listed at the beginning of each section, together with a note about any other relevant sections.

Part B focuses on activities with authentic video. It includes:

- a section on video comprehension which leads into the activities by discussing approaches to video comprehension, and giving suggestions for aiding understanding
- a bank of activities in alphabetical order, so you can find activities easily after consulting the chapters. Each entry lists: the aim; the minimum level required, e.g. lower-intermediate can be done by any students at lower-intermediate level and above; the type of video material which is suitable; the rationale where appropriate; any preparation required; and instructions to complete the activity.
- a glossary of terms used in the book, especially those to do with film

Finally, there is an index containing entries such as *grammar* and *role play*, which will help you to find activities which focus on particular aspects of language or kinds of activity.

To get the best out of the book, look through it to get a general idea of the activities and see if anything catches your eye. Rather than reading through all the activities, however, approach them either through the chapters on different types of video material or through the level indicators, e.g.

- If you have a special piece of video you want to use, consult the appropriate chapter to get ideas for activities, then look up the activities in the bank.
- If you want to use more video in general, think of what materials you can get hold of easily, and consult the appropriate chapter.
- If you would like to liven up grammar or vocabulary teaching, etc., consult the index for *grammar* or *vocabulary*. The index will refer you to activities which focus on these points.
- If you need activities for students of a particular level, look at the level indicator in each entry in the bank of activities and pick out what you want. Remember this is a minimum level, so for upper-intermediate students, for example, anything from elementary to upper-intermediate is suitable.

General guidelines for video activities

Finally, some good advice. These general guidelines apply to most activities with video:

- *Setting up* Whatever you want to do – e.g. replaying, slow motion, freezing, covering the screen, turning off sound or picture – if it's new, or the equipment is unfamiliar, try it out beforehand. Also obvious, but vital: don't forget to make sure the equipment is working, the tape or DVD is ready to go (the counter for tapes is on zero), and everyone can see and hear.
- *Breaks* Viewing should not be frequently interrupted. As far as possible, do comprehension activities before and after viewing rather than breaking up the sequence for explanations or questions.
- *Other activities* Keep writing or reading *while viewing* to a minimum – it is difficult even for expert speakers.
- *Explaining* Find the right balance between explaining too little and explaining too much. Too little help beforehand will leave learners perplexed and frustrated; too much will rob them of the surprise and pleasure that video should bring.
- *Sound only* If you want to focus only on sound, you can block viewing by turning down contrast and brightness to zero; more dramatic ways are to turn the screen round, drape a coat over it or sellotape a newspaper to it. Alternatively, persuade students to sit back and close their eyes: this is more soothing and less frustrating than staring at a blank screen; it also makes them listen really hard and is good for imaginative activities.
- *Choice* As far as possible, give students choices, e.g. they can choose which sequences to study from longer programmes, how often to view in order to understand, what roles to take in group activities, what favourite scenes to present to the class, what vocabulary to note down, etc. Personal choice is not only motivating, it is part of learning: it encourages independence and focuses on real needs.
- *Recycling* Language focus activities which encourage independent learning strategies (e.g. **Choose your words, Interactive language, Wordhunt**) should be repeated frequently: learners need to build up the habit of noticing the details of language use in real contexts.
- *Modelling* Students usually do an activity better if they have seen an example of what they are supposed to do or have tried out the activity under the eye of the teacher. Ways of 'modelling' an activity are:
  - doing an example of the activity (or the first part) with the class as a whole and then getting students to continue independently
  - studying the programmes students want to imitate

  – giving a 'worked example' for students to refer to when working on their own (there are some in the bank of activities; you can also use good students' previous products)

Some examples of modelled activities are **Dossier, Favourite scene, Interview, Lifestyle, Turning points.** Modelling gives the rules of the game, but is otherwise very 'loose': it allows free observation, choice of what to imitate and liberty about content. It is particularly important for students working independently; it also has great value for teachers as it reveals not only the language demands of the task, but also students' problems and misunderstandings about what they have to do.

- *Narrative tenses* Students usually have good instincts about what tenses to use in telling the story of a film or TV programme but it's a good idea to give some advice before they launch into an activity. Make a distinction between telling the story *from the outside* and telling it *from the inside* (see Box 1).

I wish you and your students hours of pleasant viewing and pain-free learning!

BOX 1   Narrative tenses

From the outside

The basic tense for telling the story of a film (or book) is the present simple. This is not a 'historic present' or used for dramatic effect, and can't suddenly shift to the past as a narrative alternative. The present simple is accompanied by the present continuous and the present perfect. However, the past simple *is* used for events which are clearly past in relation to the story, especially if we are told when they happened (see **A Room with a View, A**).

From the inside

If you enter the story and take on the role of the characters (e.g. by writing a diary, explaining your actions or interacting with the other characters), you see things through their eyes and use the same range of past, present and future as they would do (see **A Room with a View, B**).

   With biographies or history films, you will have to decide whether you are talking about the film story or the real story, and choose your range of tenses accordingly. If you are telling about real events in a documentary, or saying what happened in a sports match, you use the past tense.

A Room with a View

A The story of the film

At the beginning Lucy and Charlotte <u>are</u> disappointed because they <u>have not been given</u> a room with a view, and as they <u>come</u> downstairs they <u>are still discussing</u> it. When they <u>enter</u> the dining-room Miss Lavish <u>is talking</u> about San Gimignano, and this <u>reminds</u> the two old ladies of the cornflowers they <u>saw</u> when they <u>were</u> there. But Miss Lavish <u>is</u> not impressed by cornflowers ...

B Lucy's diary

When we <u>arrived</u> in Florence we <u>went</u> straight to the *pensione*, but it <u>was</u> such a disappointment! The *signora* <u>had promised</u> us rooms with a view of the Arno but as it <u>turned</u> out they <u>had</u> no view at all. But maybe <u>we'll get</u> our view after all, as Mr Emerson and his son <u>have offered</u> to exchange with us. Tomorrow Mr Beeb <u>is taking us</u> for a drive in the country.

Part A

I Video drama

Introduction

'Video drama' here means everything which tells a story about fictional characters. Part A suggests activities to exploit this kind of material. It deals with feature films, the film and the book, drama series, sitcoms, soaps, drama clips and comedy sketches. In each section all the relevant activities are listed at the beginning and given in brackets in **bold** type in the main text; you will find details of each activity in the bank of activities.

Why use authentic video?

The most obvious reason for using video drama is that language students want it. It is not an indulgence or a frill but central to language learning.

One reason why it is so important for language learning is that it is a window into culture. For instance, there are some settings which highlight particular sectors, e.g. American presidential elections, the stock exchange, criminal courts, Australian suburbia, army life, and these can be especially useful in ESP and project work (**Daily life, Organization man, Picture it**). Period settings, too, are now so well-researched that they are as good as a visit to a museum (**Place and period**). But more important are the minutiae of daily life – body language, styles of dress, table manners, gender roles, how people treat their children or talk to their bosses – and indeed the whole feeling of the social landscape, which is particularly strong in realistic soap operas (**Body language, Character network, Culture, Dossier, Fly on the wall, Lifestyle, Organization man**). The fact that this behaviour is unmarked and unremarked in film drama (just taken for granted), makes it particularly convincing. My Italian students, for example, refused to believe the English could be so eccentric as to eat biscuits with their cheese after a meal, but I showed them – in a sitcom!

Of course, much film drama is set in a fantasy world where the people are rich and white, the men are heroic and the women beautiful, boy-meets-girl ends in true love, and criminals are brought snarling to justice after elaborate car chases. But this set of formulas and clichés is also part of our general culture, copied and parodied by the media world, and can be explored with pleasure and profit in class (**Make a case, Oscar, Plan a chase, Plot idea 1, Schema, Sequel and prequel, Your movie**).

Video drama reflects major cultural movements (e.g. changing perceptions of women), but it also *creates* culture (witness icons like Mickey Mouse). Much of the popular knowledge shared by the English-speaking world comes from feature films on general release: many people would never have known about Karen Blixen or idiots savants without *Out of Africa* and *Rainman*. And this culture is now global. Many English-language soap operas and drama series have also found an international market. Thus understanding video drama is an entry ticket to the English-speaking world, on a par with reading newspapers and magazines, writing business letters, having conversations and other major language activities found in EFL coursebooks. It should, like them, be regarded as a language-learning goal in its own right.

There are equally strong arguments on the linguistic front. First, understanding is that much easier because the language is interpreted in full visual context. Events, setting, actions, expressions, gestures in a scene give a dense immediate context which highlights meaning, both literal and pragmatic. We see the angry face which says 'You'd better believe it' or the shrug that goes with 'I couldn't care less' (**Body language, Holophrases, Lipreading and mindreading, Speech acts**). Moreover, the language is directly linked to the feelings, situations and speakers which inspire it, and this full social context gives access to the full meaning (**Purrs and slurs, What's going on?**). As we watch, we also gradually accumulate an understanding of the whole story, the narrative context; this opens up the significance of the words in the action as a whole (**Jumbled statements** Variation, **Quotes, Speculations** Variation 3). This may seem obvious, but remember that language learners to some extent view life (and film) upside down. Expert speakers make use of the language to understand the action; learners frequently have to use the action to understand the language. Most listening comprehension exercises for language learners are brief, one-off and purely aural and don't provide these essential aids, the dense visual and social context and the in-depth experience of what has gone before, which make drama film the nearest thing most foreign-language students have to real-life experience of spoken meaning.

A second reason for using film drama in language learning is the *kind of language* that drama provides – interactive language, the language of daily conversational exchange (**Act along, Getting things done, Holophrases, Interactive language, Jumbled statements** Variation, **Lipreading and mindreading, Questions, Quotes, Script, Speculations** Variation 3, **Speech acts, Subtitles 1 and 2, Telephone conversations**).

13

'Interaction' is now recognized in the European Language Framework as one of the four major areas of language competence, along with Production, Reception and Mediation, but it is relatively neglected in coursebooks above elementary level. One reason is that it is very difficult to bring a wide range of interactive language into the classroom, e.g. you cannot expect teachers or students to *gloat, needle, sound people out, beat about the bush, hint, probe, flatter, fawn, threaten, stall, scream blue murder* – at least not to order! As a result, learners who have not stayed in an English-speaking country or community are often unable to produce natural spoken English. When asked to role play or script a dialogue, they frequently produce strange scholastic language, inappropriate tone, distorted idioms, unlikely collocations and above all a limited repertoire of functional language and colloquial phraseology. Another result is that students lack the metalanguage for describing speech events and acts, and the reactions and manoeuvres of conversation (e.g. *Could I have a word?; you flatter yourself; that's blackmail; I was really taken aback; take me through that again*), a major vocabulary area essential to daily conversation (**Best scene, Diary, Favourite scene, Feeling flow, Fly on the wall, Gossip, Heard and seen Variation, Speech acts, What's going on?** See also Box 13 on page 52).

Only drama can provide this range of language, and students need such exposure because to learn to speak to people they must see and hear people speaking to each other. More limited, less contextualized input such as sets of functional phrases and mini-dialogues is not in fact the best way to help students produce appropriate language or remember it well. For one thing, our intuitions about how functions are expressed are unreliable, i.e. what we imagine we might say to express doubt or disagreement (for example) is often not what we actually do say, or what our students themselves would want to say. One of the reasons is that the appropriate choice of language depends on context, situation, roles and relationships, intention and feeling, which can only be appreciated – and only learnt well – in a whole and developing context.

Finally, drama provides not only interactive language input, but also a stimulus for activities which exercise interactive language *output* (**Advice, Gossip, Lipreading and mindreading, Missing scene, Soap write-out, Scenario, Telephone conversations, What's next?**). The virtue of such activities is that they are constrained in language terms by the context, but are also highly creative and enjoyable.

To sum up, language learners need video drama because they need to understand people speaking to each other and they need extensive exposure to realistic interaction as wide-range models for their own speech.

What can we use?

But we have to go carefully. Watching drama that you don't understand is a very negative experience. You yourself may recall sitting out a foreign-language film to the bitter end after getting lost in the first half hour. If people are to learn through drama, they *must* understand it. And the fact is that, as normally viewed, most film drama is too difficult for most language students. Students need to have at least lower-intermediate level before they can cope with a full-length feature film without subtitles, and at this level it would still need to be a simple film.

What makes films easy or difficult?

What hinders comprehension is:

- high verbal density, i.e. a lot of speech with very little action (e.g. Woody Allen films)
- words which don't match the action, e.g. in smart dinner-table conversation; or words which are in conflict with the action or are an ironic commentary on it, as in send-ups and satires like *Indiana Jones* or *Monty Python*
- a high degree of naturalism in the speech, e.g. everyone talking at once, mumbled asides, actors with their backs to the camera, inconsequential dialogue
- cartoons – mouths, faces and body language are not as expressive as those of real people
- dialect and regional accents – local colour in the film generally means local confusion in the viewer, and many excellent soap operas are inaccessible to language learners as a result
- period language, e.g. Shakespeare remains difficult in spite of some wonderful adaptations; however, in film adaptations of classic novels (e.g. Jane Austen and Dickens) careful scriptwriting and clear drama-school enunciation often triumph over archaic language

What helps comprehension is:

- unambiguous action (westerns, crime), with plenty of action between speech and a close connection between speech and action, e.g. a cowboy spits out his chewing-gum, takes a long look at the saloon bar, and slowly drawls, 'I'm just gonna go in there and rearrange the furniture,' and then *goes and does it*
- clear conventional story lines: straightforward love stories aimed at adolescents (e.g. *Dirty Dancing*); children's film drama (e.g. *Babe*, the *Wallace and Grommit* series); epics (e.g. *Titanic, Jurassic Park*)

15

and science-fiction drama (e.g. *Close Encounters, Star Wars*), which have simple plot lines and time-consuming special effects which lighten the verbal comprehension burden

- stylized acting: old 'canned drama' movies are acted like plays – only one character speaks at a time, always clearly and always to camera; classics like *High Noon, Mutiny on the Bounty, Casablanca, Gone with the Wind* share this kind of clarity
- clearly enunciated speech in standard accents – this criterion rules out a lot of excellent regional films
- anything which slows down the diction: films where one of the main characters isn't able to communicate very well because he or she is an alien, a foreigner, deaf, dumb, whatever it takes to produce slow halting language which has to be interpreted both for the other characters and for us, the audience, e.g. *Nell, Rainman, ET, Children of a Lesser God, Regarding Henry, Down By Law, Awakenings, Dances with Wolves, The Piano* and many episodes of *Star Trek*

Students are the best judges of what is 'frustration level' in film drama. If they are viewing on their own, suggest that they either look for material which is easy enough to make the experience a pleasure (**Grading**), or find ways of making the viewing easier. Give them advice on what to start with and whether or how to use subtitles (see below). A checklist for discussing the use of feature films with students is given in the activity **Learning English with films**.

Subtitles and dubbing

Some films and drama series have built-in aids to comprehension in the form of dubbing and subtitling. Captioned films are also available in several languages if you have a decoder, and most DVDs give you a choice of languages for both dubbing and subtitling. How useful are they for language learners?

When thinking whether or how to use these aids we must recognize that the eye is more powerful than the ear, and (all other things being equal) will dominate. If viewers are offered both reading and listening, they will read in preference to listening, unless their aural skills are much greater than their reading skills. Indeed, people will read subtitles even if they have no need of them, e.g. when watching a film in their own language with subtitles also in their own language (or another language they know). If they are second-language learners with relatively weak aural comprehension, they will tend to substitute reading for listening.

There are four possibilities:

- *English drama dubbed into the learners' language,* with the soundtrack in the learners' language, obviously does nothing for the learners' English. If you have the original English version, it is interesting to compare it with the dubbed translation, but this is usually too far from the original to act as a 'model translation'.
- *Drama in the learners' language subtitled in English* aimed at English native speakers, can be bought in England or through big video suppliers and may also be available on DVDs. It is clearly very little use for listening comprehension and is rarely used in language teaching, but it has great potential for vocabulary extension, especially the recognition of interactive language. Provided the viewer can read English, the eye is drawn to the subtitles; at the same time the viewer understands everything, fully contextualized, and can see how it's said in English. Thousands of students swear that this was how they learnt foreign languages.
- *English drama subtitled in the learners' language* is a fairly common resource and sometimes available on DVDs. Although the film provides a running translation, there is probably very little learning of English in this kind of viewing. The viewer tends to rely on the most accessible channel, the written text, and does not process both channels equally – and may indeed 'switch off' the *verbal* sound completely. However, these versions do introduce the film, and the L1 subtitles can be covered up and used to check comprehension when necessary. They are also useful for translation exercises (**Subtitles 1**).
- *English drama subtitled in English* is available from several sources (including DVDs) and is much appreciated by students; it is also very useful for transcribing the script of a scene. It certainly improves comprehension, but unless the students' aural comprehension is very good they will almost certainly improve their reading rather than their listening skills. If this is what is wanted, fine; if not, turn off the subtitles (for DVDs) or stick a newspaper over the bottom of the screen (for videotapes) and use the subtitles only if needed, as an on-line dictionary. Advise students working on their own to do the same. Such films can also be used for good close-focus listening activities matching speech and writing (**Subtitles 2**), since the subtitles are often only an approximation of the spoken words.

1 Full-length feature films

Doing a film

At all levels we are looking for ways of *maximising comprehension*, but we also have a logistical problem with feature films: movies are long, teaching hours are short, so we also need to be able to *fit films into* a classroom schedule. How can we meet these two aims at the same time? Here are some possibilities.

Illustrated talk

Tell the story of the film yourself, illustrating it by showing three or four key scenes chosen for their comprehensibility and impact. Leave the story at a climactic point and don't tell the ending (**Film presentation**). Afterwards offer the video cassette to whoever wants to see the whole film;

18

they should come back and report to the class on what happened in the end. This is a good way of doing a number of films in a short time; after one or two demonstrations by the teacher, groups of students can undertake to present a film of their choice in the same way (**Film presentation**).

Salami tactics

'Slice up' the film into five or six episodes and do it over several lessons. Start with a lead-in (**Lead-in, Plot idea 2, Schema, Seen it before, Voice 2**). After each section do:

- a recap activity (**Adopt a character, Before and after, Character network, Cross-cutting, Dossier** Variation 2, **Jumbled statements, Make a case, Make a case for character, Sequel and prequel** (Prequel), **Schema, Summary, Why and How?**)
- a prediction/anticipation activity (**Advice, Decisions, Speculations**) for comprehension of the next section; other possibilities, depending on the film, are **Chases** Variation 1, **Fights, Missing character** and **Seen it before** Variation 2

This approach is time-consuming but worth it for a very good film which everyone badly wants to see.

Front loading

Concentrate on the introduction. The director normally uses the first 15–20 minutes of a film for 'exposition', i.e. to establish the setting and set up the characters, relationships, plot and themes. Working on this introductory part therefore really helps in understanding the whole film. Use one lesson to view the introduction only, do suitable recap activities (see *Salami tactics* above), then view the introduction again. Make sure that the recap activities are used to raise questions for the second viewing of the introduction – avoid the teacherly temptation to provide right answers. In the following lesson(s) view the rest of the film. This can be followed (or not) by activities on

- the whole film (**Before and after, Best scene, Climax, Dossier, Eye on the object, Film presentation, Issues, Lifestyle, Misapprehensions, Oscar, Place and period, Puff, Sequel and prequel** (Sequel), **Turning points**)
- individual scenes for their action (**Act along, Body language, Cross-cutting, Feeling flow, Fights, Fly on the wall, Quotes, Speech acts, What's going on?, Writing the book**)
- individual scenes for their language (**Accents, Choose your words, Interactive language, Questions, Subtitles 1, Telephone conversations, Tenses, Transcript, Wordhunt**)

Box 2 outlines a possible sequence. Alternatively, do a series of single lessons on film introductions and get students to select the one they would like to see to the end, either in class or on their own; or get groups to view the remainder of each film outside class and report back to the class.

Independent film study

If films are available for independent viewing, discuss strategies with students (**Learning English with feature films**). If students are enthusiastic, suggest a more extensive independent film study project, done individually or in small groups. The project in Box 2 has been done many times with students from 16 to 30. It is organized on the 'front loading' principle, with a break and recap activities after the introduction, then a viewing of the rest of the film and activities on the plot, characters and language. Mature advanced students can work on their own, but still need *models* of the type of product required (see page 9). One solution is to use previous students' projects as models. Younger or lower-level students need more support. Work through one film together in class, following the project outline, and together produce a set of model answers which students can refer to when working on their own. Then get students to work on their own films in groups, dividing up the activities between them. Finish with mini-presentations by each group to the class as a whole: they need this prospect to keep them going.

BOX 2   Independent film study project

Instructions for students

1 **Selection:** View a number of film beginnings to get an idea of what makes a film understandable and to help you choose your own film. Then view the introduction (the first 15–20 minutes) of your selected film and write a difficulty report (see **Grading**).

2 **Activities on the introduction:** View the introduction again, then do two of these activities: **Adopt a character, Character network, Lifestyle, Make a case for character, Summary.** (N.B. It is a temptation to go on viewing all the way through, but it will really improve your comprehension if you view the beginning twice.)

3 **Viewing break:** View the rest of the film right through.

4 **Nitty-gritty:** View the rest of the film again in order to prepare a quiz for other viewers. This helps you to become familiar with the film, and also produces exercises which can be used by other students. Choose one of these activities: **Dossier, Jumbled statements** Variation.

5 **Overview:** Review the plot or the themes of the film with one of the following activities: **Climax, Issues, Misapprehensions.**

6 **Close focus:** Select your own two scenes for a close focus on the action and the language. For the action, choose **Fly on the wall, What's going on?** or **Writing the book**; and for language study, **Choose your words, Transcript** or **Wordhunt.**

7 **Evaluation:** If you are working alone, you should do the activity **Oscar**; if in a group, do **Film presentation.**

© Cambridge University Press 2003

If your institution has a film library, self-access viewing facilities and an active viewing population, you can get students to create material for 'film files' on individual movies which can be used by other students. Ask them to grade the films for subsequent viewers (**Grading**) and include this grading as the first document in the file. Other items in the file can be quizzes on various aspects of the film (with keys) (**Dossier, Jumbled statements** Variation), questions about behaviour or issues (**Issues**), gapped dictations (**Transcript**) and critical reviews (**Oscar**).

Follow-up worksheets

Any film viewing, whether in class or independent, can be extended with independent work on reactions and interactions or on language (use part or all of the worksheets in Boxes 3 and 4).

BOX 3 Reaction and interaction

Instructions for students

1 Find three extended interactions in your film, name them and say what they are (**Speech acts**), e.g.:

Wanda introduces Otto to George.
Wendy grumbles about her day.
George briefs his team.

A Fish Called Wanda

2 Find three very clear reactions in your film and describe them (**Reaction shots**), e.g.:

Magnus is startled to realize that the house is already surrounded by police.
Mary is furious with the police for treating Magnus like a criminal.
Mrs P is perplexed when Magnus kisses her goodnight.

The Perfect Spy (BBC drama series)

3 Find a scene with a lot of clear verbal interaction. Describe it in terms of the 'speech acts', i.e. what people do with their words (**Speech acts**), e.g.:

Neil's father REPROACHES him for disobeying his orders.
He THREATENS to take him away from the school.
Neil PROTESTS.
He SAYS they don't take any notice of what he feels.
His father CHALLENGES him to say what he feels.
Neil is SPEECHLESS.
He MUMBLES 'Nothing'.

Dead Poets Society

4 Find a scene where body language shows feelings well (**Body language**). Describe what people do and what it shows, e.g.:

Helen and Paul meet on the landing.
She goes towards him and holds out her hands. (= She is pleased to meet him.)
He backs away, turns his head aside and slips past her. (= He is avoiding her.)
She moves after him, but stops. (= She realizes that he doesn't want to see her.)
She turns her head aside. (= She is puzzled.)

Howards End

---

5 Choose one whole scene and describe what's going on, bringing out the dynamic of the scene, the psychological interaction and its significance (**What's going on?**). As you tell the story, consider:

- What feelings can you see?
- What are the characters trying to do?
- Is there a turning point in the scene? What causes it?
- What is different by the end of the scene?
- How does the scene move the action forward? What is its significance?

BOX 4   Language study for drama films

Instructions for students (examples from *Groundhog Day*)

1 **Accents**: Find an interesting accent in your film. Try to identify the features and imitate the accent. Then write down ten words which sound different from the English you know and be prepared to say them, e.g. (standard American):
hog   first   possibility   talk   altitudes   thirty

2 **Questions**: Write down and classify ten questions spoken in your film, e.g.
You off to see the groundhog?
Question form, short, positive (present)
Did you sleep well?
Question form, positive (simple past)
I don't suppose there's any chance of getting an espresso?
Indirect question, negative (present)
Will you be checking out today?
Question form, positive (future continuous)

3 **Verb forms**: Find 12 verb forms, all different. Include at least two negatives, three modal verbs, one continuous form and one irregular past tense. Write down the sentences in which they occur and underline the verb, e.g.

You're missing all the fun.
Some of them have been partying all night.
It's that giant blizzard we're not supposed to get.
You should get your head examined.
I thought it was yesterday.
What would you do if you were stuck in one place and every day was exactly the same?

---

4 **Functional language**: Make a collection of 12 pieces of functional language which you think might be useful to you or your fellow students, e.g.

How're you doing?   *It's been great seeing you.*
Watch out for that step.   *Over here!*
Take a look at this.   *I'm not making it up.*

'True stories'

There is no clear dividing line between fact and fiction in feature films but some films do claim to be about real-life events and try to reflect the awkwardness of reality, with its ambiguous and unpredictable events, complex social scenery and long undramatic time spans. They are particularly useful in projects since they often centre on a theme or issue and have vivid historical, social or geographical settings.

There are two main types of 'true story': biographical films ('biopics') (e.g. *Carrington, My Left Foot, Out of Africa, Shine, Wilde*), which put one individual's life at the centre of the story; and history films (e.g. *Amistad, Schindler's List, Waterloo*), which are more interested in events and show a range of characters. Films about real contemporary events (e.g. *Alive, Awakenings, Dead Man Walking, In the Name of the Father*) are either like history films (mainly about the event) or like biographies (mainly about the people). Most of the ideas suggested for fiction films above are just as appropriate for these 'true stories', but there are some alternatives and extras you may find useful for coping with their special difficulties and potentialities.

Though 'true story' films drastically select and simplify real-life events, they are still difficult to digest. They refer constantly to events which happened before the film began ('We don't want another civil war!'), or which are outside the visible action ('My lord, France has declared war!'), or they use the dialogue to interpret the visible scene to make sure we understand what is going on ('Now here we are at Fort William, Colonel, and that is the English army'). Thus a lot of the dialogue is explanation, saying what is happening and why, and how we ought to feel about it – a much-parodied feature. This creates an extra comprehension burden. To tackle this, **Heard and seen, Why and How?** are tough but necessary overview activities which highlight the significance of events before, during and beyond the film.

History films

These in particular have to establish a complex background very rapidly at the beginning (remember those historical parchment summaries scrolling up at the beginning of old history films?). It is therefore worth spending even more time than usual on the first 20 minutes (see *Front loading*, page 19) and preparing as much as possible (**Famous people, Maps and journeys**). For a recap of the introduction do **Character network**. There may also be overview exercises which are particularly suitable. Most history films involve military or political battles (**Fights**) and a lot of moving around (**Maps and journeys**). As period pieces they can be scanned for information on life in the past (**Place and period**). They deal with themes which are found in all countries' histories – lives of great men, civil war, rebellion, invasion, social oppression, discovery, struggles for human rights – so they give rich opportunities for comparisons with students' own countries (**Parallels**) and a good basis for oral presentations and discussion.

Films about contemporary events

These benefit from the same kind of background enrichment as history films, e.g. *In the Name of the Father* cries out for a sketch of the recent history of Northern Ireland and the issues involved. Many deal with issues (**Issues**) and present cases (legal, existential, medical, moral): how to survive on a snowbound mountain, how to cope with wrongful imprisonment, what's wrong with the comatose patients, etc. These inspire the same kinds of approach as drama series episodes (see pages 35–7). They focus on understanding the important facts of the situation (**Summary, Schema, Speculations**) and the interests involved (**Character network**); they show people deciding what to do about the case (**Case study, Decisions**) and getting it done (**Getting things done**), usually in the teeth of human opposition (**Fights**).

Biographical films

Films about relatively ordinary people invite comparison with oneself in all possible ways (**Lifestyle, Other people's shoes, Turning points** Follow-up). Do any of these before, during or after the film. Since real lives are full of pointers to the future but also full of surprises, such films are suitable for predictions in the middle of the movie (**Speculations**). With biopics about famous people or public figures, use **Famous people** and **Voice 2** to give an idea of the person before launching into the film. Films about national leaders, showbiz personalities, artists or famous criminals make a good basis for comparison with national figures in other countries (**Parallels**). Unlike most fiction films, biographies of famous people usually have something to say (though not much) about the protagonist's work (**Famous people** Variation); they often also show success/failure very clearly and try with hindsight to make connections between circumstance, personality and society (**Turning points**). Films about creative artists tend to neglect the creative side in favour of life and loves, but you can often exploit the artist's music/art/poetry/prose for mood and background and use the artistic works to supply a framework for the action, moving from landmark to landmark. For example, the film *Amadeus* about Mozart was introduced with some of the musical highlights from the film (sound only) and a discussion of their mood (**Invisible music**). If there are voice-over readings from a writer (as in *Wilde* and *Out of Africa*), they can be studied separately before or after the film. For painters, you may be able to get copies of pictures which are seen in a film (try the Internet). Get students to discuss subject and mood before viewing; afterwards they can arrange the pictures in chronological order and explain their significance in the story.

Talking about feature films

Since most students have extensive experience of feature films, they need little prompting to talk about them and to create scenes and plot ideas. These activities have the advantage that they can be done without any video equipment. The standard assignment 'Write about your favourite film' produces more interesting writing if there is some preliminary discussion (try the activity **Famous films**) or a focus on a **Favourite film scene**. Also illuminating is the creation of a climactic moment from one's own movie (**Your movie**). The more elaborate film-invention activity **Plot idea 1** gets good results with advanced students (**Plot idea 2** is a simpler version); while **Plan a chase** is suitable at any level for those who enjoy the excitement of a chase. All these activities contribute to critical evaluation of films (**Film presentation, Oscar, Over the top**).

The film and the book

(Other activities for feature films can supplement work with film and book. See *Doing a film*, page 18.)

You sometimes find yourself in the joyful position of having the book as well as the film – not one text but two parallel versions of the same story, which are more or less faithful to one another. This offers rich possibilities: it gives you some of the filmscript and saves laborious transcribing; it allows you to use one text to improve literal comprehension of the other (**Climax, Twin texts**); it enables you to compare the two texts, shedding light on both (**Changes**); finally, it makes it possible to see how the film (or the book) has been created/adapted from the book (or the film) and to simulate the process yourself (**Writing the book** or the *Make the movie* sequence, page 29). One great advantage is in the study of classic literature, but most activities that can be done with *Romeo and Juliet*, *Room with a View* or *Great Expectations* can also be done with *Babe*, *Dances with Wolves* or *Michael Collins*.

When we talk about film and book, we usually think of a novel that has been made into a film or televised, but there are other relationships. Many novels are now written in the hope of being filmed and are virtually screenplays; some are written from and after the film (e.g. *Accidental Hero, Yes Prime Minister*, some of the *Star Trek* series). In some historical and biographical reconstructions the film is modelled on a specific book (e.g. *Schindler's List, 84 Charing Cross Road*), based on a stage play (*The Madness of King George, A Man for All Seasons*) or created from history books, reminiscences, letters, diaries, biographies, folklore, encyclopaedias and historical documents (*Out of Africa, Robin Hood*). These all give different possibilities.

Here are some things you may want to do:

- *Use single scenes.* You are not planning to use either the whole film or the whole book, but just work with one or two interesting parallel scenes (book and film) for the purpose of language activation.

27

- *Use the book to supplement and clarify the film.* You are mainly interested in doing the film, and plan to extend your study of the film with a few passages from the book.
- *Use the film to illuminate the book.* You are making a study of the book (or parts of it), probably as literature, and you want to use the film to throw light on it, engage interest, stimulate discussion.

Whatever your purpose, check the book for reading difficulty. A film may present problems of aural comprehension, but a novel has at least ten times as many words (a transcript of a film dialogue may reach 20 pages; a typical novel has 250 pages), and the vocabulary may be wide-ranging, so reading the book scene can be relatively long and demanding. You can, however, find easy single scenes; modern blockbuster novels written with the cinema in mind often use quite a limited vocabulary; children's books are often (not always) easier; there are some very good simplified readers adapted from books which have been filmed, and many great writers (e.g. Graham Greene, Hemingway, George Orwell, Oscar Wilde) have simple clear passages which are accessible to lower-intermediate learners. Even a rather heavy literary scene will lighten up if the comprehension demands are limited or if the film scene has been viewed first.

Using single scenes

Turning a novel into a film generally means removing many scenes, adding a few and drastically changing others, but there are usually scenes which are recognizably the same. These parallel scenes give good opportunities for observing differences and the reasons for them, and for trying one's hand at bringing the written scene to life as a film.

Comprehension, of all kinds, is the payoff. The changes the scriptwriter and director have made to the scene are there in the film to be noticed and discussed, and make for quite compelling close-focus listening comprehension and reading activities (**Changes**) going back and forth between the text and the film. You can precede or follow these with a discussion of the general differences between film and novels (**Book and film**), illustrated by parallel scenes. The activity **Writing the book** demands good aural understanding as well as a feeling for the conventions of written fiction.

Most of all, creating a film scene from a written one may well be the ultimate exercise in reading comprehension, since the director, the scriptwriter and the actors all have to understand the intentions of the writer in order to bring them to life. Experienced readers of fiction (e.g. teachers) often assume that students are as adept as they are at breathing life into the written page, but 'reading' the conventions of a novel is a learned art, and novice readers can learn a lot from the process of turning text into film. *Make the movie* (Box 5) is a series of activities in which students try out their talents as film directors on a scene from written fiction. They visualize the action (**Reading aloud**), produce a simple script (**Scriptwriter**), try out particular lines (**One-liner**), sketch the setting and test it out (**Set the scene, Walkthrough**), and decide on lighting, sound effects and shot sequences (**Effects**). The process can be halted at any stage in order to view the corresponding scene from the film and compare it with students' own directorial decisions. The complete project exercises a range of language skills. The possible sequences and combinations are in Box 5.

Choose short scenes which are explicit about settings, actions and reactions and have a fair amount of interactive dialogue.

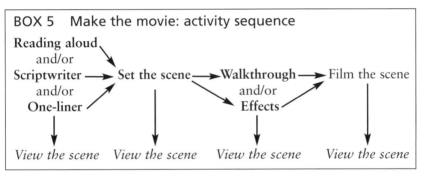

BOX 5   Make the movie: activity sequence

Don't do more than three activities on any one scene, or interest will flag. If you get as far as the final stage, and have a video camera, do allow students to film their own self-selected scenes (see also *Make your own movie*, page 33). The results are inevitably at the home-movie level but the motivation generated is tremendous. (N.B. The difference between hopeless failure and moderate success is almost entirely in the quality of the sound recording – drive home this message!)

Parallel scenes in stage plays and film offer much the same opportunities, with the advantage that the two media are closer to each other, and the script (often with stage directions) is already given. Scenes from Shakespeare are worth comparing (**Changes**) and students can easily 'make the movie' from a drama script with the activity sequence **One-liner, Set the scene, Walkthrough** and **Effects**.

Using the book to supplement and clarify the film

A book which is the source of a feature film is generally longer and more complex than the film and has more background information, more detail, more explanations and often more subtle interpretations of character and relationships. Often films make huge changes in the book: cutting whole themes, characters or story lines, introducing new characters, changing the setting or rewriting the plot, and bringing howls of protest from authors and purist readers. Nevertheless, there's generally enough common ground to give a lot of scope for using bits of the book to extend the film experience and to help with literal comprehension. The following suggestions apply to novels, drama and non-fiction books.

Bear in mind the pressure of time: it takes a long time to do a feature film and adding passages from the book may extend it. Be sure that the film you are going to work on deserves this amount of attention, and take steps to reduce the time spent in class (e.g. give the reading for homework or substitute reading an extract from the book for viewing a part of the film).

Before viewing the film, read a scene from the book to lift overall viewing comprehension. If the opening film scene is also in the book, the book scene can be used as a lead-in (**Reading aloud**) especially if it has a rich mixture of setting, action and dialogue to establish plot, character and themes. Use an early book scene to feed speculation about characters' appearance (**Casting couch 2**) before seeing them in the film.

Later in the viewing, make a difficult but crucial video scene more accessible by getting students to read it first. You can focus the reading on complicated action, motivations, or the exact words spoken (**Adopt a character, One-liner, Reading aloud, Scriptwriter**). In-depth knowledge of any written scene makes a good basis for discussing differences in the parallel film scene (**Changes**). If you are doing the film as an illustrated talk (see page 18), vary the approach by having students view some parts and read others; if you are doing it in sections (see page 19), give scenes (already viewed) from the book as follow-up reading homework, or give a forthcoming book scene for homework and ask students to report on it as the lead-in to the next section. In any case, if the book is suitable for the level, make it available to students who are interested in doing extra reading; they may also like to report to the class on the major differences.

'True stories' about famous people or historical events tend to glide rather rapidly over the historical background and rarely present unbiased accounts. Extra depth and accuracy, as well as a feeling for the time frame and the geography of the events, can be added by using extracts from encyclopaedias, dictionaries of national biography, atlases or Internet information (**Famous people, Maps and journeys**), which bring a welcome touch of factual reality.

Using the film to illuminate the book

Many school and university students study English literary classics as part of their English syllabus (e.g. *Hamlet, The Picture of Dorian Grey, Great Expectations, Howard's End*). Most of these have been made into high-quality films (some several times) which are widely available. When students are having a hard time reading extensively in English and are resorting to translations to get them through, video materials are a great gift. But what is the best way to use the video to throw light on the book and raise interest in it? If your students have some knowledge of the book but haven't seen the film, your great advantage is surprise and you shouldn't waste it. Tease your audience – delay viewing: use scenes and activities which will reinforce and extend students' knowledge of the written text *before* they see the whole film. Whet the appetite with a lead-in, then do an overview activity to get the feeling of the whole and to frame the activities which come next. Follow with one or two close-focus exercises and some activities on how particular aspects of the book can be realized on film. If you have time, plan a film scene from a book scene and then view the video version. Then, when you've got the most out of the suspense, view the whole film. Here are some suggestions:

- *Lead-ins* Try interpreting aspects of the whole book as a director would do, e.g. by getting students to suggest appropriate images to introduce the film (**Lead-in**), or to find suitable bodies for the characters (**Casting couch 1** and **2**). Simpler lead-ins are matching a video scene with a scene in the book (**Twin texts**), identifying significant utterances (**Quotes**), or focusing on details of the lifestyle (**Picture it** Variation 3) to raise awareness of the cultural realities of place and period.

- *Overview activities* Look at the plot briefly (**Puff**) or in some depth (**Climax**), or at important characters (**Make a case for character**). Or use a few short film sequences (**Before and after**) to review what students know (or don't know) about the overall action in the book.

- *Close-focus activities* As a third stage, give students a choice of scenes for doing one activity on individual feelings or character interaction (**Adopt a character, Feeling flow, Quotes, What's going on?**), and another on how the written text is brought to life in film (**Changes, One-liner, Reading aloud, Stage directions**).

- *Make the movie* All this gives a feeling for the style of the film, so that students can step into the director's shoes and choose a particular scene to use to *Make the movie* (see page 29).

Revealing the film in this way, bit by bit, means that by the time students come to see the whole film, they will have much greater insight into both film and book, will have revised the book quite thoroughly and will also find the film much easier to follow.

Independent work

If your institution has self-access listening comprehension exercises, they can easily be supplemented with activities based on single parallel scenes: The activity **Changes** is good for stand-alone comprehension, with scenes pre-selected by teachers or by students themselves.

If there are some book-film pairs in the resources library, leave some suggestions for students (see Box 6). You can run this as an advanced project, culminating in an essay or oral report.

BOX 6 Book and film

Independent work: instructions for students

Choose a book and film you'd like to study. You may have already seen the film or read the book, or you may not know either of them. Read first or view first, as you wish, and then:

- Find the place in the book where the film begins (before the book starts, at the beginning, later?).
- Find a scene which is in both the film and book and do the activity **Changes**.
- Find a character in the book/film who is not in the film/book.
- Find a scene in the book/film which is not in the film/book.
- Find a physical description of a person, place or thing and compare it with the film version.
- Look at the list in **Book and film** and find two examples of things well done in the book, and two examples of things well done in the film.
- Comment on a few of the main changes you have noticed.

© Cambridge University Press 2003

Once the *Make the movie* sequence (see page 29) has been tried out in class, students can have a go independently at making a scene from a book, culminating in filming with a camcorder if available (see Box 7 for instructions). This activity has been successfully linked with an independent book-reading project for advanced students, who themselves selected the scenes they wanted to film; lower levels can choose a scene from a class reader, a simplified reader or a drama script, or be given a book scene by their teacher. The choice of scene is crucial. One lower-intermediate class did excellent work with an early scene from *Babe*, but were reluctant to film it since some objected to playing ducks and puppies and the piglet hero refused to have his nose licked as the script demanded! They did consent to a walkthrough, however, and discussed and designed setting and lighting (**Effects**) before viewing the original scene.

Students should also be aware that this project will take some time and that it depends on everyone in the group being both available and reliable.

BOX 7   Make your own movie

Instructions for students

1   Choose the book scene you want to film. Find a scene with a fairly ordinary setting (e.g. house, garden, office), no special effects and nothing in it that your actors will refuse to do or say.

2   Organize groups and assign jobs: you will need a director, actors, a scriptwriter and a cameraperson.

3   Do a read-through of the scene (**Reading aloud**) and organize the set (**Set the scene**). Identify any necessary costumes (keep it simple) or props (= 'properties', objects you need).

4   Get the scriptwriter to produce the script in collaboration with the director (**Scriptwriter**). Aim to cut the book's written dialogue to about half and think about what else the camera will show *apart from people talking*. The script should contain stage directions and also a sketch of the setting. Get feedback on the language of your script from your teacher.

5   Organize the setting and try out the scene (**Walkthrough**). The director should decide on pauses, timing and pace, indicate where the main emphasis of the scene is and how to highlight it (stress, action, gesture, timing, pausing, etc.), and suggest how the lines should be spoken.

6   Actors learn their parts.

7   The director discusses with the cameraperson how the camera will be used: long shots, zooms, panning shots, medium shots, close-ups and where to break the action to get a change of shot. With only one camera and no editing facilities, you will have to shoot the scene in one continuous sequence, although you can stop filming to change things around or to have a break. Write your provisional decisions on the script (you can change them later). Also decide on sound or lighting effects (**Effects**).

8   Trial run. The most important thing is good sound. Try to get a boom mike and make sure the actors are near it when they speak. Film in a quiet place with no outside noise and preferably plenty of soft furnishings to absorb echoes (classrooms are NOT good places). Try out the scene once without the camera, then with the camera. View the result and get some feedback on the language from your teacher.

---

9 Do your final shoot.

10 Introduce the scene to your class. Say what book it's from, who the characters are, what point it represents in the action and why you chose it. Then play your video scene.

11 Finally, view the scene in the original film and discuss your different interpretations.

2 Other video drama

Drama series

(Most activities for feature films can also be used with drama series. See *Doing a film*, page 18.)

Drama series are usually broadcast once a week. Well-known examples are *Star Trek, ER, The X-files, LA Confidential, NYPD, West Wing*, and also older series like *Sherlock Holmes* based on short stories. Like soap operas, drama series always have the same basic cast and the same main settings, but unlike soaps each episode usually has one main story which is played out in the course of the episode and which can be understood fairly well without reference to previous episodes. This, together with the length (usually 30–45 minutes), makes them good for class use. Drama series episodes have the same kind of plot development as feature films, but unlike most movies they are often set in the working world, with professional settings, e.g. the police force, legal offices, hospitals, detective agencies, space stations, veterinary or medical practices, with visible organizational structures, relationships and procedures and all the inherent tensions of authority, obedience, insubordination and account-ability (**Organization man**). The settings are often very realistic and can provide a window into working practices and procedures (**Culture**). Getting people to do things is a constant and makes for a useful language focus on directives (**Getting things done**); things, especially documents, may be important (**Eye on the object**); there are also many dramatic decisions (**Decisions**), and much play with mystery one-sided telephone conversations (**Telephone conversations**).

Each episode in a drama series is basically a *case*: a crime, an ailment, a lawsuit, an accident; this means some predictable events and allows for a schematic lead-in to the story (**Schema**). The main plot framework is problem-solving: either there is a mystery, inexplicable events which have to be sorted out (the basic whodunnit); or there is a problem/danger which has to be overcome (an attack/capture, a natural disaster). The first part of the episode sets up the situation with a considerable flow of information in the form of events and/or talk, and comprehension can focus on summaries of the situation and speculation about the mystery elements (**Summary, Speculations**). Meanwhile, other mini-plots 'keep the pot boiling', maintain staple characters and sometimes reflect the main themes as well (**Summary**). The story usually climaxes with a crisis (shoot-out, chase, confrontation, rescue, death, recovery, revelation) (**Chases, Climax, Fights**), which is followed by a short post-mortem in which order is re-established and loose ends are tied up. There is almost always a conflict of good and evil, and good almost always triumphs – simple questions of professional ethics are raised by debating the questions of how the 'baddies' are to be recognized and how the 'goodies' behave (**Issues**).

Doing a drama series episode

Drama series episodes can be dealt with much like feature films, but I'd recommend two breaks. Start with the particular environment of the series and discuss the possibilities (**Lead-in, Schema**); go on to describe the basic situation presented by the episode then view the beginning. Make the first break when the main aspects of the problem have been presented, and do a recap to establish important information (**Before and after, Jumbled statements, Schema, Speculations, Summary**). Use this activity to raise questions, then view the first part again to consolidate understanding of the situation. If you have time, also look at character with **Make a case for Character; Organization man** helps to establish working relationships and tensions.

Make the second break about two-thirds of the way through, and answer the questions raised before. To prepare for the final part, do some work on predicting the outcome (**Speculations**) and use **Speculations** Variation 3 to resolve important comprehension difficulties in advance. You may also be able to use **Decisions** here, or, if you have time, **Chases** Variation 1, **Missing character** or **Seen it before** Variation 2.

Not many drama series episodes are good enough to make you want to study the action after it's over, so squeeze in as much as possible during the heat of the action. If interest is still high after viewing the finale, look at the development of the main crisis (**Climax**), do a character quiz (**Dossier** Variation 1) or explore underlying values with **Issues**. Looking back at the language is always worthwhile, so make use of the comprehension generated and use some scenes for language focus (e.g. **Choose your words, Getting things done, Interactive language, Questions, Subtitles 1, Tenses, Transcript, Wordhunt**). Students can select particular scenes and build up the language for *Describing interaction* (see Box 13, page 52).

Independent viewing of drama series episodes can be followed up with some or all of the activities on the general worksheets in Boxes 3 and 4. For more extensive work there is a simplified version in Box 8 of the independent film study project, adapted for drama series.

BOX 8   Drama series episodes: independent study

Instructions for students

1 **Selection:** View the first ten minutes of the episode to see if it's easy enough (see **Grading**).
2 **Activities on the introduction:** View the introduction again, then do **Summary** and **Make a case for character**.
3 **Viewing break:** View the rest of the episode.
4 **Nitty-gritty:** View the rest of the episode again and prepare a quiz for other viewers (**Dossier, Jumbled statements** Variation).
5 **Overview:** Review the plot or themes of the episode with one of the following activities: **Climax, Issues, Misapprehensions**.
6 **Close focus:** Select your own scenes for a close focus on the language, using **Choose your words, Getting things done, Questions** or **Tenses**.

Sitcoms

(Many activities in *Doing a film*, page 18, and *Drama series*, page 35, are also suitable for sitcoms.)

Sitcoms (= situation comedies) are like drama series but funny. In each episode they expose the same central characters in the same setting to a new comic situation. Some sitcoms are so good that they have become classics, e.g. *Blackadder, Fawlty Towers, Yes Minister, Seinfeld*, and *The Simpsons* in the cartoon field. Many others have excellent moments, and even old or narrowly focused ones (e.g. *Porridge, The Good Life, Absolutely Fabulous*) have highly usable individual scenes (see *Drama clips*, page 46). *Friends* and *Frasier* are full of excellent high-comprehension scenes and up-to-date language and themes.

Native-speaker teachers sometimes try to share their pleasure in their own culture's sitcoms with their students and find that they flop disastrously. This may be due not only to cultural differences in humour, but also to the nature of comedy. What makes people laugh often has to do with 'in-knowledge', with making quick connections and coming close to sensitive issues. We laugh because we are in the know when a brief cultural reference taps a pool of knowledge. We laugh when we suddenly see the hidden implications and can close the gap that the actors have set up for us. We laugh, perhaps out of a sense of protected shock, when we come dangerously close to taboos, like death and cruelty, or when we see incongruities created by juxtaposition. The important thing in a comedy show is that the audience perceptions are quick, shared and simultaneous – here comedy is a social event, and participation is indicated by the laughter. The talent of the comedy scriptwriter and actors is judging what the audience will perceive, and how quickly. Video sitcoms imitate live shows by including the recorded laughter, so that the home audience is drawn into this rhythm.

There are other difficulties. Comedy plots are often complicated; the language, even if standard, is often fast, plays with words and puns, dances about between registers, using formality and informality to exaggerate situations, and uses idioms, colloquialisms and slang, which again enhance the 'in' feeling.

In this situation, language learners are badly disadvantaged. They may not understand the references and the words. As each gag mounts to its punch line they are unable to make the necessary connections, and when the laughter comes they are cruelly excluded. This is why video sitcoms can flop so hard.

But on the other hand *getting* the joke creates a sense of social triumph, and although we have to be careful with comedy it doesn't mean we can't use it with great success. But we have to prepare our audience by bringing them *beforehand* up to the point of knowledge and understanding where they can make the final leap themselves – and laugh. This means either giving them an edited version (see *Explaining context and content* 6, page 120) or going all out for comprehension of action and words: preparing the ground thoroughly, reviewing essential vocabulary and explaining 90 per cent of the jokes beforehand. This is a long activity – a single sitcom episode can stretch over four, five or six half-hour periods. Students don't seem to mind this, perhaps because the pleasure is as much in the blow-by-blow action as in the story; if the comedy is good, they enjoy re-viewing the parts they have already covered and laughing again, securely 'in the know'; what's more, they get more fun out of retelling a sitcom story than they do with straight drama.

Going for minute-by-minute comprehension doesn't leave much time for other activities. Divide the episode into four to six parts of approximately equal length, and then follow the approach in Box 9.

Box 9 Doing a sitcom in class
Before beginning

Give students everything they need to know:

- Describe the situation and present the characters and their personal quirks – use the **Character Network** diagram. Get everyone to say the names aloud and test them on the roles and relationships.
- Explain any 'running gags' (= recurring jokes).
- Introduce key vocabulary and cultural references, especially what's necessary to understand the jokes.
- Prepare for the opening situation by doing the appropriate parts of **Daily life**, picking up the point where the comedy departs from the norm.

Before the second and subsequent parts

- Get students to recap the action so far (**Before and after, Jumbled statements, Speculations, Summary**) or to ask each other comprehension questions (see *Comprehension checks*, page 121). Identify any obscure points, then view the part again. Alternatively, look closely at one scene from the previous part, using **Before and after, Eye on the object, Fly on the wall, Lipreading and mindreading** Variation, and use this to lead into a recap of the action so far.
- Recycle vocabulary which will occur again. Write it up and get students to put it back into context, saying who used it and what it referred to.
- Give essential vocabulary for the forthcoming part and rehearse it in some way (see *Giving vocabulary*, page 121). Also explain any cultural references and wordplay.
- (For more advanced students) Ask for action predictions (**Speculations**) or prepare an obvious future scene (**Seen it before,** Variation 2).
- (For lower-level students) Explain the forthcoming situations – also explain why they are funny! Leave only a fragment to the students' own understanding. Support these explanations with **Speculations** Variation 3.

After the whole episode

- For reviewing the whole episode, do **Before and after, Climax** or **Misapprehensions**.
- Ask students to select specific scenes for language focus (**Accents, Choose your words, Getting things done, Interactive language, Questions, Telephone conversations, Tenses, Transcript, Wordhunt**).

A final word: do laugh yourself – but try not to laugh alone!

Independent work

In general, comedy viewing should be done with a teacher, but advanced students can handle it independently if given some help. In one project, political science students were given seven episodes of the sitcom *Yes Minister*, and a list of key vocabulary and cultural references for each episode. The whole class watched all seven episodes one by one for homework, and treated the series as an extended case study providing material for a final essay to be presented at the end of the course.

In another version of the same project there was also a classwork element. Groups of two or three students each took one episode and studied it in depth for presentation to the class (who had also viewed the episode). They were given instructions for the presentation (see Box 10) and divided the tasks between them (you may recognize the activities **Choose your words, Jumbled statements** Variation, **Missing scene, Summary** and **What's going on?**). The teacher presented the first episode as a model. This project was a huge success, largely due to the excellence of the video material, and became the sole topic of conversation for weeks. But these students were advanced, mature and intelligent; in general I stick to my claim that comedy programmes are best handled in class, with extensive help from the teacher.

Box 10   Presenting an episode of *Yes Minister*

Instructions for student presenters

(N.B. The whole class should view the episode before the lesson.)

1   Select three significant utterances from the episode and write them up. Ask the class to say who said them, to whom, where, when and why, and also why they are significant (5 mins).

2   Pose three comprehension questions to the class. These must be questions of fact, and answerable (5 mins).

3   Recount the episode briefly, saying who wins and how (5 mins). You may do this objectively or from the point of view of one of the characters. (N.B. Write notes to help you with this account, but DO NOT script it and read it aloud.)

4   In writing (max 150 words), report a crucial scene from the episode in detail, explaining exactly what is going on between the characters and how it affects the outcome of the episode. Get the writing corrected, then copy it, circulate the description to the class and read it aloud.

5   Ask for comments and questions on the behaviour of the characters in this scene (5 mins).

6   Present ten high-utility language items from the episode (10 mins):
   • Do not limit yourself to single words. Look also for expressions and phrases.
   • Do not limit yourself to *new* language. Often the most useful expressions to adopt are those you recognize and understand but do not use yourself.
   • Consider a range of language: tenses and verb forms, functional language, unexpected pronunciation, prepositions.

---

7 Identify a missing scene in the episode and *either* write the script *or* ad-lib the scene (5 mins).

8 Comment on the contribution of the episode to the overall case study.

Soap operas

(Many activities in *Doing a film*, page 18, and *Drama series*, page 35, are also suitable for soap operas.)

Soap operas are very different from feature films. Examples are the famous *Neighbours* and *Home and Away* (Australian), *Coronation Street* and *Brookside* (English), *Dallas* and *General Hospital* (American). Soaps seldom come round twice. They arouse addiction in some and deep boredom in others. They usually come out daily in an endless running narrative, so no matter where you start you always find yourself in the middle of the story, indeed of several stories. However, soaps recycle events more than movies do and the relationship of new to known is not as high. They always have three or four ongoing plots on the boil, so there is a lot more 'intertextuality', i.e. references to conversations in other parts of the action. There are also multiple points of view (by contrast, feature films tend to 'position' the viewer very firmly) – this leads to long conversations among soap fans about characters' behaviour.

Soaps are generally made for home viewing and often represent a perceived national, regional or social identity – Manchester, Texas, Kazakhstan. Since the cultural background and general setting are always the same, soaps can concentrate on human relationships and are generally more verbal than feature films. Unlike films, soaps have plenty of time: they can take a more leisurely view of behaviour and surroundings (culture with a small 'c'), with more attention to habits and routines, minor irritations and pleasures, little misunderstandings and small gestures, social chit-chat, gossip and pointless events (in a feature film nothing can afford to be pointless). Soaps with high social realism are often the most interesting, but also the most difficult to understand because the language is fast, colloquial and heavily accented (*EastEnders* and *Coronation Street* are unfortunately lost to EFL). But soaps can also be mindless fantasy and some are so exuberantly banal and badly acted that they become self-parodying and are taken up as cults. Such very silly soaps sometimes provide extremely obvious reactions in simple repetitive language, excellent for language learning; and soaps in general are a wonderful source of clips (see *Drama clips*, page 46).

What does this mean for language learners? A well-scripted naturalistic soap is a good way into another culture (**Culture**) and the interactive language of daily life (**Holophrases, Interactive language, Lipreading and mindreading, Questions, Telephone conversations**) – even more so than feature films. But as with any new community, it takes time to get to know the people and the background and you need to do some consolidation at the beginning (**Dossier** for soaps, **Sequel and prequel** (Prequel), **Summary** for soaps). The payoff is the enhanced understanding that follows from in-depth knowledge of character, events and situation, and this gets better the longer one follows the soap. Some things come naturally to soap viewing, e.g.: dossier creation (**Dossier**); discussing character, behaviour and relationships (**Character network, Diary, Gossip, Lifestyle, Organization man**); trying to work out what is going on (**What's going on?, Writing the book**), what might be going on elsewhere (**Missing scene**), what has gone before (**Heard and seen**) and what is to come (**Speculations, Seen it before** Variation 2). Episodes often end in cliffhanging suspense which begs for dramatic questions (**Advice, Decisions, Speculations**). It is also tempting to intervene in the action (**Advice, Adopt a character, Decisions**) especially as a scriptwriter (**Missing character, Missing scene, Soap write-out**), to extend the action (**Soap chronicles**) and to try creating your own soap (**Scenario**). Some plot lines raise issues of general concern (**Case study, Issues**). There is good scope for language work on all aspects of spoken language and reported speech (**Fly on the wall, Gossip, Script, Speech acts, Telephone conversations, What's going on?**).

Talking about soaps in general is also compulsive. Both addicts and intellectual snobs like to evaluate them and compare them with others (**Over the top, Silly soaps**), and this leads easily to debate on today's borderline between drama and reality, or to a project on what soaps mean to people. Rich input here is the whole genre of feature films *about* soaps and similar phenomena (e.g. *Tootsie, The Truman Show, Wag the Dog*), articles about soap events from the popular press and material from soap websites.

However, while some get hooked, others are bored not only by the time it takes to come to grips with the scenario but simply by the genre itself, so while students should be encouraged to view soaps, any extensive soap viewing should be a free choice. Some possibilities are:

- doing taster lessons to introduce soaps
- using clips rather than whole episodes (see page 46)
- making soaps available for self-access (the *Independent soap study project* in Box 11 can be done as an alternative to the *Independent film study project* in Box 2. For independent work also use the general worksheets in Boxes 3 and 4.

Comprehension note

The biggest single impediment to *first* understanding a soap is the proper names. Since the characters and places are not 'introduced' as in a feature film, it is difficult for learners to disentangle names from ordinary speech. Any work on soaps should start by rehearsing names of people, places, organizations and major activities involved, together with their pronunciation. Delegate the work of collecting, listing and presenting names to students if possible.

Box 11　Independent soap study project
(for individuals and small groups)

Provide four consecutive episodes of the soap, and divide the project into four phases. Give an alphabetical list of all proper names mentioned and indicate any irregular or unexpected pronunciation.

Orientation Episode 1	1 **Dossier** (for soaps) 2 **Loves and hates** 3 **Sequel and prequel** (Prequel) or **Summary**
Consolidation Episode 2	1 **Adopt a character** or **Diary** 2 **Dossier** (contd.) or **Make a case for character** or **Lifestyle** 3 **Missing scene** or **Speculations**
Digging in Episodes 3 & 4 (For groupwork)	1 **Advice** or **Soap write-out** 2 **Dossier** (contd.) or **Culture** 3 **What's going on?** (for a selected scene) 4 **Summary** (one plot line only) 5 **Silly soaps** 6 **Soap chronicles** (scrapbook or newsletter)
Language study	1 **Questions** or **Tenses** 2 **Interactive language** or **Choose your words**

3   Short dramatic sequences

Drama clips

Drama clips are short sequences from drama film – single scenes or single shots. Examples might be:

- a man burning a scrapbook in a garden (*Shine*)
- a picture of a man sitting down disconsolately on the pavement (*Down by Law*)
- two people leaving work together and deciding to go for a cup of coffee (*Awakenings*)
- a tracking shot along an American street, with fifties rock accompaniment (*American Graffiti*)
- a close-up on a pair of hands clasped behind the back (*Waterloo*)

Since all film drama has moments of verbal simplicity as well as great visual wealth, drama clips are a rich field for language learning. They are the simplest path into authentic video: they can easily be integrated into a normal teaching programme for illustration or inspiration; they are popular with students; they have high potential for teaching grammar, social language and pronunciation and also for practising notional areas to do with daily life and human behaviour. Another advantage is time-lessness – even those who are snobbish about old films don't object to watching clips from them. Use clips as models of language, as moving picture books, as samples of human behaviour and as stimuli for spoken or written production. Remember, however, that drama clips are by nature decontextualized, so always introduce them by putting them back into their context, 'setting the scene'.

Look for clips which are easy to understand and which illustrate/show any one of these:

- target language (structures, vocabulary, specific functional language)
- scripts and speech events (e.g. making conversation, bargaining, hedging, inviting, ordering a meal, quarrelling, telephone conversations, meetings, announcements)
- common native-speaker accents (UK north and south, Indian, Scottish, Irish, US north and south, Canadian, Australian) and comprehensible non-native-speaker accents
- common settings (e.g. an airport, a pub, a flat)
- arrays of common objects in close-up (e.g. goods on supermarket shelves, a dinner table, the contents of a First Aid box)
- common activities and patterns of behaviour (e.g. reading, eating, getting up, driving a car, shopping)
- runs and chases
- interesting reactions and interactions with expressive face and body language
- people talking about other conversations

Here are some of the ways you can use such clips.

For grammatical structures

Using clips to model structures lends conviction and memorability. You can recycle video material that you have used for other purposes, even after a considerable time: once it has been really well understood it is prime material for language awareness activities like **Questions**, **Tenses** or **Wordhunt**. With such 'old material' you can also focus on particular structures by asking *Do you remember how they said this?* Give three alternatives, discuss them and then play the clip again to confirm hypotheses. This is good for aspects of language which tend to be invisible to students when they are concentrating on overall under-standing, e.g. word order with adverbs, the finer tense distinctions, the use of articles, unstressed words, singular/plural verbs, etc.

Once you have become a habitual clip-hunter you will find sequences which seem to be made for illustrating particular structures. All that is needed is to: introduce the clip and show it; focus on the structure in some way; rehearse the words in some way; (possibly) explain the use of the form; and (if possible) extend the use of the form into parallel dialogues (see **Structures**). How this is done depends on the particular clips you find and the structures you are teaching. Here are some examples to illustrate slight variations on the general approach:

- *The verb to be* A short scene was chosen for an elementary class because it illustrated the different forms of the verb *to be* in the phrase *I'm sorry* (see Box 12). The teacher first practised the forms, asking for the negative, the plural, the negative plural, the question form, the imperative. He introduced the clip and asked students to notice the forms while it was playing. On the second viewing, students counted the questions and the negatives, then divided into groups of three, adopted the parts and viewed again until they could reproduce the dialogue (**Act along**).

Box 12   Example of a scene focusing on the verb *to be*
(Arnie and Gilbert are delivering groceries to Becky's caravan. Arnie drops the groceries.)

Gilbert:	I'm sorry, I'm sorry.
Becky:	It's OK, don't worry about it.
Gilbert:	(*picking them up*) I'm sorry.
Becky:	It's OK.
Gilbert:	I'm sorry.
Becky:	Don't be sorry. (*To Arnie*) Are you sorry? (*Arnie shakes his head*) No. I'm not sorry. He's not sorry. We're not sorry. Don't be sorry.
Arnie:	(*triumphantly*) I'm not sorry.

From What's Eating Gilbert Grape?

- *Questions with long subjects* Students are often led astray when the question subject is longer than normal and leave the auxiliary stuck to the main verb (*Why the Prime Minister of Sweden has resigned?* instead of *Why has the Prime Minister of Sweden resigned?*). To lend conviction to her corrections the teacher introduced and played a scene from *The Importance of Being Ernest*. She asked the students to listen *only* for the question with a long subject (*Where did the charitable gentleman who had a first class ticket for this seaside resort find you?*) and write it down. Students then invented similar conversations modelled on the dialogue, generating more questions with long subjects.

- *-ed and -ing adjectives* To introduce adjectives ending in *-ed* and *-ing*, the teacher pre-taught the verb *appal* (= shock, horrify), then introduced and played the opening sequence of a political satire in which senior civil servants lamented (frequently) that the news was *appalling* and they were *appalled* by it. The teacher asked simple comprehension questions (*How do they feel? What do they think about it?*) and discussed the two forms. Students repeated the lines with the actors (**Act along**), then thought of other situations which might provoke similar adjective pairs (*thrilled* at winning the lottery, *depressed* by *depressing* rainy weather) and acted out similar short scenes.

- *Definite articles* The significance of zero article in English is often lost on learners. A scene from *The Life of Brian*, set in the Roman Empire, shows Palestine citizens talking about what the Romans have given their country. The zero article suggests that 'peace' and 'public order' have actually been introduced by the Romans, whereas '<u>the</u> wine' and '<u>the</u> roads' are improved versions of what was there before. The teacher introduced the situation and played the clip, making sure the students understood it; on the second playing, students listed what the Romans had brought; on the third playing, they listened for the definite article. Finally they had to say why some items had definite articles and some not.

Searching for structures, counting them, writing down the words, repeating them and acting along (**Wordhunt**) are simple but compelling activities and powerful mnemonics: learners can recall a structure months later by referring to the video clip that featured it. You can lead in to focusing on a particular structure (or several) through transcribing very short sequences (see **Transcript**) or through impromptu gap exercises – just write up some of the words as they come up in the video and get students to fill the blanks.

As well as modelling language, drama clips can be used to prompt production of particular tenses and other structures. Any description of the action (e.g. **Chases**, **Fly on the wall**, **Stage directions**) will practise the simple present extensively, since drama action is conventionally described in the present tense (see page 11). For the present perfect and the imminent future (*going to, about to*) use clear action sequences with predictable outcomes, freeze the picture and do **Before and after**, concentrating on the 'after'. Slow-motion pictures of impending doom or danger (e.g. an approaching steamroller) can be used for speculating about the outcomes using future passives (*He's going to be flattened!*), *will/could/might* (*He might still escape*) and *unless* and *not unless* (*Not unless he can get out of the way fast*), which are quite hard to generate spontaneously. An activity for concurrent actions (*when, while* and the contrast of present simple and continuous) is **Long and short**. At elementary level, **Completions** builds up word order with adverbial phrases. Question-formation can be practised in any of the quiz formats (**Dossier, Picture it**); at lower levels quizzes can be restricted to (for example) questions with *to be* about colours, numbers and positions of things.

For interactive language

Drama video is particularly valuable as a source of interactive language, both for ordinary life and for ESP situations. Collect samples of useful one-off utterances, short exchanges, routine exchanges or speech events which are relevant to your students, keeping an eye open for those which will fall into place alongside your other materials/activities.

Reuse sequences which have already been well understood to focus on aspects of interaction. General activities here are **Choose your words, Getting things done, Interactive language, Purrs and slurs, Questions, Speech acts** and (for monolingual classes) **Subtitles 1**. These all need to be done several times: first to get to know the activity and then to develop the 'noticing' habit.

Clips with single functional utterances, well-highlighted (e.g. different ways of saying goodbye or sorry), can be the basis of absorbing lessons (**Holophrases**), which can also be set up and run by students if they have personal access to English-language video. If you find a scene with predictable responses (an indignant denial, acceptance of an offer) play it and pause to discuss the exact formulation of the upcoming response (**What next?**); this improves comprehension of the context and concentrates attention on the target form.

Everyday 'scripts', i.e. the fairly predictable conversations we have every day in shops, at service stations, with friends, etc., turn up frequently in soap operas, sitcoms and feature films, though always with slight distortions for the sake of character, comedy or plot. Start by establishing the standard dialogue (**Script**). This improves comprehension of the clip, which will in its turn introduce interesting variations (how to do it rudely, hesitantly, etc.). Business telephone calls of course have a language all of their own. This is well covered in published mini-courses on telephoning, which also provide audio practice, but video examples add interest and conviction (**Script, Telephone conversations**), as do extracts from novels (techno-thrillers are particularly good for word-for-word telephone conversations).

Awareness of interactive language becomes productive when there are also plenty of opportunities to use it actively. Drama clips can stimulate production and extend interactions beyond the normal social limits of the classroom. Learners can exercise their imaginations scriptwriting possible dialogues (**Lipreading and mindreading, Tone up, What next?**) or producing scenes with self-created settings and characters as in the activity **Scenario**; this is easy to set in motion and extremely motivating. Such scenes can be linked into a loose narrative sequence, a kind of do-it-yourself soap opera reflecting students' language needs and interests.

For describing and reporting speech and interaction

'Talking about talk' is an important element of conversation. It is a potentially elaborate linguistic task which requires correct choice of speech verbs (*say, tell, promise, suggest, mumble, snap,* etc.); accurate handling of their associated structures (a fertile area of error); appropriate reaction vocabulary (*really taken aback, couldn't get a word in*); expressions for extended speech behaviour (*he was having me on, we tried to calm her down*); appropriate tenses; and, overall, interpreting the interaction by highlighting some parts and telescoping others.

Wherever possible, help students find *names* for speech acts, speech events and extended speech behaviour (**Speech acts**). Speech verbs and their structures can be practised in any interactive scene with **Speech acts**; build up reaction vocabulary with **Body language, Reaction shots** and **Stage directions.** You can study 'talking about talk' in accounts in 'the book of the film' or in clips which refer to other conversations (frequent in soaps) – sometimes the original conversations can be reconstructed from them (**Gossip**). Recounting film conversations follows naturally, but to avoid blow-by-blow accounts (*she said – he said – she said*) give students some general purpose for the account, e.g. explaining why one of the participants was angry/moved/offended/scared afterwards – this gives shape, direction and motivation to the account. These exercises can lead up to the more taxing activities **Writing the book** and **What's going on?** which call for a full interpretative account of a scene. Box 13 is an example of a mini-project which practises the various aspects of describing interaction and leads up to a full description of the events in a single film scene – quite a sophisticated task. The component activities are **Feeling flow, Fly on the wall, How it's done, Reaction shots, Speech acts** (in any order), and **What's going on?, Gossip** and **Writing the book** can also extend the project.

Box 13   Describing interaction: a mini-project

A class of intermediate students studied their own films independently in groups while they worked on describing interaction in class. At the beginning they checked the meanings, forms and dependent structures of some of the commonest speech verbs (see **Speech acts**) so that they could use them throughout the project. They then viewed three film scenes in class and did various activities on each, building up the vocabulary for describing speech acts, interactions and reactions (**Reaction shots, Speech acts**) and also adverbs of manner (**How it's done**). Using scenes from their own films they produced simple blow-by-blow accounts of scenes (**Fly on the wall**), and looked at the overall dynamic of scenes with **Feeling flow**. Finally they practised giving a full description of the interaction which brought out its significance in the action as a whole (**What's going on?**). The whole project took eight class hours.

At the end students did an exit test using an early scene from *A Room with a View*. They watched the beginning of the film to establish the context, then viewed the scene as often as they wanted and were given any help they needed with understanding. One of the responses is given below, with the teacher's comments (but not corrections). Some of this work was used as a model for other groups working on **What's going on?**

A good response: *A gentleman Mr Emerson sitting at their table hears Charlotte and Lucy discussing their rooms and tells them he has a room with a view that he occupies with his son George. Kindly he proposes to Charlotte to exchange their room. Charlotte is very embarrassed and she decidedly refuses. Lucy seems to be very happy about Mr Emerson's proposal and tries to say something but Charlotte immediately stops her. Mr Emerson urges George to persuade Charlotte but she is impassive. Mr Emerson explains to Charlotte and Lucy that he doesn't need a room with a view because all the beautiful visions he could see out a window are inside his heart. At this point Charlotte stands up and goes out and she orders Lucy to follow her. Charlotte is very worried and seems to be offended by Mr Emerson's behaviour, so she nervously says to Lucy 'What an impossible person!' But this is not Lucy's opinion.*

Teacher's comment: Why does Charlotte leave the room at that point? And why is she so offended? You could interpret and bring out the dynamic of the scene a little more. You could also add more about what Mr Emerson says as the women leave and about George's behaviour through the whole scene. Try and find different words for *kindly*, *impassive* and *decidedly* – perhaps also *nervously* isn't quite right in this context. But it's a nice clear account with a lot of appropriate language and good grammar.

For pronunciation

There is a tendency for students to pick up a 'reading pronunciation' when they meet new words in their written form – quite reasonably they pronounce them as they are spelt (you will recognize old friends like *sword, doubt, castle* and *higher*). The fascinating fact is that the mistaken pronunciations students generate by reading are often not over-ridden by the heard form, however often it is heard. A simple and effective activity for the pronunciation of new words, especially those with irregular spelling, is to write them up before viewing, *without* saying them, and ask students to notice how they are pronounced when they view; if they get it wrong, go back and do it again. This makes learners depend upon their ears and, more important, realize how important it is to do so. Focus on small stretches of dialogue with **Act along**. To improve comprehension of fluent speech, do awareness-raising activities on unstressed words and morphemes (**Wordhunt**) – just counting the words in short stretches also concentrates attention. These are activities which can also be done with audio, but imitation is improved by video, since students can see how mouth and movements fit with voice.

The social significance of accents is also enhanced by video, because accents are the signature tune of a culture and should be heard in their social context. For most students, however, the first problem with accents is comprehension. Lower-level learners need to be able to understand at least two major standard varieties of English (e.g. Standard English English and Standard American English), while advanced students should be able to identify a few important non-standard accents, as well as understanding a range of non-native expert speakers. Phonological familiarization can be helped by focusing on some of the more obvious sound differences (**Accents**) and by imitating the accents (which students enjoy).

For specific vocabulary and prepositions

New vocabulary which comes up in the dialogue can be presented before viewing in a number of ways (see *Giving vocabulary*, page 121); a good way to review vocabulary items is to write them up a week later and get students to put them back into context, asking who used them and about what. Get them to notice structures which go with the words (e.g. constructions with verbs, prepositions with adjectives). Encourage them to notice not only new items but also those which are frequent and of high utility *which they don't use themselves*: this is the purpose of the activity **Choose your words**, which should be done often.

Use the pictures in the clips for all kinds of concrete vocabulary. For physical behaviour and expressions try **Body language, Body parts, Reaction shots** or **Stage directions**. These also open the way to finding interesting adverbs for human behaviour, which can be enjoyably reinforced by **How it's done**. Any scene with an array of common objects is good for a game (**I spy**) – find clips which show plurals and uncountables too; use **Picture it** for areas of vocabulary such as furniture, clothes, food, buildings, toiletries, street furniture, vehicles, office equipment. Clothes and dress and the set of associated verbs are practised in **Dress** and **Fashion parade**. **Make a case** is also useful for items of vocabulary related to a particular environment and particularly for weather and related vocabulary. If scenes show a different physical or cultural reality they make a good basis for comparison with students' own environments (**Panning**).

I spy and **Picture it** can also be used for prepositions of place, especially preposition quizzes (*Where was the hairbrush? What was on top of the cupboard?*). For prepositions of movement, which are difficult for learners, **Runabout** is worth doing several times and can build up to **Chases** and **Plan a chase**, which call on a range of vocabulary for actions and places.

Use obviously prejudiced or partial speakers to bring out the overtones of words, e.g. *Why does he say 'smelly' rather than 'perfumed'?* This 'loading' has to be recognized and learnt as part of the meaning of words (many of the funniest mistakes result from clashing connotations) and is best recognized in the rich context of video (**Purrs and slurs, Voice 1**).

Common human activities such as shopping, going to the bank, travelling and eating out feature heavily in language coursebooks, partly because of the spoken language they demand but also because they are constant topics of daily talk. Fortunately, they also turn up regularly in film drama and it is easy to find sets of sequences showing the same activity (I have eleven 'getting up' scenes!). Of course they always have a twist: film life is never quite normal, otherwise we wouldn't watch it. The activity **Daily life** generates talk about everyday processes but also emphasizes the differences between expected norms and idiosyncratic reality. It is also a good way in to comedy sketches based on ludicrous variations on normal processes (see below). The combination of vocabulary building, video illustration and talking about oneself is a good classroom cocktail. But don't swallow it all at once! **Daily life** is meant to be used selectively.

For stimulating production

Drama clips can be used in other ways to stimulate language production. Use **Panning** as a basis for students to write about their own environments as if they themselves were cameras. Imaginative speculation can be stimulated by removing some kind of input, if only the before-and-after of an image (**Enigmas**); in the same way a single scene with a powerful interaction can be studied (e.g. with **Body language, Cross-cutting, Feeling flow, Speech acts** or **What's going on?**) to raise speculation about what happened before or after. The sound-only activities **Voice 2** and **Invisible music** generate descriptions of people's appearance and character or of settings and action. The beginnings of many feature films set up evocative moods and settings which can inspire storywriting (**Plot idea 2**). Some kinds of action make good models or stimuli for one's own imagined sequences – apart from the highly creative **Scenario, Plan a chase** is stimulating for those with an aggressive streak, while **Plot idea 2** takes off from a single scene. Many scenes of everyday experience can spark personal reminiscences or comments (**Lifestyle, Trigger**). And everyone can imagine a scene in which they star themselves (**Your movie**).

Comedy sketches

Act along 123   Completions 146   Daily life 149
Puzzle 221   Script 234   Tone up 255

(Most of the activities recommended for *Drama Clips*, page 46, can also be used for comedy sketches.)

Traditional comic turns in theatres and music halls consisted of a comedian telling jokes, a few songs and dances and some comic 'sketches' – short dramatized situations, complete in themselves. All of these have transferred easily to TV and cinema, but sketches have been particularly

versatile and enduring. Classic and modern English and American com-
edians have all depended on sketches: Charlie Chaplin, W.C. Fields,
Buster Keaton, Laurel and Hardy, the Marx Brothers, the Two Ronnies,
Tony Hancock, Morecambe and Wise, John Belushi, Eddie Murphy,
Monty Python, Mr Bean. Comic sketches are the backbone of satirical
TV programmes like the long-lived American *Saturday Night Live* and
the English spoof news hour *The Day Today*. Some sketches (e.g.
Hancock's *The Blood Donor* and the Monty Python *Dead Parrot* sketch)
have become immortal. Stand-alone sketches can also sometimes be
found in comedy film drama: some of the most famous scenes in Buster
Keaton, W.C. Fields and Charlie Chaplin movies are comic sketches;
there are sequences in *Dr Strangelove* which will last till Doomsday
finally arrives; and later film drama (e.g. Monty Python films) continues
to sandwich self-contained comic scenes into the plot. There are a few
examples in Box 14, which have all been used for language teaching. It
is not suggested that you use these particular ones – they are only here
to illustrate the range.

BOX 14   Comedy sketches

1 Starving gold prospectors, stranded in a log cabin in a blizzard,
cook, serve and eat a boiled boot with great refinement, filleting
the sole from the upper, delicately removing the nails, pulling out
the laces and twirling them up like spaghetti. (Charlie Chaplin,
The Gold Rush)

2 An immensely dignified French police inspector is disaster-prone
with ordinary everyday actions: he cannot put out a light, go to
bed, put on a coat, open a door, without an accident. (*The Pink
Panther*)

3 A senior civil servant is approached by a man seeking public
funding to develop a silly walk. The civil servant (who also has a
silly walk, as does everyone in the Ministry) considers the
proposal seriously but decides that the proposed (and
demonstrated) silly walk is insufficiently silly. (*Monty Python's
Parrot Sketch not Included*)

4 A man, late for an appointment with the dentist, gets dressed,
washes, shaves and brushes his teeth while driving his Mini
through the morning traffic. (*The Terrible Tales of Mr Bean*)

5 A sultry female cat sings about love in a nightclub populated by
other cats and dogs. The young dog who is in love with her
manages to evade the bouncer and (literally) falls into her arms by
the end of the song. (*My Baby Just Cares for Me*, a Nina Simone
soundtrack animated by Aardman Animations)

---

6 Two extremely stupid upper-class young men, Tim Nice-but-Dim and Dick Nice-but-Thick, meet at a party. They have great difficulty exchanging names, but finally achieve it, only to forget the names immediately. 'Goodbye, Tony!' they chorus. (*Harry Enfield and Chums 1997*)

How to use comic sketches? For a start, watch them *for fun* – that's what people normally do! You don't need a linguistic excuse to share something funny with a class. Tell your students about a sketch you like, describe it in detail, ask if they want to see it (they will), give some key vocabulary and show them the clip. Tell them why you like it and play it again. Do **Act along** if it's suitable – students will often memorize sketches that catch their fancy. If you have self-access viewing facilities, leave some sketches for students to view and get them to vote on their favourite. Rather than putting a selection on a single tape, direct students to find specific sketches on the original tapes. This will involve them in hours of inadvertent extra viewing!

Sketches can also of course be used, like other short sequences, for specific purposes: as stimuli, for description or comprehension, as language models, as collections of pictures and as models for activities (see pages 46–55); they often do better than more naturalistic sequences. Different sorts of sketch lend themselves to different purposes and approaches. Parodies of everyday situations (most of the examples in Box 14) drive ordinary life to absurdity and fit nicely into a syllabus which deals with the activities of normal life (eating out, getting up, etc.). So do visual gags (e.g. 1, 3 in Box 14), and many slapstick and mime scenes depend on distortions of everyday actions. Introduce them by establishing the *norm*: the usual sequence of events and elements, problems and solutions, dialogue/script (depending on what the sketch is playing with) – use **Completions, Script** or the appropriate parts of **Daily life**. Then speculate on how else life could be managed, and view the sketch. Or use **Daily life** to predict what could go wrong with a simple action (such as opening a door or exchanging names, e.g. 2, 6). Or focus on the bizarre element (**Puzzle**) to get students speculating; after viewing, ask them to think up similar wild scenarios (e.g. cooking, serving and eating a handbag; getting dressed underwater). In music sketches (e.g. 5) the visual element generally overthrows the expectations set up by the music. Build up the expectations with **Invisible music** (also a good writing stimulus) then show the clip.

Highly verbal sketches (e.g. 3, 6) often present the same problems as sitcoms: exaggerated accents, puns and wordplay, idiomatic language, high-speed diction, cryptic cultural reference. But they are often also very clearly articulated, with exaggerated reactions and excellent timing (and pauses for laughter), and the linguistic games they play can be a plus rather than a minus, good for focusing on structures, vocabulary, pronunciation or aspects of interaction. Prepare your students well to understand the joke: rehearse the interaction, sort out puns and word-play, even give the punch line if necessary. The trick is to anticipate the game – do what the characters do, but in advance. If characters persistently misunderstand, preview the words to see how this could happen. If they are talking at cross purposes (see Box 15 for an example), get students to try out the 'normal' interaction before viewing the send-up (**Script**). If the sketch plays with tone or register, write up some key utterances beforehand, discuss who they would expect to say them and where, and how the message could be reworded in a more formal/colloquial way (**Tone up**).

BOX 15   Smoky bacon ice cream: a lesson

This lesson was based on a Two Ronnies sketch, set in an ice cream shop where the customer insists on ordering ice cream with the flavours of potato crisps. The honest indignation and incomprehension on both sides, together with some impossible flavours recited at breakneck speed, make it very funny.

Students practised a normal dialogue for buying an ice cream, discussed the range of flavours and their personal favourites and practised reciting them at great speed (as in the sketch). They then rehearsed a similar dialogue for potato crisps, with appropriate flavours. The teacher gave a mock test, calling out flavours while students called back *ice cream, crisps* or *neither*.

Students discussed what would happen if someone ordered a smoky bacon ice cream – how would the ice cream man react? What if the customer insisted? Then the class watched the sketch. On second viewing they formed pairs; each pair had to note and remember one exchange (*I tell you we don't have those flavours – But you used to!*). The class then tried to reconstruct the whole sketch, viewed it again and tried again.

(The Two Ronnies, BBC Enterprises Ltd)

II Non-fiction video

Introduction

What is non-fiction video?

Non-fiction video isn't easy to define, since the boundary between fact and fiction is blurring. *Life is your film!* proclaimed a recent poster addressed to teenagers. There are now many staged documentary effects in drama film (e.g. grainy shots, real historic footage, authentic-sounding talk) and some extended (and brilliant) fakes, e.g. computer-animated documentaries about dinosaurs with all the gestures of an authentic wildlife programme: the hushed voice-over, the camera tracking rockily after a speeding animal. At the same time, more and more factual material (life in an airport, a council eviction) is being shaped into dramatic form with clever editing. In 'reality TV' real events are staged for the media, e.g. people living in Stone Age camps and 1940s houses act out their lives in front of the camera. Private life is hijacked for TV: people find partners, get married or shout at their in-laws, sometimes with gleeful audience participation.

But we can still usually tell the difference between fact and fiction and this gives non-fiction viewing a special edge. Whether it's the news or *Big Brother,* we recognize reality and respond to it.

What is it good for?

Although there's a huge variety of non-fiction video programmes, they share some qualities which suggest how they can best be used for language learning:

- Live events, real feelings, unpredictable interactions are compelling in ways that fiction can't be, and naturally excite observation, comment, extension, imitation, description, comparison; there is a host of ways to exploit this response (**Ad angles, Commentary/ Copywriter, I spy, Letters to the editor, Other people's shoes, Picture it**).

- Non-fiction video often talks directly to us – to persuade us, sell us things, find out what we think – or implicitly includes us, as in interviews and talk shows, so that we are a silent part of the show. This makes us respond more directly to the messages (**Over the top, Purrs and slurs, Rhetoric, Voice 1**).
- Non-fiction video deals with topics we know about personally (**Experts, Issues, Parallels, Picture it, Stand by it, Talk show, Trigger**). It appeals to our knowledge of the world, which in turn helps us understand it (**Famous people, Follow the news, Maps and journeys, News leads, Summary**), and supplies us with the images and language of everyday life in real contexts (**Body language, I spy, Racing, Reaction shots, Weather words**). Although it doesn't show the same range of reaction and interaction as drama, it is more interested in pure talk and fuels debate on current issues (**Follow the news, Issues, Talk show, Voxpop**).
- The formats are familiar all over the world. Non-fiction programmes (talk shows, game shows, documentaries, ads, news, live sports, etc.) are all managed with different rules, tones and styles, but we know them through and through and can respond to them, imitate them and parody them. Many activities in this book exploit this knowledge.
- Non-fiction video has just as many things to play with technically as drama does (talking heads, pictures, voice-over, sounds, music, silence, dramatization) but has more choices about the mix. The relationship between the words and the pictures is full of possibilities: the pictures can show us what the words are talking about, or give us clues, illustrate a point (simply or subtly), create puzzles and then resolve them, make pointed contrasts, or tell a different story altogether. Pictures can be synchronized with the words or not: the picture can arrive before we hear about it in words (this seems to make the words more convincing), or we can hear a speaker apparently commenting on the picture before he or she appears in person. The 'revelatory' camera can establish causal connections all on its own. For example, in a documentary the camera moves from the UN flag blowing in the wind to flowing muddy water, then pans across to floating corpses – suggesting that the UN is somehow responsible for local genocide. Activities which play with these possibilities are **Commentary/Copywriter, Cross-cutting, Labelling and linking, Matching, News script, Quoting and illustrating, Themes, Viewshare, Voice 2**.
- There is a lot of writing *about* TV programmes which can be used as back-up, stimulus and models. Newspapers have regular TV critics to review the week's TV and there are books which

supplement popular documentary series. The TV channels generally have their own magazines and websites, with programme trailers and programme news, interviews with media personalities, letters, competitions, articles, reviews, profiles, opinion columns and photographs. Some websites give transcripts of live chats and interviews, which can help the teacher immensely (it is much quicker to read a script than to view a video and you can write on the transcript, cut it up, blank out parts, etc.). All of this gives possibilities for reading–writing–viewing–speaking connections (**Famous people, Interview article, Letters to the editor, Preview, Programme proposal**). You don't necessarily have to have the text that actually goes with your video material, you can do a lot with material that doesn't match – use it to reconstruct the programme described (**Letters to the editor**) and as a model for students' productions (**Interview article, Preview**).

A word of warning. Perhaps because non-fiction is closer to reality, it appeals to strong loyalties and partialities. Whereas most people are glad to watch feature films, it's harder to find common ground with non-fiction – some love the news, some hate sport, some are bored by game shows. This is something we have to handle by distributing time reasonably, consulting students and individualizing as far as possible – see **Experts, Grading, Learning English with film, Pick of the news** and the various suggestions for independent work in this book.

There is probably more falsification in non-fiction than in drama. We are more likely to be convinced that what we have seen is true – and of course it is never completely true. Most of the activities here improve students' English, but they also help to raise awareness of how the media shape reality – which should be part of everyone's education!

1   Programmes about real life

Documentaries and educational films

Documentaries are quite long, highly-planned programmes which present facts and opinions about single subjects. Educational films are much the same, but are generally more serious and often accompanied by a book to increase the information content (as are major documentary series). 'Docudrama' is a close dramatization of real-life events.

The content, style and purpose of documentaries vary enormously. You have probably seen ones about famous people, institutions, events and places; history and social history; travel and other cultures; music groups and sports; the making of other films; topical issues and social problems; work and hobbies and the lives of ordinary people; art, music, culture; science, nature and wildlife. Like the news, they are put together from moving pictures, graphics and stills, commentary, talking heads, excerpts from interviews, music and sound effects. They have a huge range of mood, tone and style (and difficulty). Compare, for example, a relaxed and beautiful, virtually wordless, tour of Ireland with a hard-hitting exposé of criminal carelessness in the health service. The style is of course governed by the purpose, which may be to exhibit, narrate, discuss, investigate or expose. What you can do with a documentary reflects all these different parameters, so there aren't as many catch-all prescriptions as for drama films.

What documentaries do have in common is high focus. A documentary is the TV version of a newspaper or magazine article, a kind of essay in words, sounds and pictures, with *sustained interest in a single topic*. The overall structure is generally the same. They start with a 'teaser', to whet the appetite and set the tone; then they voice their concern in a statement, a question or a claim, and generally tell us explicitly what they plan to do. The rest of the programme pursues this point: presents and explains, tells the story, supports the claim, airs the sides of the case, seeks answers or makes a bid to reveal the truth. Just like written articles, documentaries tend to divide naturally into paragraph-length sections, except that the links are marked in many different ways: with pauses, words, images, sounds, music, even captions. They make points and support them with 'quotations' and 'illustrations', just as in writing, and the more serious ones give copious 'references' in the form of acknowledgements at the end.

For language teaching, documentaries have a lot of scope. They may be topical but they are not ephemeral like most news – they can be stored and used again. They are easy to find. Some (e.g. wildlife programmes) are spectacular; some have been acclaimed as feature films (e.g. *The Buena Vista Social Club, Microcosmos, Looking for Richard*) or won Oscars (e.g. *Woodstock*). They have a good mix of spontaneous and scripted language and a lot of usable short sequences. On top of that, they aren't very difficult to understand: they are shorter than feature films; the commentary usually has a sober style with standard phraseology and a standard English accent (generally the more serious the programme the more standard the accent!); the pace is slower than the news, the information less dense and the visual element more supportive; there are generally only four or five main points. Most upper-intermediate students can cope with most documentaries, and at intermediate level they can manage edited versions.

What are they good for?

Some are useful in ESP: travel documentaries for tourist schools, management training videos for civil servants and business people, educational programmes for students of all subjects. Some provide a basis for comparison with one's own country (**Parallels**) or for discussion (**Issues**). Some inspire imitation, e.g. a film about South African children moved a class to interview and record other young children and put together a collage of their picture of life (**Labelling and linking** Follow-up). As 'essays' they can serve as models for writing: making clear the parts and the links, supporting points with illustration (**Labelling and linking, Quoting and illustrating**). Some are good for learning about things (**Experts**). And some are just interesting.

Why don't we use such programmes more?

One reason is that, though shorter than feature films, at 30–60 minutes they still take up a lot of class time. Some answers to this are to make a feature of them (see *Documentary of the month*, page 66), or to set up enticing self-access activities with some tutorial back-up (see Box 16). Another objection is that they are simply too in depth for EFL, which (it is said) normally flits lightly from topic to topic. This is something which has to be squared with your students' interests and capacities and your own teaching style, but again an element of individualization and personal choice may help to keep both students and teachers happy. Finally, it must be admitted that documentaries really are quite heavy on the attention. They are not quite as compelling as feature films – there's less narrative curiosity, emotional excitement and glamour; more of the important messages are in the words, the sentences are longer and the pictures not always as self-explanatory. Even for an advanced class an undiluted 45-minute documentary in another language is tiring.

So to promote documentaries:

- discuss the value of documentary viewing with students (**Learning English with films**)
- give choices and consult preferences
- make a range of material available for self-access, with doable and attractive activities and 'taster' sessions in class (with **Lead-in**)
- get students to assess difficulty and to leave their comments for others (**Grading, Preview**)
- do everything you can to lighten the comprehension load

Comprehension

Here are some suggestions to lighten the comprehension load:

- *Select with care and consent* If you are not sure of students' levels of documentary tolerance and understanding, start out with **Grading** and do a taster series to find what appeals. This will help both you and your students to orient yourselves and may save a lot of pain and labour.
- *Get briefed* Having chosen your documentary, get students to assemble everything they know on the subject and to check reference sources (e.g. encyclopaedias, history books, Internet, articles from TV magazines or websites) – this doesn't take long if the work is shared. Students can prepare quizzes or briefing sheets for each other on essential background information. **Character network, Famous people, Maps and journeys** can help with preparation for many programmes.

- *Do preliminary vocabulary work* Review the names of people, places, organizations, acronyms and their pronunciation; establish key words, drill phraseology; and start on a vocabulary map.
- *Anticipate* For most kinds of programme you can pose the main questions before you start, get some speculative answers or personal opinions and seal them in envelopes to be opened after viewing; or encourage a preliminary overview of the main parts of the programme with **Labelling and linking**. If you have a summary of the programme from a website, present it with gaps and get students to speculate on how they are completed. For all documentaries, do some intensive work on the first five minutes, which set up the tone, scope and purpose of the whole (**Lead-in, Matching**). Also whet the appetite with some early sequences (talking heads, silent footage or graphics, arresting shots or an interesting sound sequence with a darkened screen) and invite speculation about what they show and their significance in the programme. If students are able to work independently, an interesting lead-in is to show several very brief enigmatic shots from the programme without sound (**Enigmas**), discuss what they might mean, assign them to individuals or groups for homework and ask them to explain them in the following lesson before the class watches the whole documentary.
- *View lightly* To lighten the viewing of the whole, try the 'illustrated talk' approach, as with feature films (see page 18): tell the story yourself, play three or four sequences to illustrate, and entice students to view other sequences on their own. If students can view outside class, ask individuals or groups to prepare to talk about specified sequences (give them the first and last words), and do your narration with contributions from the class. Small groups can also view the programme outside class and constitute expert panels (**Experts**) to answer questions prepared by the rest of the class. If some students have already seen the programme, this is a bonus not a drawback – exploit it (**Seen it before**).

  With 'salami tactics' (see page 19), you can cover a documentary in two or three episodes, recapping the previous section each time and preparing for the next. Students can share out the comprehension load each time by concentrating on words *or* pictures, people *or* events and then pooling their information (**Viewshare**).
- *Reviewing comprehension while viewing* Some types of reading comprehension exercises extend naturally to many documentaries (**Labelling and linking, Quoting and illustrating**). For reviewing each part, get the facts straight with **Summary**, and **Why and How?** if there is explaining to be done. **Before and after** or **Matching** can be used for quick recall.

Other review activities depend on the type of documentary. If it's about people, explore facts, interactions, behaviour and motivations with **Adopt a character, Advice, Case study, Character network, Famous people, Other people's shoes, Speculations**; for history and travel, **Maps and journeys** may come in useful; if a conflict is represented, lead in and follow up with **Fights**; if an argument or issue is being aired, pull out individual opinions before more general debate (**Issues**). Many descriptive documentaries are basically a guided tour round a country, a place, a picture or a group of people, visiting different aspects in turn, and can be understood and imitated within this framework (**Labelling and linking** Follow-up); information about processes and work programmes can be collected in a flow-diagram, as in **Daily life.**

- *Follow-up* After viewing, descriptive films can be chunked and written up by groups as paragraphs in an account. Discuss stories about individuals with **Other people's shoes** and perhaps **Turning points.** Stories of daily life may inspire an imaginative **Diary** for the day. Some social themes lend themselves to comparisons with other countries or times (**Parallels, Place and period**) and others to analysis (**Case study**); for controversial programmes, discussion can come before or after (**Issues**) and can result in a round-up of opinion recorded on audio or video (**Voxpop**) or in recorded interviews with opinionated class members who would like to have taken part in the programme as players (**Adopt a character** Variation 2).

  Extension activities are: dreaming up ideas for similar programmes (**Labelling and linking** Follow-up, **Programme proposal**); producing programme trailers/previews (**Preview**) or a simple rating (**Grading**); and writing enraged or appreciative **Letters to the editor.** For advanced students, the programme may provide sensational material which will inspire a newspaper **News story.**

- *Language work* Get students to select a section they would like to study for vocabulary (**Choose your words**), and pick useful short passages for studying tenses, structures and pronunciation (**Structures, Tenses, Wordhunt**); if you have programmes with subtitles in either English or the first language you may be able to do some close-focus language work with **Subtitles 1** and **2.**

Documentary of the month

A really good documentary with wide appeal deserves a full three-hour afternoon slot for several classes conducted as a mammoth 'sandwich':
- preparation, discussion, viewing of first part
- recap/review/preparation, viewing of second part
- recap/review and final discussion or debate

Make it a social occasion. Get individual classes to organize the event, invite prepared contributions (with a time limit) for the debate, and leave room for a refreshment break between the first and second part, as in the cinema.

Independent work

If there is the possibility of independent viewing, get students to make their own choice of documentary and prepare written work, presentations or expert panels (**Experts**). An outline for independent work is given in Box 16 – for a lighter load omit the reviewing (steps 5 and 8).

BOX 16   Independent work with documentaries
Instructions for students (individuals, pairs or small groups)

1 Choose your documentary. Write down briefly the reason for your choice.

2 If possible, research the subject before you view – in an encyclopaedia, on the Internet. List the names of people, places and organizations and check the pronunciation.

3 View the introduction (the first five minutes).
   a What is the mood/tone? e.g. serious, indignant, interesting, light-hearted, neutral, chatty?
   b What is the main idea/purpose of the programme? Is it a question or a statement? Write it down.

4 View the first 15–20 minutes, then make a break. Make some notes on these questions.
   a What are your feelings? Are you interested/bored/indignant/ horrified/amused? Why?
   b What does it *say*? What is the most interesting information/point?
   c What does it *show*? What are the most significant or interesting pictures?
   d Who are the *players*? Which is the most interesting?
   e Does it answer any *Why?* or *How?* questions? Write down the questions and the answers.
   f Is there any important new vocabulary? Check the meanings.
   g Is it worth going on? (If so, go on to the next stages.)

5 View the first part again and extend your notes. How many main points are there? If you have time, write a brief summary of the ideas so far (**Summary**).

6 Play the second part and answer the same questions.

---

7 (Optional) Take a position. Do one of the following:
  a Select one of the players and adopt his/her point of view.
  b Pick a player and think what you would like to say to him/her.
  c Think how you would behave/have behaved if you were there.
  d Decide if you would like the place/period/society/occupation and why/why not.

8 Play the second part again and make a few notes on your position. Write up your notes, e.g.:
  The programme is about … Its main idea/purpose is …
  My main reaction was …
  Briefly, it says that … and it shows …
  The most interesting part/person/fact/picture/moment/idea is …
  If I was/had been … I would/would have …
  I would/would not recommend this documentary because …

9 Do one of the following:
  • Present a written report to your teacher or to other students.
  • Present your report orally in class, with short sequences to illustrate.
  • Write a letter to the TV channel giving your opinion of the programme (**Letters to the editor**).
  • Write a short documentary preview (**Preview**).
  • Produce a basic rating form or difficulty report and attach it to the cassette (**Grading**).

The TV news

(For other uses of news items and for general language work, see *Nonfiction clips*, page 99. Many activities in *Documentaries*, page 62, can also be used with major national events.)

Many teachers (and students) shun the broadcast news. This is a pity. It is true that some news is parochial, some is controversial, and a lot is about politics, which bores a lot of people. It is also true that the news is difficult to understand. It is heavy with references to people and situations which may be unknown to viewers; dozens of proper names, unrecognized in their English forms, obscure word boundaries for learners. The pictures are often not self-explanatory. The text is dense with information and is spoken rather fast, and has its own journalistic code (diseases are *scourges*, events *herald* revolutions, situations are *fraught* with danger). A lot of news is about bizarre or violent events with rare and specialized vocabulary which would not get priority in most EFL syllabuses, e.g. *massacre, mourning, curfew*, and teachers often feel it does not have obvious links to other classwork.

On the other hand, there is nothing like the TV news! It is the most accessible (and most frequent) TV programme available; it is backed by four parallel news media (newspaper, radio, Internet and teletext); it comes in neat little labelled packages; it has compelling images and is an open window on the world and on the country of the language. Above all it is real, and 'hot', and there really is something for everyone. Moreover, it *is* possible to link news items to other classwork, and there are many ways of mediating understanding. The news also deserves attention for itself: just like feature films, conversation, service encounters, correspondence, etc., it is a discourse which can't justifiably be neglected in a language syllabus. As with movies, the learner's main desire is usually just to understand, but it is also motivating to look at what news is and how it is composed and to try one's hand at inventing it oneself.

Structure

TV news items are composite creatures, put together from several sources. They have a standard structure (much parodied) which to some extent follows the pattern of newspaper stories:

- The *lead* (a few sentences) summarizes the story. It is spoken by the newsreader/anchorman(woman) in the studio, usually with a still picture of the news item in the background and a caption (for examples, see **News leads**).
- The *expansion* repeats the story in more detail, giving the who, what, when, where, why and how. This is often done in a *location report* by a reporter, whose voice comments on *footage* of the events, places or people. The footage itself may be cryptic or illuminating – it may make no sense without the words or it may be full of landmarks and symbols revealing action, location and

players. It may also be highly relevant and up-to-date or only loosely connected to the topic (e.g. a still shot of the location).

- Included in the location report are *quotations* from interviews with interested parties, experts or witnesses – usually just a few words – and often *graphics* presenting simple information.
- There is a short conclusion in which the reporter *winds up* and *signs off*, usually speaking to camera.

Using individual news items

Use news items on a day-by-day basis just for their topical interest. Make a list of the main items for the day, ask students to choose one, view it and air the issues it raises (**Pick of the news**). There is plenty of topical material for ESP teaching, e.g. for business people and civil servants (takeover bids, government spending, taxation), for lawyers and legal students (trials, civil suits and international law), for doctors and medical students (new cures, the state of the health service, epidemics) and of course for political science students. Here, too, choice is important: if possible, give individuals the option of preparing the item outside class and bringing it back with an expert opinion (**Experts**). In mixed-nationality classes this also gives students the chance to explain their own country to others, as does **Parallels**, e.g. How does *your* country deal with drunk drivers? Are your schools like this? – Tell all!

But news doesn't have to be immediate to be interesting. You can use stand-alone news items for their interesting visual sequences and in projects as one of several kinds of source. Historic footage (e.g. the Berlin Wall, the assassination of Kennedy, the release of Mandela) will make a series of lessons in itself (**Pick of the news** Variation 2). Many coursebook themes (e.g. war, famous people, smoking, the environment, education, crime, jobs) can be reinforced by news clips. Collect high-interest items which could belong to many times and places. Very valuable are the year-end retrospectives which assemble great quantities of usable material, important or just spectacular. Also collect items dealing with general human experiences, which can unleash personal reminiscences. Everybody has their own horror story about driving, hospitals, crime, neighbours, bureaucracy, shoddy goods or bad workmanship; use news items to pull them out and stimulate discussion, debates and essays (**Trigger**) on topics.

Understanding news items

As we saw, news is difficult and dense. Despite its visual back-up, it is highly verbal, and it really does pay to understand as many words as possible. If this is what the students want, how can we achieve it?

For a start, if students are unused to the speed and density of the news, they will need to view any given item several times, often far more often than most teachers would let them – one class demanded to watch an item five times. Use a variety of comprehension aids to lead in. An essential preliminary is to brainstorm all relevant proper names and practise recognizing and producing them. Add information – get students to share all they know about the topic (including the obvious) and then predict what is in the item. Or read the parallel newspaper article, teletext or Internet texts before viewing (**Twin texts**); gather vocabulary and speculate on what footage will be shown, who will be approached for comments and what they will say. Equally, you can use a TV news item to 'illustrate' the newspaper, and ask students to make matches between the written word and the TV pictures (**Twin texts**).

Alternatively, exploit the basic components of news items as lead-ins: the lead, footage, 'quotations' and graphics are all natural entry points. Focus on the lead systematically to anticipate the rest of the item (**News leads**). Pick up new vocabulary in the lead and get students to find it 'illustrated' in the footage (**Matching**). Footage, quotations and graphics can all be easily isolated and used to speculate about the content and wording of the item before viewing it as a whole (**News leads**). Take care that the footage is 'illuminating' rather than 'cryptic', that quotations are in standard English, and that graphics are clear and informative.

On first viewing concentrate on difficult vocabulary (see *Giving vocabulary,* page 121) and do other partial comprehension activities, such as matching pictures and sound (**Matching**) or writing down words heard and extending the strings of words on each viewing (**Transcript**). Once there is some understanding, go to standard comprehension activities which supply logical frameworks for catching content and interaction, such as taking notes under the headings *Who, What, When,* and *Where* (**Situation report**), recreating a chronological narrative, mapping the relationships between the players (**Character network**) or visualizing the geography (**Maps and journeys**). As self-tests or recaps, get students to prepare comprehension questions or to explain the (silent) footage, picture by picture (**Before and after** Variation 1).

Language work

Grammar work can be done after the news item has been quite well understood. The news has traditionally been used to demonstrate the contrast of past and present perfect because it often starts with the 'updating' present perfect and moves into the past tense for details. But also look at the whole range of tenses in the item: often there is a clear

71

sequence of present perfect, past, present and possible futures (see **Situation report**), with a sprinkling of passives and continuous passives, otherwise quite rare (e.g. *The ground is now being cleared for construction*); get students to notice where one time frame moves into another (**Tenses**) and any related time expressions. There are usually some useful verb-dependent structures (e.g. *prevent the bulldozers coming in*) and a few long noun groups (e.g. *the 10,000-seater volleyball stadium*) (**Structures**). Do **Choose your words** for useful vocabulary, but warn students about the special news idiom: talk of *mercy dashes* in *fleets of ambulances* for *bloodstained victims* rings rather oddly in intermediate conversation!

Independent work on news items

The independent work outlined in Box 17 concentrates on comprehension, but leaves the choice and analysis to personal interest.

BOX 17   Independent work on news items
Instructions for students (intermediate and above)

1 View the whole news programme and select one item you would like to understand better.

2 If possible, read up on the subject in newspapers, on teletext or on the Internet. Gather essential vocabulary and background information. In particular, find out how the names are pronounced.

3 View your chosen news item again. Make a list of all the names. Study the pictures, the 'quotations' from interviews and the graphics and see how much you can understand.

4 Go back to the news lead (the short introduction spoken in the studio). This summarizes the item and gives a good idea of its content. View it several times and transcribe it (**Transcript**).

5 View the rest of the news item several times, trying to understand the words. If you don't understand everything, try some of these:

   a find places where the words match the pictures and write down the words
   b identify the people who are interviewed
   c take down a 'quotation' as dictation
   d collect details under the headings *Who, What, When, Where,* and *Why*

---

6 Once you have understood the words quite well, you need to grasp the whole picture and try to explain what has happened. Do **Character network** or turn down the sound and talk through the pictures, explaining them to yourself.

7 For language study, do **Choose your words** for useful expressions or **Tenses** (looking for passives and continuous forms, and the sequence of present perfect, past, present and future).

8 Write an account of the news item. Explain briefly what has happened, why you chose this item, why it is interesting/ significant, what questions it raises and how the situation might develop in future. Give your work to your teacher *or* present the item in class in the same way, playing the item at both the beginning and the end of your talk.

Following the news

Of course, the best way to understand the news is to follow it as one does in real life, pursuing a developing situation as it unfolds day by day. Once students are familiar with the situation, comprehension is cumulative: each news item adds only a small amount of new content, background information and vocabulary, and the news idiom gradually ceases to sound strange.

Some news stories go on long enough and are sufficiently absorbing to make them worth following in class, e.g. O.J. Simpson, BSE and 11 September had world audiences and won't be soon forgotten. Some stories are virtually permanent (e.g. the Middle East) and some surface regularly (e.g. the environment, genetic engineering); some have so fascinated journalists that they have become books (e.g. *Alive*[1], about the air crash of the Ecuadorean football team and *Into Thin Air*[2], about botched ascents of Everest). For ESP learners a relevant ongoing news story can be used (**Case study**) to bring learners closer to raw data in their own fields. For ordinary classes the time needed to 'follow the news' is considerable but can be justified if the topic has general appeal, if the activity breaks the comprehension barrier and swells confidence, and if it generates successful independent work. The project **Follow the news** can be done in the mini or the maxi version according to the time

[1]*Alive*, by Piers Paul Read, Avon Books, New York, 1974
[2]*Into Thin Air*: a personal account of the Mount Everest disaster, by Jon Krakauer, Anchor Books, Doubleday, 1997

available. Finding the right story is not easy: it needs to last at least a week (most don't), to have rapidly accelerating events, and a foreseeable end if possible – rescue stories are a good bet and so are stories with pre-fixed dates (e.g. elections and referenda, trials, international meetings). You have to be able to seize a good story as it breaks, and be prepared for unpredictable events and some unplannable lessons. As far as possible delegate the search for materials to the students – there are many of them and only one of you!

Independent work on following the news can follow the lines of the project. Students choose their own ongoing news story and work through Box 18.

BOX 18   Independent work on Following the news
Instructions for students (upper-intermediate and above)

1 Choose an ongoing news story which interests you and which will last at least a week.
2 Decide what questions it raises, i.e. what the issues are, and write them down.
3 Follow the story over 5–10 days. Use more than one medium: TV, radio, newspapers, teletext and Internet. Put your sources into a dossier (include tape recordings if possible).
4 Write a summary of the news over this period, as if you were a historian. Tell it as a narrative, in the past tense, with a clear time frame. Try to integrate your sources and not just repeat what each one says separately. Use a plain non-journalistic style (this will mean a lot of rewording).
5 Do a little research into the background: past history, important players, relevant issues. If a map is necessary, find one. Put photocopies of your source material into your dossier.
6 Select one player to focus on (a person or an institution) and try to understand his/her/their motivations, actions and relationships with the other players.
7 Present your work to the class. Briefly give the background and say why it is interesting/important and what questions it raises. Outline the recent events, then analyse the issues (i.e. try to answer the questions you raised). Illustrate with brief clips from the TV news. Finally, explain the position of the player you selected and predict what will happen next. Answer any questions.
   or
8 Do 7 in writing, check it, and give it to your teacher for comments, along with the dossier.

Creating the news

It is easy to put together something which looks or sounds roughly like a newspaper story or the radio news, but no one can make convincing TV news items without good camerapeople, high-quality sound recording equipment, editing facilities, a reference library and video archives – so classroom productions are not a real option. On top of that, most language learners have no desire to be journalists, and newswriting is a highly specialized task which is not much use in normal life. But as long as some glamour hangs around the TV news, most students are quite motivated to play reporter and there are some news-producing activities which are fruitful as well as fun. They can also be tied to projects about the news itself (see the next section).

The four main components (lead, location report, quotations and footage) can all be used for practising summary, speaking and writing. Students can: produce a news lead after viewing the location report (**News leads**, Variation 2) then try their hand at playing the anchorman; recreate the interviews and add on 'quotations' from interested parties (**Comment**); expand the lead with their own (messy but creative) location reports; and at an advanced level simulate the rigorous process of fitting a script to existing footage (**News script**). Stretch students' imaginations by sending them back into the past to interview participants at famous historical events (**Interview**). For those who want to try their hand at writing newspaper stories, any piece of video drama (the simpler the better) which shows a newsworthy event (there are plenty) can act as a stimulus. Turning a TV news item into a newspaper story is also (unfortunately) an authentic journalistic practice, and much easier than writing a story from scratch (**News story**). But it takes time to unlearn the habit of chronological narrative and to develop a journalistic style: activities like these are fun but hard to justify except for students of literature, politics, journalism and mass communication.

Studying the news

People tend to take the news as a fair picture of world events except when it is flagrantly distorted. But the popular image of news-gathering doesn't recognize how derivative news is and how distant from first-hand experience. Even the most responsible news coverage is seriously partial: ethnocentric, highly constructed and a forum for competing interests. News is increasingly seen as entertainment: important events may be downplayed because news programmes seek the sensational and dramatic to improve their ratings, while trivial events with picturesque footage get more time than they are worth. Many note-worthy events do *not* become news, simply because they have no channel of communication; or they become news later only because they were not news sooner, i.e. when it's too late.

An understanding of how news comes into being is a valuable antidote to myths about the news. For relatively mature students, exploring the questions *What is news? Where does it come from? What makes it 'good'?* makes the basis for an intermediate/advanced project to which students can contribute their experience of their own countries' news services (see Box 19). Strand A of the project, the classwork core, looks at items of TV news. Strands B, C and D are optional. Strand B is individual work modelled on Strand A; Strand C uses feature films about the TV news to raise and discuss the same questions; Strand D proposes subjects for debate.

BOX 19   Good news!
Strand A   Classwork

1 **Vocabulary** Start with some terms: the uncountable word *news* (+ *an item of news*), *scoop/exclusive*, *bias/biased*, *sources*, *propaganda*, *broadcast*.

2 **What is news and what is not?** View a complete news programme and get students to list the items. Discuss and decide why these events made the news and whether it would be the same in their country. Which items (in their opinion) could be left out, and why? And what is missing? Discuss why there is no news

(for example):

- about literature or showbiz
- about global warming or AIDS
- about new slimming diets
- about crops and harvests
- about oil in the Caspian Sea

Build up criteria for what makes news (e.g. accessible, odd, interesting, relevant, important, negative, close to home, well publicized, official, about money, *new*). In particular bring out the fact that an event, however important, cannot become news if it has no access to the media.

3 **Where does it come from?** Select a few news items which appear to have a range of sources (archive footage, new footage, interviews, agency information, press conferences). View each item and discuss how many sources the reporter used and where he or she found them (this can demand very attentive viewing and some speculation).

Does the news really reflect the important events of the day or does it simply take what it's given by various publicity machines? Discuss this in relation to the analysed items.

If there is time, get students to try their hands at putting TV news items together themselves, as in **Comment** and **News script**.

4 **What makes it good?** Discuss criteria for good news coverage and reporting, e.g. should it be important, worldwide, packed with information, very up-to-date, objective, balanced, interestingly presented, very clear? Students evaluate some news items on these grounds.

Strand B (optional)   Individual work

1 Students select and study a news item, as in Box 17.
2 They list the sources they think the reporter used for each part.
3 They select three top criteria for good news reporting and evaluate the item in terms of these criteria.
4 Each student shows the item and reports to the class.

Strand C (optional)   Classwork or individual work

The class chooses one of the following films or any other film which deals with the making of the TV news (more stars mean more language difficulty).

> *Wag the Dog*****   *Accidental Hero***   *The Broadcast News****
> *Godzilla***   *Network***   *The China Syndrome***

The series *Yes Minister* also has some good scenes dealing with the political role of the TV news.

Do the film in episodes, or arrange for independent viewing, or just select scenes which focus on gathering, creating, manipulating, suppressing or delivering the news (there are excellent sequences in all these films). Discuss the questions: *What is the news here? Why is it news? How is it created? Where does it come from? What is the idea of 'good reporting' in this film?*

Strand D (optional)   Questions for class discussion

• Is the news worth watching? Why/Why not?
• Is our news manipulated or manufactured? If so, by whom?
• What news should we have more/less of?
• Do we still have fearless investigative reporters? If so, where?
• When are governments justified in suppressing news?

Weather

TV weather reports have changed dramatically. The geographical scope is now far greater: CNN and BBC reports cover the world. The visuals are more glamorous and also more informative – the graphic weather maps really do speak for themselves. This makes them a natural stimulus for oral production and has relieved the weather reporters of some straight reporting – they now give information in a much chattier style and sometimes very fast.

Weather reports also seem to be rarer in EFL textbooks! Increased difficulty could be a reason; or it could be that the weather reporters have abandoned the *will* future which made them so popular with structural courses; or perhaps weather forecasts are just not very interesting except as they relate to your personal tomorrow.

However, weather reports are still good for language work. Everyone needs to talk about the weather, and they are ideal for practising and extending weather vocabulary (**Weather words**) at all levels. They are rich in geographical vocabulary and locations (*low-lying valleys, high ground, on the coast, in the south-west*) and good as a moving atlas for catching place names and noticing their grammar (**I spy** Variation 2). With the new colloquial tone there are often a lot of modifiers and 'hedges' (*a bit, quite a bit, just that little bit*); picking these up (**Interactive language**) is a sensible preliminary to listening comprehension work.

To understand authentic weather forecasts, students need either simple texts (try regional forecasts) or good strategies. Help them to make full use of the graphics in order to understand the words (**Weather words**) and to develop listening strategies for pulling out the essentials (**What weather where**).

Many weather reports have a striking lack of main verbs (*Quite a mobile situation here – a lot of thunderstorm activity in the north, and high pressure just beginning to build up ... plenty of showers too coming in from the west ...*) but more old-fashioned ones have the predictable cluster of tenses typical of the **Situation report**. Use them to study this pattern of tenses and to model other situation reports. Or use the words and/or visuals to help students generate a quiz with *going to*, e.g. *What's it going to be like in Lusaka tomorrow? Where is it going to rain? Is it going to be sunny in Spain?*

Major national events

As English becomes an international language, students are less interested in the idiosyncrasies of national culture, e.g. Beefeaters, Thanksgiving, kilts, shamrocks, digger hats and the difference between tea and dinner. But some (e.g. trainee teachers or students of tourism) still need or want to learn about the home culture of English-speaking countries. Live coverage of major national events is a window onto some of its more picturesque aspects: regular ceremonies like the opening of the UK parliament or the swearing-in of the US president; national festivals like the Notting Hill carnival, Hogmanay, St Patrick's Day, the Australian Mardi Gras; big sporting/cultural/political events which are also major social occasions, such as the Oscars, the Oxbridge boat race, the razzmatazz of the Rugby League Final at Twickenham, political party conventions and conferences; and one-off landmark occasions like the opening of the Tate Modern or the ritual handover of Hong Kong.

These programmes are distinguished by ceremonial elements, display, rhetoric and an unreal sense of real time (the length of it all!). They generally arouse faint puzzlement in viewers from other cultures and cry out to be explained. But since there's a lot to look at and the words are usually not too difficult, the mysterious events can be quite successfully treated as cultural explorations. One in-service teachers' group were fascinated, if bemused, by the 'last night of the Proms' in which they identified several national symbols, tuned in to the extraordinary combination of passion and irony in the audience and learned to sing along with *Jerusalem, Rule Britannia* and *Auld Lang Syne*.

What is important is that events and mood are correctly interpreted, and viewers are free to express their reactions. Aim for them to: get some strong impressions; recognize and name things, events, people and places; describe atmosphere, events and details, and be able to explain them to others. Check that you yourself have all the information you need to make sense of the event, and decide how much you want to edit the programme. Then try the procedure in Box 20.

BOX 20   Major national events

1 **Introduction:** You need to give an overall frame for interpretation of an alien ritual! Before viewing tell students about the event; the background; the major players (and their social status); the structure (and rules, if any); the location. Short information articles about the event or the players (e.g. the role of Black Rod in the opening of Parliament) are useful both to introduce the event and for follow-up. You may also want to discuss appropriate attitudes, e.g. it is important to know that the endless standing ovations during the US President's address to the Union are regarded as routine.

2 **First view – impressions:** Play the video just to give an impression of the occasion. While viewing, write up the names of people, things and actions which are seen or mentioned.

3 **Identification:** Go through the list, establish pronunciation and ask students if they can identify the named things and give some details. Explain where necessary.

4 **Atmosphere:** Ask students each to write one or two adjectives to describe the atmosphere, and one or two comments or questions, and read them out.

5 **Second view – details:** The second viewing, ask each student to notice one of these:
   a one or two details about the *place* (e.g. decorations, features, colours, shapes)
   b one or two *events/actions*
   c one or two *people* or aspects of people (e.g. clothes, behaviour)
   d one other detail of any kind
   They should write each detail on a separate strip of paper.

6 **Groupwork:** In groups, students match their strips (e.g. place – event, action – people) and arrange them in chronological order. Circulate to check accuracy and language.

7 **Discussion:** Discuss: whether they would like to have been present; what the event reveals about the culture and the people.

8 **Writing:** In groups, students discuss and write a general opening comment, and then a brief account of the whole event, concluding with comments on the aspects in 7. They may target it at a tourist brochure for visitors to the country/city. OR individuals write a description of a similar event in their own country.

Speeches

Speeches are not at all like the news: most make no pretence at objectivity. They are included here because many are given at major national events and are covered in news programmes. There are party political speeches, ceremonial speeches, harangues at rallies and conferences, ministerial addresses to the nation, famous historical speeches like Martin Luther King's 'I have a dream', Parliamentary Question Time (full of little speeches), after-dinner speeches. For an insight into how such speeches are set up, there is nothing better than the parodies in *Yes Minister* and *Saturday Night Live*.

Speeches can be rabble-rousing, inspirational, formal and ceremonial, tightrope-walking, policy-making, but all speechmakers are very aware of their audience and purpose and most are as interested in the *interpersonal* effect as in the *ideational* messages: form, style and technique are as important as content, or more so. Speeches are therefore ideal for appreciating how body language, prosodic features and words work together for effect, and how the audience is involved in the process. And there is so much to appreciate: gesture, loaded language, figurative language, wordplay, other 'voices', use of known trigger words as 'claptraps' to stir up applause, exaggeration and high emphasis, pointed contrasts and climactic build-ups, irony and sarcasm, pathos and indignation, point-scoring, sheer bitchiness, insinuation and accusation, anecdotes, special personas projected for the occasion. There is excellent scope for stress recognition and imitation in 'tub-thumping' speeches when speakers bang out their point on the rostrum or wag their fingers rhythmically in the air. Describing all these things is an essential aspect of daily life (*He makes himself out to be so quiet and reasonable, but he really does exaggerate; she does a lot of tub-thumping, but she gets them on her side because she's so sincere*). For a reversal of the normal comprehension process, start with the body language (**Body language, Reaction shots**, the non-verbal parts of **Rhetoric**) and continue with the ideas and the language (verbal parts of **Rhetoric** or **Purrs and slurs**). Then get students to summarize the content, decide if they would like to support or oppose the speaker and do a roundup of opinion (**Voxpop**).

Parliamentary debate

This is televised in the UK and is great fun because the issues are completely overshadowed by gamesmanship. There are rules, a referee (the Speaker), time-honoured tricks and techniques, strong partisan feeling and enthusiastic audience response. Each speaker aims for maximum impact and has his/her own style and techniques, and most are very practised; it can therefore be riveting to watch even if you are not at all interested in the people or issues. As regards content, it can also be used for inference, since the debate is fairly inward, and for summarizing facts and taking sides; but use a light hand, since most of the debates don't have great intrinsic interest for people outside the UK.

Some sequences are usable at intermediate level: the speaking is fairly extempore but clear and slow, with excellent sound quality, and the speeches are short. Find topics which are not obscure or parochial and which may have parallels in other countries (e.g. the national lottery, military service). The debate usually divides neatly into sequences by theme: use one sequence to establish the rules of the game, then go on to look at rhetorical styles and content in other sequences.

Establishing the rules
- *The context* Before watching, do **Picture it** to establish how the Houses of Parliament are organized; or just explain that main parties are on opposing sides, the Speaker is seated high in the centre and the party leaders are on the front benches, with the Cabinet and the Shadow Cabinet.
- *The rules* Play the sequence and ask students to work out the rules, e.g. for Prime Minister's Question Time the Prime Minister starts with an outline of what he has done that day and questions are supposed to be in response to this; questions can be pre-scheduled but seldom are; the Speaker allocates the floor and keeps order; speakers must refer to other MPs as 'My honourable friend' or 'My Right Honourable Friend'; responses are booing, groaning, shouting (but not clapping), etc.

Looking at the techniques
Students:
- say what they're talking about
- identify any good points that are made
- say who's winning and which speakers are strongest (**Fights**)
- find examples of rhetorical techniques (**Rhetoric, Purrs and slurs**)
- compare speaker styles (**Describing speech style**)
- give their own opinions if they wish

Interviews and talk shows

Answers 127 Awkward answers 128 Body language 131
Celebrity interview 137 Character network 139
Choose your words 142 Describing real interaction 154
Describing speech style 155 Famous people 162

Face to face, in a pool of light, round a table or in after-dinner chairs, people chat, swap stories, fence or battle it out in interviews and talk shows, the most verbal events on TV.

Talk shows have many forms: one guest or several; games, songs, sketches as well as talk; home or studio settings; studio audience or none; theme-based or people-based; serious discussion or 'cat fight'; light or heavy, sensational or soothing. The only constants are the well-known host, the invited guests and the live unscripted conversation. Examples are Oprah Winfrey, now a major industry in the USA, Parkinson, who has returned to the UK, and programmes which start the day, like *Good Morning, Australia!*

Interviews also have various agendas: to provide expert opinions, political soap boxes, informal trials, opportunities for self-justification, sympathetic biographies or just photo opportunities for media personalities. Examples are press conferences, interviews with celebrities, or encounters on CNN's *Larry King Live* or BBC World's *Hardtalk* (transcripts from the channel websites). There are also fictitious media interviews in films (e.g. *Godzilla, You've Got Mail, Accidental Hero*), parodies of celebrity interviews in comedy programmes, and many satirical skits of political interviews (for high clarity and hilarity I personally recommend the BBC's *The Long Johns*).

What have they got to offer?

What these shows have in common is also what makes them good for language learning:
- *They are topical and aim to catch popular attention* They focus on three high-interest areas: people (*Tell us about yourself*), issues (*What do you think about that?*) and important events (*What happened? What was it like?*) (**Famous people, Issues, Interview**).

Some are good for a wide audience, e.g. whether Madonna is more conservative than her image.

- *They put people under a spotlight* Character, attitudes and feelings are on display (**Make a case for character**); people's enthusiasm, fury, affectations rouse our responses and there are some vivid personality contrasts Faces and expressions are in high focus; appearance, clothing, accent and speech style illuminate personalities and interactions (**Body language, Describing speech style, Fashion parade, Loves and hates, Reaction shots, Voice 2**).
- *They focus on talk* Exchanges range from sympathetic chat and discreet probing through spirited argument to hostile grilling so there is plenty to react to and describe (**Answers, Fights, Floor, Purrs and slurs, Question types, Speech acts, What's going on?**). Language study can deal with ways of giving opinions, agreeing, disagreeing, qualifying, hedging, etc. and many of the features of spontaneous unplanned talk (**Holophrases, Interactive language**).
- *They are based on question and answer* The simple exchange of information can take many forms: questions can be roundabout, loaded, or straight, and answers can be evasive, indignant, or vague (**Answers, Purrs and slurs, Questions, Question types**). This makes for interesting work on literal and interpersonal meaning, while the questions provide a skeleton for anticipating or recapping content (**Summary**).
- *They play to the audience* The audience is part of the show, the third party, and knows that its opinion counts. Even if there is no studio audience, host and guests take time to tell each other things they already know, to keep the audience in the picture (*Now you've often said the next film is your last – is this actually true?*). The guests are talking to the public as well as to each other; the host asks questions on the audience's behalf as well as his/her own. So it is natural for viewers to express their feelings about the subject and react to the people (**Letters to the editor, Loves and hates**). By the same token, viewers are captivated by the roles of questioner and questioned and want to enter the arena themselves. Luckily the shows are highly imitatable: formats are easy to set up and a lot can be learnt by looking at models (**Celebrity interview, Interview, Problem, Talk show**).

Difficulty and divisibility

How difficult are these programmes? Long stretches of non-stop talk with only faces for visual support make for quite heavy viewing. Programmes with intellectual pretensions are particularly hard work:

they pack in more information, have longer more complex sentences, fewer pauses, more metaphors and more showing off. Less highbrow programmes are often easier, especially if there's a studio audience which also has to hear and understand. The guests are on display, so the articulation is good and the accents shift towards standard. There's a clear view of mouth, gesture and facial expression; the turns are well controlled; the pace is not too fast; and the topics are clearly stated and generally have to do with everyday experience.

Moreover, all these programmes are manageable. They don't generally have tight overall coherence and there is no special reason to view them whole – they segment easily and can be used in bits. Interviews generally divide clearly into topic sequences of three or four questions, each led by a 'main question' (more if the interviewer is taking the guest through a story, or insisting on an answer). Talk shows also divide up by topic and may break to introduce a new guest or have a game, a song or a commercial break. Hosts are expert at fitting into these frames, and the pauses may well improve the programme by allowing the talkers to draw breath.

This allows many different approaches. It is easy to use salami tactics (see page 19) and view piece by piece, or present the show as an illustrated talk, showing the simpler bits and narrating the rest; you can do the beginning of the show as a taster, or only one interesting part, e.g. good discussions were stimulated by extracts where an Indian writer talked about arranged marriages (*Hardtalk*), four Americans discussed whether they work harder than Europeans (*Greenfield at Large*), and Dennis Tito talked about being weightless in space (*Now, Dennis, what is it like to float around?*). **Issues**, **Picture it**, **Trigger** are all useful.

How do you use them?

If possible, offer students a choice, or do a quick check to find what appeals. Decide the amount students can cope with, what approach you're going to take, and select excerpts if necessary. If you are doing a whole show, do a lead-in, break for first impressions, then view the rest, review overall content, and focus on a few short sequences. If you are doing parts, select freely from the following techniques.

Lead-in

Ways of leading in are:

- *Pooling knowledge* For interviews with (and about) well-known people, get students to put together all they know about them (**Famous people**). For important events, explore the background

(**Character network** or **Maps and journeys** may help). With issues, identify the central questions and get students to take up personal positions (**Issues**). In all cases, do preliminary work on recognizing proper names.

- *Anticipating questions and answers* Ask what *main* questions students would ask if they were hosts, and write them up. Or write up the first three 'main questions' that are actually asked, get students to suggest short answers (**Answers**) and (if appropriate) say how they would answer themselves.

- *Sneak preview* (teach *looks/sounds, looks like/sounds like, looks as if/sounds as if* as a preliminary):
  - With well-known or representative guests (e.g. a film star, a bishop), start with a brief clip of the voice only (**Voice 2**); students guess who or what they are, and where they're from.
  - For guests with strong visible personalities, choose a revealing brief sequence, play it without sound, freeze on the person (blow up the image if it's a DVD), get descriptions of dress and appearance and speculate on character (**Fashion parade, Make a case for character**).
  - If there are strong visible interactions, view them speeded up and speculate on what's going on between the people; if there are any striking reactions view them slowed down, without sound (**Body language, Reaction shots**) and speculate on what they show and what caused them.

Break, recap, preparation

After about 10 minutes, make a break and get reactions to one of these questions:

- How do they feel about the participants' personalities, attitudes, opinions, appearance or speech? (**Describing speech style, Fashion parade, Loves and hates, Make a case for character**). Ask for illustrations and replay any moments mentioned.
- What are the relationships between the participants: friendly, flattering, challenging, hostile? Again, re-view any significant moments.
- What new information is there on people/issues/events?
- What main questions have been asked, and what answers have been given? Clarify with **Answers** or **Jumbled statements** Variation.

Prepare for the next part:
- Ask students what questions they themselves would ask next.
- (For talk shows) Anticipate with some upcoming utterances (**Speculations** Variation 3).

- Give the forthcoming questions or topics (**Labelling and linking**), discuss answers (**Answers**) and speculate on what will be said.
- Suggest that groups adopt one participant each and concentrate on the new information, and reactions and interactions.

View on, making further breaks as necessary.

Review

After viewing, review the content. A quick recap for any topic is **Quotes**. Or do a rerun of the show to see how much everyone has grasped: get students to identify the main questions (**Labelling and linking**) (or give them out) and use them as a framework to talk it through (**Summary**), re-viewing if there is disagreement. Round off with an activity which relates to the type of programme:

- For personalities, recap the information about their lives (**Character network, Turning points, Why and How?**), discuss how they come across (**Loves and hates, Make a case for character**) or what they have in common with us (**Other people's shoes**).
- If an event is the centre of interest, look at how it affected the person (**Other people's shoes**) and discuss its causes (**Why and How?**), its significance and the questions it raises (**Pick of the news**).
- For issues, we are interested in how our opinions compare with those of the participants (**Issues**). With controversial topics, the trick is to avoid a 'slanging match' – sometimes students need practice in separating people from opinions and acknowledging the importance of evidence.

Close focus

Ask students to select one or two short sequences from the whole. Do intensive comprehension work on them and use them for what they're good for: take strong opinions apart inch by inch to see who agrees, ask students to reply to a speaker as if they were there, recall similar experiences (**Trigger**). For language study, look at patterns of verbs (**Tenses, Situation report**), at **Interactive language** and reduced words/morphemes (**Wordhunt**) and get students to collect expressions they could adopt themselves (**Choose your words**). If reaction and interaction are particularly interesting, analyse and describe them with **Answers, Awkward answers, Body language, Character network, Fights, Floor, Purrs and slurs, Reaction shots, Speech acts** or **What's going on?** It may be fun to describe the whole show in terms of what happens between the participants, selecting one sequence for close focus (**Describing real interaction**).

Sometimes participants break the rules spectacularly by bragging, breaking down or being drunk, and some talk shows rejoice in this kind of mayhem; but the real skill is to wield the words: to woo, needle, tell a story, hedge with aplomb. Seize opportunities for describing what people do when they talk: losing one's temper, rising to the bait, getting off the point, exaggerating, prevaricating. And keep your own ears open for specific functional language (**Holophrases**).

Independent work

If you have a number of high-interest interviews and talk shows and facilities for independent work, get students to evaluate programmes and report on them for others (**Grading, Preview**). Any interview or talk show can be viewed with **Describing real interaction**. For celebrity interviews use the questions in Box 21 – the work can be done individually or in groups, and delivered in writing or as a class presentation.

BOX 21   Celebrity interview
Instructions for students
1 Find out something about the celebrity before you view: ask around, or look on the Internet (**Famous people**). Then view as much as you want of the show, and answer these questions:
   - What do you learn about his/her life?
   - Does he/she reveal any important opinions/attitudes? Do you agree with them?
   - Are there any surprises?
   - Appearance – what does he/she look like? What do clothes say about him/her?
   - What's your impression of his/her personality? Do you like him/her? Why/Why not?
   - Select the three most interesting moments, describe them and say what they reveal.
   - Say something about the difficulty of the programme and whether you recommend viewing.

2 Write up your comments, and/or prepare to present them in class, with two or three extracts from the video.

Extra options: If you are inspired, write an article about the person (**Interview article**) or use material from the interview to prepare a scene for a biographical film (**Gossip**).

Follow-up

Letters expressing opinions (**Letters to the editor**) follow naturally from these programmes, but the most enjoyable follow-up is do-it-yourself (DIY) talk shows and interviews. Students are generally happy to ask and answer questions about their involvement in important events (imagined or real) (**Interview**), their practical problems (**Problem**), their own lives (**Celebrity interview, Interview article**) and topical issues (**Talk show**). They usually have TV role models in mind – often models unknown to their teachers!

With these activities, a lot of learning is achieved not just during and after, but *before*, in preparing personal contributions and looking at models. There are specific suggestions for model study and preparation in the four DIY interview activities (**Interview, Celebrity interview, Problem** and **Talk show**). Before launching into their own shows, learners can view sample programmes to look at:

- Major moves (e.g. welcoming, introducing, signing off).
- Main questions and follow-up questions. Professional interviewers 'follow up' to clarify, get details, develop the story. This is not a high-level art but learners need the confidence to do it. They should practise spotting main questions (**Labelling and linking**), observe follow-up in action and discuss how they would handle it themselves (**Answers**).
- Different ways of asking and answering questions, both the forms (**Questions**) and the functions (**Answers, Question types**). If you have good examples of evasive answers, it's fun to practise 'wriggling off the hook' (**Awkward questions**).
- Ways of expressing opinion, agreement and disagreement. Not many expressions are needed to carry people through a discussion, and you can go a long way with *I think, In my opinion* and *What about ...?* But it's important to know (for example) that *agree* is a verb, not an adjective, that the usual negative of *I think* is *I don't think* (not *I think ... not*), that *I wonder* is a useful formula and *maybe* a good softener. Get students to observe how people express these functions, or work on specific language with **Holophrases**.
- Tense patterns. Look for the set of tenses for **Situation report**, and the narrative tenses in anecdotes and accounts of major events.
- Supportive listening. Many don't realize the importance of audience support and the huge value of nodding, smiling and making encouraging noises. Get students to collect expressions of interest and practise giving audible/visible attention.
- The preparation that goes into the show on both sides (e.g. selecting topics, thinking of questions, pre-interviewing, recalling anecdotes, gathering information). Looking at this will help students with their

own preparation and help them realize that it's the combination of planning and spontaneity that makes these shows work.

Be careful about the activity format. It has to involve everyone, maintain interest, ensure learning and create a satisfying product. A good way in is to have the class interview the teacher, then move other class members into the hot seat, letting the rest of the class share the role of interviewer. For small classes, one-to-one interviews in front of the class are fine: have one 'interview spot' a week and give it a good build-up. With bigger classes, split them into three at interview time, and circulate round the groups, or sit in on one and get reports on the others; or get small groups of three or four to interview each other one by one. If there are recording facilities, students can film their interviews for homework and play excerpts in class. Or they can interview each other by letter or e-mail (as in **Problem**). The same options apply to talk shows, but these are easier to manage because they absorb more people and the class can participate as a studio audience (see **Talk show**).

Sports programmes

Body language 131   Enigmas 159   Experts 160   Feeling flow 165
Fights 167   I spy 177   Jumbled statements 185   Matching 196
Picture it 209   Place and period 211   Racing 225
Situation report 240   Sports highlights 246   Sports quiz 246
What's going on? 266

In any language class, many people are interested in some sport, a few are interested in all sport and some are not interested in sport at all, and there is a high degree of mutual incomprehension between them. Teachers too are people with interests and preferences (a fact often forgotten). 'My students would love to talk about Formula One,' said one, 'but I *hate* motor-racing.' Because of these partial passions there's a limit on how much TV sport we can use. It's also hard to profit from one of the most motivating aspects of sport, its immediacy: live events are seldom an option – too long, wrong day, wrong time, many students aren't interested. Sports news too is not very usable in itself: it generally covers too much too fast, and relies heavily on inside knowledge and interest. Then there are a lot of language activities few teachers would want to do, e.g. full comprehension of long TV commentaries or news-paper reports, which can be quite arcane. Writing about sport is also not much in demand, although one does occasionally find a budding sports writer in class.

But there is still great scope for using sports TV. Sport excites great passion, is a metaphor for a lot of life, has a huge world role, develops great knowledge and expertise and sparks passionate and informed debate. The TV resources are abundant. Many games and races divide up neatly into watchable segments; matches also have very usable slow-motion replays (or you can do your own). The sports news provides edited game highlights, discussions and interviews. There are plenty of commercial videos (e.g. about the history of Ipswich football club, the 1960 Olympics in Rome, 100 years of Wimbledon). TV sports language ranges from almost wordless interviews to fevered machine-gun commentary and special ornate sports reporting. A lot of sports have a man-of-the-people image – this makes regional accents and colloqui-alisms almost obligatory in English national programmes, but there is more standard language on American TV and world channels. More-over, most of the meaning is in the pictures, so we can also use TV sports in any language with the sound turned down.

Talking about sport

Thus, there are huge resources, but what can we do with them? For most people, when they're not playing it or watching it, sport is a *talking job* – they want to talk about their passions and understand other lay enthu-siasts talking about theirs. Language-wise, this is not a rarefied activity. Much sports vocabulary is generalizable to other walks of life (e.g. *rules, points, fans, goals, cheering, tyres, bats, boots, trainers, supporters, race, competition, records, drug tests, sponsors, speed, catch up, overtake, give up, win, lose,* etc.); there is a world of sporting metaphor (e.g. *an own goal, a level playing field, no holds barred*); and the functions are the same: explaining, describing, asking, answering, narrating, evaluating, commenting and predicting are the name of the game (so to speak).

In this perspective, the great value of sport film is that it helps people to talk about things they know and care about. It illustrates brilliantly, it adds reality and it conveys excitement with powerful images. These powers can be harnessed for general work (see the next section), but the job of talking about sport is best handed over to the student experts, who have the interest, the knowledge, and probably the equipment and clothing in a cupboard at home (see page 93). An advantage is the built-in information gap since many people in the class don't know what the 'experts' do know. By the same token, of course, you have to judge carefully the amount of sporting life the class as a whole can tolerate. One possibility is to make sport just one of the options in a programme of student-led activities (group presentations, demonstrations, etc.). Another is to promote independent work (see page 95).

Sports for all

When sport or leisure come up in the syllabus, here are some ways to supplement the coursebook:

- *General sports vocabulary* Use the nicely edited 'match highlights' (one- to two-minute summaries) on the sports news to pull out general sports vocabulary (**Sports highlights**). For a quick naming exercise, show the montages which lead into sports programmes: get students to list the sports, their locations and their main equipment in three columns and find the appropriate verbs (*do, play, run,* etc.). Alternatively students guess the sport from mystery shots (**Enigmas**). In guessing games push students to say *how* they know – it pulls out the vocabulary as well as exercising the brain!

- *For specific sports*, discuss what you expect to see before viewing (**Picture it**) (e.g. a ring, umpires, boxing gloves, ropes, hitting) and then view. This can be joyfully varied if you have any good sports parodies, such as the Monty Python philosophers' football match or the Queen Victoria race (a dozen Queen Victorias hurtling along Aintree race track). Pick up sports metaphors (e.g. *no holds barred, pass the baton*) when you come across them in other texts.

- *Racing language* Squeeze in some extra time to talk about racing, since it is a metaphor for business, jobhunting, elections, schoolwork and (for some) most of life. All forms of racing (e.g. sculling, swimming, Formula One, sprinting, hurdling, horse racing) have a common vocabulary and students at all levels can build this up with video sequences (**Racing**) – most races (except marathons and cross-country skiing) fall easily into a lesson schedule. For extra participation and partisanship place bets on the results, 'adopt' competitors or wave flags.

- *Basic action vocabulary*, e.g. *catch, run, pass, kick, hit, throw,* can be taught first and then identified by students in video sequences (**I spy**, Variation 2, **Jumbled statements, Matching**). Or vary the activity **Body language** by asking students to note down (in any language) the actions they see as they view, then act them out for the class to name; follow up with the game *Simple Simon Says*. Give some special attention to behaviour at moments of great rejoicing (**Picture it, Variation 4**) – this is also a good way to lead in to a sports project.

- *Comment* If you deal with a single sports sequence in some detail, you can follow up by simulating brief follow-up interviews with players, managers, etc. Tell students who is going to be interviewed, ask them to think of three questions they would ask (or give the actual questions), role play the interview, then view the real one.

Experts

Before calling on students as 'sports experts', get them to indicate their interests on a form (see Box 22 for an example).

BOX 22   Sport and you

NAME ....

Sport	Watch	Do/Play	Interest (1 to 3)
Football	✓		2
Cycling	✓	✓	3
Basketball		✓	1
(etc.)			

Fill in your own form on the board and invite questions and comments, then get students to fill in their forms, talk them through in groups and report back (collect the forms afterwards). This will show them who shares their interests and will help you to match interests with video resources and to organize the work. If you find you have a good collection of 'experts' in the class, divide them into 'expert teams', one for each sport. Below are some ways they can share their expertise – the choice will depend on the class's interests and talents, the time available, and how many sports you want to cover.

The 'knowledge'

Establish basic knowledge about the various sports with **Sports quiz**, a series of structured question and answer sessions run by students, adaptable to most levels.

Illustrated talk

Ask expert teams to prepare one of the talks below, illustrating it with video clips, objects, pictures and diagrams, and answering questions from the class. They should introduce their talk with ten items of essential vocabulary and use an appropriate array of tenses. Give a time limit.

- Show a recent video sequence of the sport and put it into its overall game context (**Experts**).
- Explain the main rules, strategies, techniques and equipment of the sport (**Experts**).

- Outline the competition structure and categories, say where we are in the championships and who's big at the moment (**Situation report**).
- Tell a little about the history of the game and how it's changed – addicts may have access to old footage on sports videos (**Place and period**, archive footage) (N.B. Tell speakers to focus on what they personally know and not to deliver a full history, memorized, translated or copied).
- Present a technical point (**Experts**, Variation 1) – this is quicker and slicker than the previous activities and allows everyone to have their say in a fairly short time.

Unplanned question and answer

Give the expert team an appropriate sports sequence beforehand, so they can understand it and anticipate questions (or put the experts on the spot with previously unseen footage). The class view the sequence and ask questions which the experts answer to the best of their ability. Urge the class also to ask questions about the reactions (verbal or non-verbal) of the commentators or the audience (**Matching** Variation 3) – or ask them yourself.

Live events

When an important event is coming up, get experts to provide (with the consent of the class as a whole), a blow-by-blow commentary in phases:

Before the event

- a picture of the tournament structure and how it stands at the moment (**Situation report**)
- a discussion of the odds (as in **Fights A**)

After the event

- a summary report of the match, illustrated with video highlights, as in **Fights B** – if necessary, students can use clips in other languages, turning the sound down and substituting their own comments
- simulated post-mortem interviews OR comments on the press write-ups

Follow-up

For follow-up to the preceding activities students can:

- produce written versions of any of the illustrated talks
- compile mini-dictionaries with the terms from their own sport
- expand the contents of the form they completed to write about *Me and sport*

- describe a sporting event they attended, focusing on the setting, the feelings, the spectators or the game itself
- predict the outcome of the current league table and give their reasons
- study a long match and try their hand at producing the script for a 'match highlights' news item, indicating alongside what clips they would illustrate it with
- read and comment on sports reports after viewing the event

But be careful to give alternative activities for students who hate sport in all forms!

Independent work

For independent work with sports video, limit the verbal comprehension and the production and give quite a lot of attention to vocabulary building, as in Box 23.

BOX 23   Independent work with sports video
Instructions for students

1 Choose a sports event you'd like to watch. Write a few words to say why you've chosen it: because it's interesting and significant? out of curiosity? because you're a fan?
2 View the event.
3 Chart the emotional impact of the event as it develops (**Feeling flow**).
4 Collect vocabulary. Choose a part you'd like to see again, view and collect some useful vocabulary from what you *hear* (don't try to understand all the commentary). Classify the vocabulary in three columns, under *actions, people* and *things*.
5 View again and find words for important actions, people and things you *saw*. Add to your lists.
6 Significant moments. Pick out three significant or exciting moments from the event (e.g. *Coulthard overtaking Schumacher on the last lap*) and describe them briefly in writing.
7 Choose the most significant sequence and describe the action in detail (use the present tense), saying what happens and why it is important or interesting (**What's going on?**).

Game shows

Rules 230   Situation report 240   Speech acts 244

Game shows are TV quizzes and competitions. They can be slow-minded, sharp, tough, funny, greedy or satirical; the contestants may be celebrities or ordinary people. The pleasure in watching them comes variously from trying to work out the answers, rooting for one of the sides, admiring other people's cleverness or laughing at their antics, getting excited (or jealous) about the prizes and (most recently) from seeing naked self-interest at work in no-holds-barred competitions like *The Weakest Link*. Some long-running game shows are remembered with affection (*Mastermind, Charades, Jeux sans Frontières, Twenty Questions, Double Your Money, Whose Line is it Anyway?, Who wants to be a millionaire?*), but not many last long. They depend a lot on the personalities and the game structure: the best are simple, dramatic, witty and full of surprises. Many are easy to understand, as the rules become evident quite quickly, the essential language is clear and repeated, and the general formats are internationally recognized. However, the performances are geared to national tastes and students don't often choose to watch them independently. But they have their uses. You can:

- adopt the games and use them in class
- watch and participate
- video the whole show
- do language study
- make up your own game show

Adopt the games

You can add some games to your teaching repertoire either without using the original TV show or using it as a model. A few examples are given in Box 24. Games on students' own national TV have the advantage that everyone from that country knows how to play: in mixed-nationality classes one national group can teach the others their national TV games. (N.B. Be careful that the game *does* involve language, and not just mime or physical activity!)

Participate

Even boring shows can be fun if viewers have a stake in them. Use a show which is within your students' comprehension and do only a few rounds in case interest flags. View the first round to work out the rules (for appropriate language see **Rules**) then ask students to declare loyalties (*I* *want x to win because ...*). In successive rounds, pause the tape in appropriate places so that students can guess answers, suggest advice for contestants, calculate the score and sum up the situation (**Situation report**).

Run your own show

Use the show as inspiration for activities students can do in class. View a few rounds, work out the rules (**Rules**) and play the game. If you want to rerun the entire show (e.g. to challenge another class), ask students to note the main moves and the appropriate language (welcoming the audience, introducing the contestants, explaining the rules, leading in to the first round, announcing the score at the end of each round). Get the class to appoint a questionmaster.

Language work

Games vocabulary is widespread and useful: add five minutes to any viewing of a game show to focus on the language used and the language needed for talking about it. In particular, look at:

- expressions with *get* and *have*, e.g. *get it right/wrong, get the right answer, get a point; have a go, have a shot at it, have a try, have a break*
- expressions with *go, turn, lead* and *worth*, e.g. *have another go, it's your go/turn, in the lead, take the lead, worth three points, not worth it*
- question forms in quiz games (**Questions**), in particular, questions with *What* and *Which*

Get students to describe the game (**Rules**). Review speech-act vocabulary with **Speech acts** (e.g. *whisper, hesitate, explain, ask, exclaim, swear, consult,* etc.) or focus minutely on contestants' behaviour when they are working on answering a question, doing a slow-motion replay if possible (**Body language**).

Make up your own

Any kind of quiz can be a model for your own class. The students should invent the quiz, but give them examples to establish that the questions must be clear, answerable, not too easy or difficult, and grammatically correct (none of these can be taken for granted), and check them before they are used. More elaborate but also more fun is to use puzzle video clips, another staple of quiz shows. Just three or four clips on a theme, selected by students, will do. The whole class can answer, or a team of class 'experts' on film, literature, sport or politics can volunteer for trial by their peers. Stipulate that the exercise should involve language, either in the clip or in the words which introduce it. A few possibilities for 'clip quizzes' are:

- 'Quotations' from news items: Who is this? What is he/she talking about?
- Very short film clips: What's the name of the film?
- Shots of parts of famous people – hands, back of neck, hair (or voice only) – Who's the star?
- Moments in literature: What's the book and who's the writer?
- Famous places from documentaries: Where is this?

BOX 24   Games from game shows

1 **Numbers** Students select six numbers under 20, then are given a large number and have 30 seconds to work out how to make up the big number from the others by multiplying, adding, subtracting, etc. Good for the language of arithmetic. (*Countdown*)

2 **Props** Teams are each given a large object with no apparent function (e.g. a large flat cone-shaped basket, a big square of card with a round hole in it); they have ten minutes to think of what it could be and then act out mini-scenes using the object, e.g. the basket becomes a Chinese hat, a small pond, a cauldron, Snow White's mirror, a satellite receiver. Good for idiomatic language. (*Whose Line is it Anyway?*)

3 **Crosswords** Students are given a mini-crossword of six numbered words: a team picks a number, is given a clue and has ten seconds to work it out. The next team picks a number and so on. These simple crosswords are extremely easy to invent – get students to prepare them, but vet the clues and spelling before they are used. (*Crosswits*)

---

2   Short sequences and promotions

Non-fiction clips

(Many of the activities outlined in *Drama clips*, page 46, can also be
used with non-fiction clips.)

'Non-fiction clip' here means any short sequence which is not scripted
drama: it could be a sequence from a documentary, interview or talk
show, part of a news item or ad, a programme trailer. Other short
promotional sequences are music videos, which although not dealt with
in this book, can lend themselves to successful exploit-ation in the
language classroom.

Many ideas for using drama clips apply just as well to non-fiction
clips, so when you find a good sequence, consult the drama section first
(see *Drama clips*, page 46). There is also little to choose between drama
clips and non-fiction clips for highlighting and generating particular
structures, pronunciation, specific vocabulary and prepositions,
although some kinds of non-fiction sequence have particular strengths,
e.g. some sports shots lend themselves well to speculating about what
has happened or *is about to* happen (**Enigmas**); archive material in documentaries gives good opportunities for comparing past and present
(**Place and period**); and many ads highlight particular structures or
vocabulary neatly (*Promise you'll call me! – I will. I promise.*).

But some kinds of sequence, typical of non-fiction programmes, have
their own special values and uses:

- *Images*
  - pictures of real people, places and things
  - thematic sequences
  - images of movement and feeling
  - enigmatic images
- *Words and pictures*
  - quotations and illustrations
- *Words*
  - live unscripted interactions
  - opinions and attitudes
  - narratives and other 'long turns' within conversations

Images

Real people, places and things

Programmes about real life constantly show people, places, things and events which are famous, typical or representative, e.g. the Grand Canyon, a German castle, a war crimes tribunal, the interior of the Houses of Parliament. To develop the ability to describe people and places, or to extend cultural or factual knowledge for a theme or project, build up expectations of what will be seen (**Picture it**): ask questions (e.g. *What is the Statue of Liberty standing on? What exactly is on its head? Does it light up at night?*) and get speculative answers, then play the clip and compare expectation with reality. It is particularly enjoyable if the image does not answer to the stereotype, e.g. the predicted tall, dignified, pin-striped, umbrella-carrying English peer on the news turns out to be tubby, purple-faced, balding and scruffy, and clutching a carrier bag.

This activity sharpens observation and creates enduring memories. It also makes a good basis for comparing one's own country's landmarks, landscapes or institutions (**Parallels**). For preparing to view famous people, offer pairs of adjectives, e.g. do they expect him/her to be *confident* or *nervous*? *relaxed* or *restless*? *loud* or *quiet*?, then view and discuss impressions of personality. Or use a snatch of the voice (sound only) (**Voice 2**) so students can guess the identity, and then view. For elementary students, write up a few words said by the person and let them speculate who it is before viewing.

If students have access to video resources, they can choose their own famous-place-or-person clip and run their own *Twenty Questions* game; or write a short physical description, and read it out to the class for them to guess; or show mystery shots of well-known people (**Body parts,** Variation 2) – in all these cases the clip provides the final 'right answer'.

Warn them not to: give the game away too soon; choose adored nonentities or favourite places that no one else will know; simply reproduce existing reference material in their descriptions. Model the activity before students do it.

A simple stimulus for writing a story is to provide a setting, some characters and an event on separate clips (a castle, two small bright green frogs on a lily pad, a bolt of lightning), discuss possible developments and hand over the story to the students. Such ingredients can also be worked into more extensive film scenarios (**Plot idea 2**).

Thematic sequences

Some programme trailers and lead-ins, ads, documentaries and news items have compelling sequences of images built around a theme, with music and sound effects. A collage of sports shots introduces the sports news, scenes of street violence punctuate a rap music video. These can be used to practise noun-phrase participle structures and specific vocabulary, or as a prompt for creative writing (**Themes**).

Movement and feeling

Game shows are excellent for illustrating small physical expressions, e.g. defeat (hands spreading wide), nervousness (fingers twisting), thought (head and chin rubbing), triumph (thumbs up). Use these (speeded up, slowed down, frozen or magnified) for the language of body movement (**Body language**) or for reaction adjectives (**Reaction shots**). Sports programmes have more extreme gestures and expressions, often breathtaking – we see the ball go straight through the goalie's arms and legs, fans behind the goal cover their faces with their hands, the goalie looks round in disbelief, the trainer's mouth falls open and the scoring side goes wild with joy – all in ten seconds. Vivid sequences like these can inspire a mini-write, focusing on movements and emotions (**Reaction shots** Variation); again, slow-motion replays, freeze-framing (and zooms on DVDs) help a lot.

Enigmatic images

Documentaries rejoice in shots which arouse curiosity. A wildlife programme begins silently with a slow-motion shot of a large bird leaping vertically from the long grass – again and again. The idea is to catch and puzzle the eye first and then satisfy the mind. Graphics also have this effect – we start to puzzle them out before we hear them explained. Other vivid shots from live events (e.g. sport) become enigmatic if we isolate them from context or commentary (**Enigmas**). This gives us a great store of intriguing visual puzzles, some with only one possible interpretation, others with many. They can be used simply to stimulate discussion – speculating about the meaning starts the brain turning on any chosen subject (e.g. genetic engineering, pets). If the commentary is easy enough, turn it into a comprehension exercise: viewing without sound, speculating, then turning the sound up. If possible, discuss the puzzle in class and give the video as comprehension homework to groups or individuals. Or ask students to write an appropriate voice-over (**Commentary/Copywriter**) – realistic or fantastic – and to try it out on the clip before they hear the original.

Words and pictures

Quotations and illustrations

Documentaries and news items are splendid examples of 'illustrated discourse'. The news headline is supported by direct quotations from the people concerned; the commentator's spoken point is directly illustrated by what the viewer sees on the screen. This link between words and images can be a great help with improving students' writing, since writers at all levels have to learn to illustrate. Whether it is an elementary EFL composition, a Proficiency essay or an academic dissertation, there are rarely enough examples, details, quotations or concrete evidence, and this leaves the writing foggy and unconvincing. Use video clips to introduce the idea (**Quoting and illustrating**) and then transfer the practice to written work.

Words

Live unscripted interaction

Some documentaries have 'scenes' of spontaneous unscripted interaction – more casual, unplanned and informal than interviews or chat shows (see Box 25 for an example). They are often hard to understand because of voice overlap and movement, but they are real language, real interaction and do inspire the desire to understand, especially if they are well-edited and the speakers are well known or interesting. Any course which gives high priority to natural talk can use them for comprehension, study and extension just like drama clips (see page 46), looking for speech acts, interactive language, pronunciation features, and building up to describing the interaction with **What's going on?**

BOX 25   Who gets the bathroom?

A brother and sister argue about who should have the bedroom with the ensuite bathroom. 'I bag it,' says the girl. 'Girls need privacy, it's a *girly* bedroom.' 'Who says a girl needs a bathroom more than a boy?' says the boy. 'It's a myth, you know it is.' They toss for it. 'It fell heads! I won!' says the girl.

Opinions and attitudes

Often pithily expressed, these turn up everywhere: in news quotations, documentaries, interviews, talk shows. It's worth building up a collection of provocative statements, e.g. a politician proclaiming that prison works (news), a judge deciding for the natural mother over the adoptive parents (documentary). For opening up classroom debate (**Issues**), they are most useful if they can be lifted easily out of context, to avoid a lot of explaining. Examples of discussions which can easily be enlivened with video opinions are old favourites like: *Should smoking in public places be banned? Is capital punishment immoral?* One can also often find material closer to home: I have useful clips on whether Shakespeare (or any other national literature) should be taught in school, whether parents should be allowed to slap their children and how to stop dogs fouling parks and pavements. If you have time and a camcorder, round off your debate with a **Voxpop** opinion sequence – the prospect of being filmed focuses both mind and grammar wonderfully!

Many short interview 'quotations' in documentaries or news reports are selected specifically because they express very clear single attitudes or feelings, e.g. enthusiasm (for a project), scepticism (about a new policy), retrospective terror (about a near-death experience). Build up a collection of these and use them for verbal comprehension and for identifying feelings (**Reaction shots**). Gather clips from discussions, interviews and chat shows with expressions of opinion, agreement and disagreement (**Holophrases**) and turn-taking language (**Floor**) and look at them before or during class discussions.

Narratives and other long turns

Anecdotes, reminiscences, explanations – little stories about personal experience – are part of everyone's repertoire and you'll find them in many genres, including news, documentaries, interviews, consumer shows, chat shows (see Box 26 for an example). They are fairly self-contained, structured, often easy to understand, spontaneous (but also rehearsed by time), and usually have some special 'point'.

For comprehension you may need some scene-setting or background information or a vocabulary skeleton; narrative anecdotes lend themselves to various forms of visualization (enactment, drawing, model-making, walkthrough, rearranging objects) and are often short enough to be written down (**Transcript**).

BOX 26   An anecdote

Dai Jones remembers an unwelcome visitor

The CID came to my house – I wasn't home – and rang the doorbell. My elderly mother – a wonderful woman – came to the door and they said 'Mrs Jones?' 'Yes?' 'We're here about Dai Jones.' 'Yes? And who are you?' They took out the card and showed it to her. 'CID!' Well, Mum did something which I wouldn't have thought a gentle little elderly lady would do – she slammed the door in their faces!

Many personal narratives make excellent models and stimuli for recounting similar personal experiences (**Trigger**): most people have a story of an unexpected visitor, a clash with authority, a great local event, a revelatory experience of music/literature/film/art, a difficult decision about one's career. After viewing, discuss what details make the account particular and interesting – capping others' anecdotes not only prods the memory but seems to draw out detail and increase the particularity in students' accounts. Sometimes an outline is enough to stimulate the imagination: e.g.:

> *You work for a big film mogul, very powerful and wealthy. One day he invites you to his house, shows you round his estate and shows you a special private project of his own (nothing to do with films). You finally find out what he invited you for.*

In this case the original clip was played *after* students had imagined and produced their own anecdotes. (The film mogul was breeding chickens and wanted the narrator's advice!)

Tales of experiences which students are *unlikely* to have had (going to prison, seeing a train fall off a bridge, visiting Buckingham Palace) open up other possibilities because they are usually *not* what you would expect, e.g. it's interesting that what one witness remembers most about an urban explosion includes litres of milk running down the gutter, choking dust and a chorus of car alarms. In these cases, anticipate with **Picture it** to open up expectations with questions, e.g. *How do you think prison would affect you most psychologically? socially? physically? What would you miss most?*, before hearing the original story. Reminiscences on great events from people who were there can inspire convincing fantasies about other historical events (**Interview**).

If the story involves several people, there may well be other ways of looking at it, e.g. an encounter with the CID could very well be retold from the point of view of the CID agent. Set the scene, give the bones of the story, view, then get students to consider it from the other point of view (**Adopt a character**, Variation 2) and retell the episode. Filming the counterpoint anecdote is a nice extra.

There are other recognizable and imitatable 'long turns' which have the same potential uses as models and stimuli as anecdotes do, e.g. saying where you would like to live, describing a plan, demonstrating how to do something. Any interesting speech styles will also give good material for **Describing speech style** or the related exercises **Body language, Over the top, Purrs and slurs, Rhetoric, Tone up** and **Voice 1.**

TV commercials

Ad angles 124   Ad language 125   Adopt a character 125
Best image 130   Commentary/Copywriter 145   Describe an ad 152
Fly on the wall 170   Lipreading and mindreading 192   Matching 196
Over the top 207   Picture it 209   Purrs and slurs 221   Rhetoric 229
Situation report 240   Speculations 242   Speech acts 244
Stand by it 248   Voice 1 261   What's going on? 266

(Many of the activities in *Drama clips*, page 46, and *Non-fiction clips*, page 99, can also be used with TV commercials.)

Why use ads?

If you have access to English-language TV you probably see a lot of TV ads – 'commercials'. Don't switch off! They are wonderful material. Apart from being profusely available, they are short, vivid and highly crafted; they have shock, beauty, atmosphere, glamour, drama, comedy, all in the space of 15–30 seconds. They are generally easy to understand – they have to be. They are a playful genre with a vast repertoire of verbal tricks: wordplay, puns, catchphrases and slogans, jingles, hype, 'voice', rhyme, rhythm, accent – and these are matched by visual jokes, arresting images, artful logos and clever interplay of sight and sound. They are very high quality: more money is spent on one good TV commercial than on a whole language coursebook. As the 'pretty' part of globalization, they stand on international common ground, so they are easy to predict, imitate and parody. On the other hand, each country's TV advertising is culturally distinctive, so comparisons come naturally. All this gives TV ads great potential for general comprehension, for fun, for language study and as a stimulus for speaking and writing. At a wider educational level they are worth studying in themselves, just to expose their techniques.

How do ads work?

Showing, telling, playing

The techniques ads use will suggest a lot of the activities we can do with them. There are just a few basic sales pitches or techniques in TV commercials – most are illustrated in the examples in Box 29 on page 115. TV is particularly good at just *showing* the product or how effective it is, or the difference between haves and have-nots, or before and after ('I was a seven-stone weakling until ...'). It's also good at the old-fashioned 'client testimonial' where someone with high credibility *tells* us how good it is. Men in white coats have gone out of fashion but we have other pundits: glamorous professional women, famous sportsmen, green goblins, nice guys, even horses. This approach is constantly revamped, e.g. in the celebrated Creature Comforts ads, the testimonials were given by animated animals with real human voices; there are also *anti*-testimonials, e.g. from threatened bacteria who fear for their lives. If commentators do the telling, they have to establish their credentials quickly, so TV ads specialize in the rapid creation of attitude, mood and context through 'voice'. Another approach is to *play it out* so we can see how others are impressed by the product – this can be just a hint of a story or a complete mini-drama, with words or without. All these forms are the breath of life to TV and are parodied endlessly – indeed a lot of advertising is self-parodying and some of it works simply by pretending to be different from other ads.

Angles, associations, expectations

TV ads work as all advertisements do, by establishing an angle and making associations, but TV provides many more ways of doing it. The *angle* is a way of grabbing the attention: a new selling-point or a new way of selling, e.g. a joke, visual or verbal. TV ads can:

- arouse curiosity by not revealing the product until the very end (e.g. 6 in Box 29)
- parody media programmes and films (e.g. 1 and 2 in Box 29)
- use special voices: a reverent tone, the sound of a wildlife commentator, the commonsense voice of the man in the street, the menacing voice of organized crime, a scientist (e.g. 1, 2, 3, 4, 5 in Box 29)

- set up a special relationship with the viewer: intimate, persuasive, authoritative (e.g. 3, 4, 5 in Box 29)
- manipulate the relationship between sight and sound: it is easier to convince (or deceive) the eye than the ear and generally the sober reality is in the words and the fantasy in the pictures (e.g. 4 in Box 29); some 'bifocal' ads carry completely different messages in the words and pictures
- associate the product with the sort of people they assume the customer wants to be (e.g. 1, 6 in Box 29)
- link the product to atmosphere, physical or emotional satisfaction, professional or sexual success, beauty, a glamorous lifestyle (e.g. 1, 3, 4, 6 in Box 29)
- 'borrow a mission' from a fashionable cause, e.g. the environment
- use anything else which makes them memorable: jingles, slogans, animation, trick photography, special sound effects (e.g. 1, 2, 3, 4, 5, 6 in Box 29)

But ads still have to fulfil certain *expectations*, so many are highly predictable. For example, if the product is a washing powder, we are likely to see a washing machine, dirty clothes, clean clothes, possibly a housewife and a family. For cars there have to be high speeds, dirty weather, cornering and rough roads. For frozen fish we can expect sea, boats, fishermen, nets, live fish, cooked fish – though never, never just dead fish!

What are the issues?

Some burning questions come to mind when we enter the advertising world, e.g.:

- What are ads really selling? (or what is the customer buying?): chocolate bars or the right social group? washing machines or a clean environment? a car or a new personality?
- Do these sales pitches actually work? How many people admit to being influenced?
- Can advertising be honest? Does it matter? Should it be controlled by law?
- Is it possible to justify (in any terms) the amount of money spent on advertising?
- What is the future of a genre which jades the appetite it tries to stimulate?
- What is the value of a genre which devotes huge creativity to a single commercial purpose?

Language teaching should not ignore questions like these, which beg for discussion. They can be raised in any discussion on advertising, or just brought up when advertisements come into the classroom.

What kind of ads should we look for?

Generally, look for ads which are just very effective, attractive or funny, or have any of the following:

- connections with other classwork, e.g. airline ads for travel, household goods for discussing furniture or housework, programme trailers for talking about TV
- useful language in the words or in 'picture dictionary' images
- simple actions and interactions of normal life
- common everyday settings, e.g. homes, pubs
- particularly evocative sequences of images
- images which suggest the product without revealing it
- very different messages in the words and the pictures
- an effective punch line, slogan or catchphrase
- a clever angle or sales pitch for presenting the product
- wordplay of some kind
- different 'voices' or accents for special effect
- a special atmosphere
- highly conventional (and therefore predictable) formats
- really good parodies

Get students to help build up your collection. Include a few non-English ads: wordless ones can be used for description; ads with other-language text are good for scripting in English (see **Commentary/Copywriter**), or can be used with sound for translation, description and evaluation.

What can we do with ads?

- Use them initially for general interest or to supplement coursework – they don't take long. Do a lead-in, some comprehension activity and a language follow-up (see below).
- If your students are interested, do some advertising follow-up involving description and discussion and perhaps some independent work.
- For extra fun, create ads at any time and with any level.
- Finally, you may want to run a bigger project on advertising in general.

Use the guidelines below to help you.

Lead-ins, comprehension, language follow-up

Lead-ins

- Guessing the content. This works well with conventional ads. Tell students the product (e.g. antiseptic soap, shampoo) and ask them to list what they expect to see (encourage the structure *someone doing something*). This pulls out a lot of everyday vocabulary which can be checked off when viewing (**Picture it**). If the text is short and revealing, give the words as well as the product and ask students to predict the pictures. With very evocative words or 'voice', ask what mood the words suggest and get them to try out different voices (at different speeds) before viewing. Or play the sound only and speculate on the images.
- Guessing the product. Give some key words (e.g. *rinse, bounce, shining*), discuss their meaning and ask students to guess the product (**Ad language** Variation) before viewing. If the images are associated with the product, but not too obviously, play without sound as often as necessary, get a list of images and ask students to guess the product using the visual clues (this sometimes produces *could* and *might* but don't bet on it!). After guessing, students predict a few words they expect to hear, and finally view with sound. For ads which don't reveal the product until the end, pause before the end to discuss what the product might be (**Speculations**) – since many are extremely difficult to predict, the interesting element here is the reasoning.

Comprehension

Comprehension activities can focus on the words, the product information, the sales message, the relationship with the audience or generally on what happens:

- To catch the words, students do a gapfill or build up the whole text (**Transcript**), then check on meaning. With direct ads which mention things as they show them (e.g. mud, oil stains, rinse, pieces of polyester – see 3 in Box 29), give the 'matching' words beforehand and get students to infer meanings by close viewing (**Matching**).
- A simple summary can be done with conventional ads which tell or show clearly what the product is, has and does (e.g. *Delta Airlines IS comfortable and quiet; it HAS personal videos and laptop power supply; it GIVES personal service and it FLIES more passengers worldwide than any other airline*). Students 'shrink' the product information in this way, taking account of messages both seen and heard.

- Do a 'double summary' with 'bifocal' ads which deliver different messages in the words and pictures: students first listen without vision and summarize the message they hear, then view and summarize the message they see (this can be a revelation!).
- For the relationship with the viewer, give a set of speech verbs with a few distractors (e.g. *describing, making a claim, boasting, urging, recommending, hinting, suggesting, explaining*) (**Speech acts**), ask which the speaker(s) is/are doing, and what their own responses are.
- Retell the ad in some way: for dramatic ads, students take on different characters and tell the story from their point of view (**Adopt a character** Variation 2), or just recount the action (**Fly on the wall** or **What's going on?**); for other kinds of ads, get an account of the action which covers the main images, sounds and spoken messages. Use the sentence heads *We see ..., We hear ...* and *A voice tells us ...* in any appropriate order.

Language follow-up

For generating language, modelling language or studying language use, TV ads can be used in the same ways as clips, with the advantage that they can stand alone and don't have to be put back into context to make sense. Ads are very here-and-now; they seldom contain passives or past tenses or generate them in description, but they do have a characteristic range of tenses centred on the present (**Situation report**), they are rich in simple noun phrases, interactive language and positive adjectives, and the descriptive language they can generate is huge. Another advantage is that objects, settings, actions and language items are often beautifully framed and highlighted (e.g. oil stains, the seaside, washing one's face, the word *promise*), making TV ads powerful illustrators. Scan your ad collection for its value as a picture dictionary, for usable language and for its potential for generating language (e.g. discussing what makes an aeroplane comfortable or what you find in a kitchen). There are plenty of ideas for specific language work in the chapters on Drama clips and Non-fiction clips.

In addition, focus on the special language of advertising:

- *Catchphrases* Double meanings in slogans are common ('Delta Airlines – on top of the world', 'Woolworths is right up your street'). Students have to find the catchphrase (easy), write it down exactly (not so easy), and explain it in relation to the whole (quite tough – drives them to their dictionaries).
- *Wordplay* Tell students what to look for (**Rhetoric**), e.g. visual puns, tricks, jokes, songs, jingles, alliteration, rhymes. Discuss meanings and use dictionaries.

- *Product vocabulary* If the words describe the product (they often don't), students can classify the vocabulary under product, message and evaluation (**Ad language**).
- *Hype, loading and voice* A lot of rapturous adjectives will help to introduce the idea of advertising hype (= hyperbole) (**Over the top, Rhetoric**). Ads which describe the undesirable as well as the desirable ('No more fiddly bits of string! No more tatty pieces of brown paper! Use Paddibags for your parcels – fast, handy, clean') lead into the idea of vocabulary 'loading' (**Purrs and slurs**), especially if the feelings are visible in the pictures. Introduce the concept of voice (**Voice 1**) and discuss what the voice conveys.
- *Words and pictures* If the relationship between words and pictures is particularly interesting, look at it closely (**Matching** Variation 1), or do a 'double summary' (see *Comprehension*, page 110).

'Advertising' follow-up

To focus on the visual element, get students to comb ads for good images (**Best image**). Detailed work on ads can build up to a short writing activity (**Describe an ad**) which can be done at most levels and covers most of the aspects above. The worksheet in Box 27 gives an expanded version which can be used to raise awareness in class or for independent work. Choose elements appropriate for the level, the ad and your particular purpose, or get students to make the selection.

BOX 27 Worksheet for TV commercials
Instructions for students

FIRST VIEW

1 Choose your commercial and study it. Write the name of the product and what it is.
2 Give some information about the product:
   It is .... It has ....
   It (does) ....
3 Who do you think it's aimed at? (Women, young people, rich people, etc.)
4 Is there a slogan/catchphrase? If so, write down the exact words and explain it.
5 What kind of commercial is it?
   - Is there a story of some kind? Is it a drama?
   - Is it a parody?
   - Does it have a comic idea? } Give details.
   - Does it create a mood/atmosphere?

---

6 What's the angle? How does it try to get your attention? What's new/different?

SECOND VIEW

7 Write down one or two phrases you hear. View again and add to what you've written. Try to build up the whole text.

8 What kind of voice is used? Is there anything special about it?

9 What and who is the product associated with – and how?

10 Formulate the main message – what is the ad telling you *explicitly*? (e.g. this product will clean your hair better)

11 Formulate the indirect message, the intangible idea (usually in the pictures). What is the ad telling you *implicitly*? (e.g. this product will make you irresistible)

THIRD VIEW

12 List the words which are associated with the *product* (e.g. electrical appliances, dishwasher), with the *message* (e.g. quiet, luxury, whisper) and with *evaluation* (e.g. unbeatable, superb).

13 Is there any wordplay (puns, rhymes, alliteration, jingles)? Is there any loaded language? Any wild exaggeration (hype)? Use a dictionary.

14 Are there any visual jokes or tricks? Describe them.

15 What does the music/sound add to the ad?

16 Are there any really good images? Describe them.

FINALLY

17 Would this ad be different in your country? How?

18 Give the ad a rating (0 to 3) on these scales:

original	0 1 2 3	corny
persuasive	0 1 2 3	unconvincing
memorable	0 1 2 3	easily forgotten
attractive	0 1 2 3	uninteresting
honest	0 1 2 3	dishonest

19 (Optional) Describe the whole ad. Start with the product and the general angle, then go through the action in order (use the present tense), showing what we see and what we hear and what effect it is intended to have. Finish with a general evaluation as in 18 above. For models, see the IKEA and DELTA descriptions in **Describe an ad.**

Creating ads

TV ads are excellent for inspiring short bursts of creative or guided writing:

- Use ads with clever angles/punch lines to spark students' own ad ideas (**Ad angles**). Follow up with the original to see how the pros did it (students appreciate the artistry but may also express disdain!).
- Try imitation or parody with some simple ad formulas (**Ad angles Variation 1**).
- Allow time for honest advocacy of products that students really believe in (**Stand by it**); this can be extended to a **Voxpop** survey.
- Let students script existing ads – possible at most levels and great fun (restrain wilder imaginations by introducing a professional note). Draw attention to the appropriate range of tenses (**Situation report**), find appropriate ads and do **Commentary/Copywriter**; realistic dramatic ads in domestic settings can be rewritten to fit other countries and cultures. This also works with short dramatic ads where students take on the parts (**Lipreading and mindreading**).

Advertising project

A project on advertising, building up to TV ads through personal ads, picture ads, telephone sales and the Internet, has great potential for language practice (see the outline in Box 28).

BOX 28   Project on advertising

1 Start by looking at the <u>issues</u> (see page 107). Ask students which they would like to discuss, and make this the basis for a final class debate, presentations or essays/compositions. Urge students to seek real ads to illustrate their opinions, and come back to the issues briefly after each phase of the project.

2 Present some <u>essential terms</u> and discuss how to use them (e.g. *advertising, ads, advertisements, blurb, brand* and *brand name, catchphrase, commercials, commercial break, hoarding, hype, logo, marketing, poster, publicity*). Many of these have 'false friends' in other languages.

3 Use <u>small ads</u> (personal advertising for sales, jobs, accommodation) to study standard abbreviations (e.g. c.h. = central heating); for devising questions (*How much is the three-quarter-length fur coat?*); as models for students' own ads briefly describing goods, apartments, lost pets (give a word limit); and as prompts for role-played telephone calls enquiring about goods/jobs.

4 For <u>telephone sales</u> or 'cold calls' to unknown clients, discuss various ploys to keep clients on the line (e.g. offering prizes,

---

referring to mutual acquaintances, using discreet flattery, pretending to be doing a survey, asking questions, asking *for* questions, whetting curiosity); propose some products (a subscription, a course, a holiday); get groups to invent details of the product and an infallible script to 'hook' and hold the client, then role play the 'cold calls'.

5 With <u>picture ads</u> (magazines and posters), separate the pictures from the text, raise speculation about what the pictures are advertising, then bring text and pictures together. Ask students to explain the connection, to describe the ads in detail and to summarize the explicit and implicit messages. More advanced students can look at voice and wordplay. A good class exercise is a competition for best ad, based on agreed criteria; and an excellent exam question or essay is an analysis of an ad, its general strategy, its messages and how the design and the text convey them.

6 <u>Internet sales</u> have many format possibilities: look at some examples, then get students to design a (very simple) hyper-text ad and an e-mail making a special offer.

7 Culminate with <u>TV ads</u> as above, looking for visual and verbal messages, and creating own ads.

8 Finish off with a <u>debate/presentations/essays</u> on the issues raised at the beginning.

BOX 29   Some TV ads

1 Biactol (notice the wordplay on *spot*)

Words	*Pictures*
Every morning at watering holes the adolescent males gather.	The camera tracks through tropical vegetation to find a young man washing his face over a basin.
Some specimens, still washing with soap and water, aren't hard to spot,	Three fingers point to the spots on his face, the last finger being clearly that of a gorilla.
while the more successful males wash every day with Biactol,	The camera moves across to a clean-faced young man, smirking a bit, then focuses on his hands as they squirt out Biactol and apply it.

because unlike ordinary soap Biactol kills the bacteria that build up daily and cause spots,

A magnifying glass enhances the close-up on his clean chin, and we cut briefly to a green animated bacterium which is knocked out by a tide of Biactol and washed away in a wave of water.

giving these lesser spotted males a clear advantage,

The camera backs off to show the spotless young man next to the spotty one.

especially when it comes to finding a mate.

A female hand appears and fondles the clean chin; the boy growls appreciatively like a panther.

Biactol – knocks spots off soap and water.

The Biactol bottle is placed on a table as the ad finishes, and the slogan appears on the screen.

2 **The Godfather, Part 3** (jokey use of 'voice')
Three sinister Mafiosi approach the camera – dark glasses, hats, raincoats. One produces a microphone and says in a voice heavy with menace: 'Here's someone *else* who would recommend that you buy *The Godfather*, Part 3'. The head of a horse nods dumbly and rolls its eyes like an intimidated witness.

3 **Ariel** (a nice conventional before-and-after ad)
(Setting: a large middle-class house with garden)

Older brother: Remember the story of Cain and Abel? Well, I know that feeling. (*to younger brother, eating breakfast*) Tell me I'm hallucinating, tell me this isn't my tiger shirt! You stole it! (*He picks the shirt out of the laundry basket.*) Look! Mud, mayonnaise, burger, ketchup – and what's this? (*showing a greasy hand mark*)

Younger brother (*shamefacedly*): My bike broke.

OB: Dirty oil!

Mum (*coming in*): For goodness sake, stop it!

OB: Ruined!

Mum (*looking at the stain*): *That* won't shift.

YB: But, mum – (*holding up the product*) this improved Ariel says it *does* shift oil stains.

OB: Creep!

Mum (*putting the shirt in the washing machine*): We can but try.

Voice: New improved Ariel Ultra's got revolutionary oil dispersants (*graphic*). Watch what they do after you've been using it. (*Two samples marked 'Oil' are lowered into two beakers.*) Both these pieces of polyester have been stained with oil. (*The two samples are removed and rinsed; on one the oil stain disappears.*) Improved Ariel Ultra disperses the oil stain and rinses it clean away like never before.

OB (*in clean T-shirt*): It did it! (*threateningly*) And if it did it on filthy oil, it'll do it on blood! (*He chases after YB. Mother raises her eyes at the noise.*)

(*The product is shown on the table, with the caption.*)

Voice: On many a soil, even oil, Ariel gets it clean.

4 Heat electric (contrast between words and pictures)

Words	*Pictures*
(A real recorded voice with a no-nonsense northern accent, evidently a serious sportsman)	A real house setting with electric radiators in the background.
Oh, it's good to come back into a warm flat after you've just been for a run, and it's always nice to come into somewhere warm if you've been freezing to death out on a ten-mile slog.	An animated model tortoise is speaking into a mike. He is serious and self-possessed, like the voice.
Yes, it's easily controllable and it *needs* to be easily controllable as well. I don't have much time, I'm a very busy person and I have to have everything just as I need it ...	He points to the radiators and wiggles fingers to demonstrate. He spread his hands.
They should be something fairly modern in design and they've got to be easily turn-off-and-onable.	He gestures turning on a switch.
Voice-over: For all your creature comforts, heat electric.	

5 **Sleepytime rat control** (a pleasant parody)

Words	*Pictures*
Voice: Sometimes it seems no matter how hard you clean, no matter how hard you scrub, you just can't rid your home of – (*sepulchrally*) SEWER RATS!	A housewife rubbing and scrubbing.
Housewife 1: Oh no! (*She shakes her head.*)	She goes into the bathroom and discovers rats in the toilet.
Voice: Who needs it? Not you. Not any more. Not with Sleepytime Rat Control.	The salesman appears, showing the product.
Housewife 2 (*stepping elegantly around to avoid milling rats*): Sleepytime? How does it work?	
Voice: It's not a poison. It's not a trap. It's a powerful sedative that puts rats to sleep – DEEP SLEEP. (And so on ...)	A rat on a table nibbling a tablet. Same rat asleep, with ZZZZ ... rising from it.

6 **Golf** (good for language work and imitation)

Gentle music. A series of slow-motion black and white pictures of people in public, each with a caption, each with a certain style. A man in a restaurant brandishing a Rolex watch – 'I'm loaded'; a man in a café reading philosophy in French – 'I'm intellectual'; a skinny half-clothed teenager on a monocycle in a crowd – 'I'm eccentric'; an Afro-American in a suave leather jacket adjusting his shades – 'I'm cool'; a man restraining two fierce dogs – 'I'm hard'; an election candidate pulling his family into the picture – 'I'm a family man'; a man in a leather waist-coat with heavy nose, lip and ear piercings – 'I'm different'; a girl in school uniform putting on mascara – 'I'm grown-up'; a man in a speedboat eyeing up a pretty girl – 'I'm well endowed'; finally, an ordinary young man getting into a car, and the caption – 'I'm going down the shops.' The screen clears to show the Volkswagen logo, the word GOLF and the caption *A car, not a label.*

Part B
Activities with authentic video

1 Video comprehension

Understanding video

One of the main complaints about authentic video is that it is too difficult. There's a lot of justice in this. Obviously students learn best when they understand most of what they hear and comprehension is therefore a top priority. We need to develop a good feeling for what students can manage and how to help them with it. We also need to be sympathetic to what they want to understand.

Clearly the level of language is very important. The elements which make for comprehension difficulty are: high verbal and lexical density; high-speed speech; little support from the visual scene; background noise; dialect or strong regional accents; and 'natural' features like indistinct articulation and overlap. If you want to decide the difficulty of a particular sequence, consult your students: they are the experts.

Understanding the whole

We should be aware that comprehension of authentic video is different from (for example) comprehension of coursebook audio-cassettes, where the material is mainly verbal, self-explanatory, short and complete. First, the visual element provides its own layer of comprehension, which can affect the verbal messages in many different ways, highlighting, supplementing, contrasting with them or overriding them. There is also a layer of sound and music which carries its own messages, reinforces verbal or visual messages or sometimes even interferes with them.

This of course is also true of coursebook videos. But with authentic material, there are no concessions to learners' knowledge of culture or ideas and this too may present problems. Moreover, we are sometimes working with a whole programme, far longer than normal classroom input, and we have to think about how learners grapple with such long structures: how do they recognize the parts? or the significance of utterances in the whole? If on the other hand we are using decontextualized clips, then facilitating comprehension will mean we have to explain or reconstruct the context adequately.

So with authentic video, comprehension of the whole seldom comes from the words alone. As teachers, we must always aim at and check for understanding of the whole *as well as* comprehension of the words themselves. If we do this, we will discover that students come to many strange, interesting (and sometimes justifiable) conclusions quite different from our own about the meanings of what they have seen.

At the same time we need to encourage global comprehension strategies. For language learners, because so much is obscure, the attention is forced down to details far more often, and when this happens they tend to lose sight of the overall meaning: they often complain that they 'understand all the words but can't answer the question'. Activities which make them look 'upwards and outwards' will help to overcome their fear of not understanding every word. Many activities in this book aim to do this (e.g. **Before and after, Character network, Labelling and linking, Matching**).

Understanding the parts

Comprehension of the whole does not mean that the details (including the words themselves) do not matter. When viewing in our own language we tend to go for the general idea, 'get the message', but it's also natural for us to monitor closely for anything which disturbs our overall grasp, and we may bend our attention to small points (a word, a sound, a single visual detail) at will. Effective comprehension seems to be 'interactive', calling on global or close-focus strategies at need.

Telling students to just relax and listen for the general meaning helps to overcome tension, but it doesn't always keep them happy as learners. There is a great desire to *understand the words*, and perhaps this is natural too, an important language-learning strategy which should also be encouraged as long as it doesn't increase students' tendency to focus on individual words at the expense of the whole. So there are also many activities in this book which aim at comprehension of the words themselves (e.g. **Ad language, Choose your words, Holophrases, Interactive language, Lipreading and mindreading, Matching**). In the next section I also suggest some general techniques for close comprehension.

In the end, comprehension is a very individual process, and we shouldn't be too dogmatic or prescriptive. Try lots of approaches, observe what students do, consult them about their difficulties and give instinct its head. Learning has a will of its own!

Understanding the words

Many of the activities in Part B are aimed at understanding the full meaning of video material in context. The suggestions here concentrate instead on close comprehension, mainly of the words themselves, and can be used as lead-ins or supplements to the other activities. With a variety of such comprehension aids, students can understand, at some level, a good range of video material. There is no suggestion that you *must* do any or all of them – they are just options which will depend on the material, the level of the group and the other activities you are planning.

Explaining context and content

1 Give plenty of background information before viewing, e.g. explain the situation, describe the characters involved, get students to research the background and brief each other, use parallel texts (e.g. newspaper articles mirroring TV news items) to prepare the ground.
2 Give all proper names and cultural references beforehand and practise the pronunciation. As a recap, go through all the names after viewing, asking for more details.
3 Describe the actual content of the video before playing it (this way students hear everything twice).
4 Play the really difficult sequences one by one, explain them, play them again, then play the whole.
5 (For drama) Supplement the preliminary explanation with role play before watching the scene.
6 Take on the role of the narrator yourself. Play the easy bits and paraphrase the rest, fast-forwarding through to the next easy bit.

Anticipations

1 Give the subject, or the opening sentence, and have students anticipate what they'll see and hear: what people will say and what kind of information they will give.
2 View the pictures without the sound and guess what the sequence is about and what the people are saying. Then view with sound.
3 Play a short stand-alone sequence (e.g. a news 'quotation', an interview clip, an anecdote) for comprehension, and speculate on its role in the whole.
4 Play the sound without vision and have students speculate on what they will see.

Giving vocabulary

1 Give a few key words and expressions in advance. Teach the meanings or get students to find them out beforehand. Ask which ones go together and how. View first just for students to pick up the key words and put them back into context after viewing (e.g. to say who said them and what they refer to).

2 Write up key words with irregular pronunciation but (for a change) don't give the pronunciation. Ask students to notice the pronunciation when they view.

3 Pick out the most important phrases and collocations, discuss them, then drill them (or get students to do so in pairs), giving the first half and demanding the second.

4 Give some vocabulary which gives the skeleton of the story/commentary. Discuss any new meanings, speculate what the sequence might be about, then view.

5 While viewing, write up a number of essential words and expressions and after viewing get students to copy them down. Ask students which ones they know and what they mean, then view again and discuss what the others might mean.

6 With tricky accents, pick out some of the important accented words beforehand and draw attention to how they are pronounced.

Looking for vocabulary

1 After viewing to identify the topic, ask students to view again to find the words which gave them the clues to the topic. Build them into a vocabulary map, then add any that the students have missed and get them to listen again to pick them up.

2 After one viewing, choose some collocations, write them up with one part missing (e.g. *[fan] the flames, [put out] the fire*) and ask students to listen again for the missing words.

3 Give definitions of a few key words (but not the words themselves) and get students to view to find the words represented by the definitions.

Comprehension checks

1 Ask very simple comprehension questions after the first viewing, more difficult ones after the second viewing, and so on.

2 Get the students to prepare comprehension questions (on what they've seen as well as what they've heard). Check their grammar while they are preparing them, then have them ask each other the questions from group to group. View again to check the answers.

3 If the content can be represented visually, get students to do this by (for example) moving objects around, walking through the actions, doing a sketch of the scene, etc.

4 Get students to identify the three worst 'black spots' (patches of incomprehension), explain them, and then together try to work out what the problem was.

5 Ask students each to concentrate on one speaker and follow what he/she says, then select anything he/she says which isn't clear to them and which seems important. Review these parts and explain them.

Dictation/gapfill

1 Do very small difficult portions of the text as a gapfill: write them up as you hear them, leaving out a few words for students to complete on second viewing. If they are longer than a sentence or two, prepare them beforehand.

2 Do a 'progressive dictation' of a small part of the text (maximum two or three sentences). Students view, then call out as much of the text as they can remember. Write up the words, leaving appropriate spaces between for the other words. View again and again, filling in more and more gaps. Alternatively, write up the first words of each natural word group and get students to view again until they have the whole. A good preliminary is simply to get students to count the number of words they hear.

2   Activities

(N.B. The level indicated (elementary, lower-intermediate, etc.) is a *minimum* level, e.g. an 'elementary' exercise can be done at any level from elementary upwards.)

Accents

Aim: recognizing and interpreting major accents of English

Level: lower-intermediate

Rationale: Recognizing accents is important not only for comprehension but as a clue to cultural identity.

Material: clips

Preparation: Choose three short clips which feature the target accent and are quite easy to understand. Select two or three distinguishing pronunciation features, e.g.

Standard American	*Northern English*
the sounded /r/ in *hard, forty, thinner*	the short /ʊ/ sound in e.g. *cup, love*
the voiced medial *t,* e.g. *madder* for *matter*	the short /æ/ in e.g. *bath, pass*

Procedure

1 Play one clip for comprehension, then view again. Students note down all words which exemplify the special pronunciation features. Do **Act along**, trying to imitate the accents.

2 View two more short clips; students 'translate' selected utterances by changing the accent into the variety of English they know.

Act along

Aim: focusing on language forms and pronunciation

Level: elementary

Material: drama clips

Preparation: Select very short sequences containing useful language.

Procedure

1 View once for students to select a speaker – one each, or one for all.

2 Play the sequence several times. Students 'shadow' their chosen speakers, i.e. speak the words a split second after hearing them.

3 When they have the feel of the sounds and stress patterns, turn the sound off and rerun the sequence. Students substitute for the actors as if dubbing.

Variation

The karaoke version is for natural actors or learners working alone. Students choose a scene which features their favourite star, learn his/her part and then act along with the star, imitating voice, gesture, emphasis, expression.

Ad angles

Aim: creative writing: inventing and imitating TV ads
Level: lower-intermediate
Material: TV commercials
Preparation: Find an ad with a simple clever angle or a single significant line/catchphrase.

Procedure

1 Don't show the ad, but tell students the product and the angle or catchphrase, e.g.

Your product is ...	*You want to ...*
apple juice	show the product dozens of times without boring the audience
a dark beer	create a dark, secret, mysterious atmosphere
furniture	use the phrase *You need some new furniture!* (no other words)

2 Ask students how they would present the product in a 30-second ad. In groups, they work on an 'ad idea' and present it; the class chooses the best.
3 Show the original ad and invite comment.

Variations

1 Show an ad for imitation. Use simple ads which associate products with intangibles (e.g. a glamorous lifestyle). Students identify the product and the associations. Suggest a different product (e.g. boots, beer, biscuits), discuss what associations could be activated, then together devise the text and the images. Sophisticated students may enjoy producing parodies.
2 Use realistic dramatic ads in domestic settings for cultural transposition. Discuss what would change if the country was different (house, people, clothes, behaviour, even the product), and ask students to produce a version for their own country or a country they know well.

Ad language

Aim: comprehension of the advertising message
Level: elementary
Material: TV ads

Procedure

After viewing, students view again to pick up vocabulary to do with the *product* (e.g. shampoo, rinse), the *message* (e.g. light, bouncy), or the *evaluation* of the product (e.g. fantastic, beautiful) (see Box 30).

Variation

Before viewing, give students the vocabulary, mixed up, to classify into *product, message* and *evaluation*.

Note

Use this activity to lead in to loaded language and advertising hype (**Purrs and slurs, Over the top**).

BOX 30 PME: product, message, evaluation		
Product	tea	washing maching
Product words	blend, aroma	washing machine, engineering
Message words	choice (adjective)	economical, conserving resources, saves water and energy
Evaluation words	posh, choicest	advanced, best, precious

Adopt a character

Aim: recapping whole or part of a film/programme; close comprehension and oral production of shorter sequences; really understanding the characters
Level: intermediate
Material: drama films; documentaries with a strong cast; dramatic TV ads; anecdotes

Procedure

1 After viewing, individual students (or groups) each adopt one of the main characters and assume their identities. They view again and think about 'their' situation, current mood, motivations/desires, and feelings about the other characters.

2 Students present their new selves to the whole class, covering the four aspects outlined in step 1. Students answer questions from the class and ask questions of the other characters. If working alone, students write about 'themselves' from the four points of view.

Variations

1 *Hotseat* Students prepare their characters in small groups then select one person from each group to sit in the hot seat and be quizzed by the audience on his/her behaviour, background, character, relationships, feelings, etc. OR students interview the 'characters' one-to-one in front of the class, asking three questions of each. (If you are dealing with documentaries, record these interviews if possible, replay them and get the class to decide what short excerpts could be included in the documentary and where.)
2 For TV ads or personal anecdotes, get individuals/groups to retell the story from the point of view of the various people involved, as a check on comprehension.

Note

Character network can be done as a preliminary to this activity.

Advice

Aim:	stimulating discussion and producing interactive language
Level:	intermediate
Rationale:	In a lot of drama there is someone who clearly needs to be advised or told what's going on.
Material:	drama, especially soap operas and TV drama series; some documentaries

Procedure

Stop viewing at a suitable point and ask students to imagine that they intervene and enlighten the person who needs advising. Discuss the best way to do it and what the reactions of the person might be, then role play the scene and/or script it.

Variations (very suitable for soap operas)

1 After viewing a sequence where there's a lot of bad or stupid behaviour, view the scene again, pausing frequently and asking for comments, advice, suggestions for alternative replies, etc.
2 Students rerun the scene the way they think the character(s) should have played it.

3 Students set up a counselling session with the erring character as in **Problem.**

Answers

Aim:	comprehension of questions and answers
Level:	intermediate
Material:	interviews or talk shows
Preparation:	View the programme and write down some questions that were asked where the answer is not simple or explicit (see Box 31 for an example).

Procedure

1 After viewing the programme, replay the selected questions, or display the words, or get students to write them down (**Transcript**). Ask what kind of *short* answer each question expects (see Box 31 for examples).

2 Re-view the answers given in the programme and decide which short answer comes closest to the speaker's meaning.

Variations

1 Students focus on two or three questions and answers and decide whether the answer is a straight answer (direct or indirect), a 'hedge', or shifts the ground.

2 Pause after each answer and discuss whether students (as interviewers) would regard the question as answered, or push for more. If they would push, what follow-up question would they ask?

3 Give the questions (or rough paraphrases) and discuss possible answers *before* viewing, as an aid to comprehension. Follow up by discussing the answers.

BOX 31 *Hardtalk* interview with Mikhail Gorbachev

Tim Sebastian: How much do you share the concern of many people in Russia about how the loss of the Kursk submarine was handled by the authorities?

Possible answers:
a a great deal
b quite a lot
c not much
d not at all

Gorbachev: August was really tough – you could say we went through a kind of crisis. The explosion in the underpass in Moscow, then the nuclear submarine catastrophe, and the fire in the Ostankino television tower – all this put the spotlight on some poor media management.

= Answer b) quite a lot

Straight answer, but indirect. The interviewer pushes for a clearer answer.

TS: So the information was handled badly, the information handed down to the public?	Possible answers: a yes, very badly b not very well c not so badly d quite well
MG: I think the authorities initially – in all cases, but particularly with the submarine – well actually, things were pretty clear straight away with the blast in Moscow – the authorities didn't give out the full information. I even felt that the president himself didn't get all the facts. And that's really bad.	= Answer a) yes, very badly Straight answer and direct, but shifts the ground a bit.

Awkward questions

Aim: identifying awkward questions; recognizing and practising evasion

Level: intermediate

Material: tricky questions from interviews, with evasive answers

Procedure

1 Recall famous 'tricky questions', e.g. (for Hollywood scriptwriters) *Are you or have you ever been a member of the Communist Party?*
2 Introduce the vocabulary *tell the truth, lie, tricky/awkward question, put someone on the spot, get off the hook, wriggle out of it.*
3 Tell the class the tricky question from the interview (e.g. *Was the match fixed?*); get pairs to think of how to wriggle out of it (assuming the true answer is *Yes*), and come up with a response, e.g.:

   • return the question (*You tell me. Your guess is as good as mine.*)
   • respond to the questioner, not the question (*Now why are you coming back to this again?*)
   • evade (*It's really amazing how the press exaggerate.*)
   • answer a different question and then sidetrack (*It's possible that the qualifying rounds were fixed – it's difficult to check standards in so many different countries ...*)
   • react indignantly (*I'm sick and tired of these accusations!*)
   • sidetrack with a long rambling story (*Well of course when this was first suggested we went into it thoroughly – and it was an expensive enquiry, which we had to pay for out of our own pockets ...*)

- go into terminology (*It depends what you mean by 'fixed' ...*)
- question the assumptions (*Is it really possible to fix a match?*)
- imply a (false) answer (*Oh come on, Sid, you know us better than that!*)

4 Play the clip and discuss how the interviewee wriggles out of it.

Before and after

Aim:	reviewing the action so far
Level:	lower-intermediate
Material:	drama films; film and book (Variation 2)
Preparation:	Choose three or four short visually striking sequences which represent important moments in the plot (or get individual students to do this).

Procedure

After viewing part of the film, go back and play each short sequence, freeze, and pose the questions: *Who? What? Why? What has just happened? What next?* Get an oral report using an appropriate spread of tenses (**Situation report**) as in the example in Box 32.

Variations

1 Choose sequences randomly by fast-forwarding the film, stopping it every few minutes and viewing ten seconds of film. Or fast-forward on *Play*, so everyone is reminded of the events: individuals decide which are the important moments, freeze them and explain why they are important.
2 For film and book, use the same technique to review the book plot before seeing the film. Students studying the book then locate the scenes in the book.

Note

The same procedure is used for different purposes in **Enigmas** and **Reaction shots**.

BOX 32   An important moment in *Shine*

A middle-aged man is burning a scrapbook in his back garden.

Oral report: *This is David's father. He's burning the scrapbook about David's musical career. David has decided to defy his father – he's going to leave home to study music in London. As a result his father has rejected him. The next thing we see is the Royal College of Music in London.*

Best image

Aim:	describing images, dress, scenes, actions, etc.; understanding descriptions
Level:	elementary
Material:	TV commercials (a selection must be available to students outside class)
Preparation:	Choose one striking image from the sequence and prepare a description, setting it in context (see Box 33 for an example).

Procedure

1 Read your description to the class.
2 Play the video; ask the class to shout *Stop!* when they see the image.
3 Announce a competition for 'Image of the Month'. Volunteers should describe their own favourite images in writing (avoiding any which might offend) and present them in the same way, first reading out the description, then playing the video for others to spot the image.
4 After each presentation, display the description.
5 When there are no further volunteers, re-read the descriptions, replay the images and vote on the new champion image.

Variations

1 Presenters use the opportunity to write down all the words they can hear as they prepare. The teacher checks (and extends) this transcript while the class is viewing.
2 Run similar competitions for the funniest moment, the best outfit, etc. Students can think up some more.

Note

This makes a good series of ten-minute lesson fillers.

BOX 33   Best image

My best image is in an ad for a news programme. There's a series of flashes – a man doing some mysterious sign language, some kind of army conflict, then a big car containing an African potentate, surrounded by the Press. The car window closes slowly, the chief turns his dark glasses to the window and then for a moment he raises his hand, with enormous silver rings on all the fingers.

Best scene

Aim: evaluation; discussion
Level: intermediate
Material: drama films

Procedure

After seeing the whole film, individual students decide which was the most memorable/interesting scene, then propose and support their choices. Re-view the most popular scenes and have a vote.

Variation

Before re-viewing, recap the chosen scene with **Fly on the wall**, or follow on with **Favourite scene**.

Body language

Aim: recognizing and describing significant reactions; vocabulary of the body and body movements
Level: lower-intermediate
Material: Any sequence where gesture and body language are very clear and reveal significant feelings and reactions: drama, speeches, sports, competitions. (N.B. Game shows are good for micro-movements – head-shaking, nodding, chin-rubbing, head-scratching, handwaving – revealing indecision, reflection, triumph, disappointment.)

Procedure

1 View with the sound off, then view again, getting students to observe carefully and say what the characters do with body, hands, legs, face and head. (N.B. Speeding up or slowing down the film makes the body movements more pronounced – but allow for the comic effect!)
2 Ask students to imitate the body language and then write down in two columns what the person does (e.g. *He looks down at the table and runs his finger along the edge*) and what this reveals (*He's suppressing his anger*). Do an example on the board first.

131

Body parts

Aim:	vocabulary of the body
Level:	elementary
Material:	clips showing body parts in close-up
Preparation:	Collect one or two clips showing one body part (see Box 34 for examples). If students have access to video, challenge them to find rare close-ups such as noses, knees and elbows.

Procedure

1 Say that the focus today is on *feet* (or *fingers* or *necks*). Before viewing, ask students to imagine some feet and say whose feet, where they are, what they are wearing, what they are doing and why.

2 Students write down their ideas, check the language, and read their ideas out or write them up (e.g. *I imagine bare feet in cool water on a hot day*).

3 Play each clip and compare with the speculations. Students who know the film can explain the role of the shot in the action.

Variations

1 Collect clips of several body parts and allocate each body part to one group. Each group views their clip and speculates on who, where, why, etc. before the whole class views the clip.

2 Students collect glimpse shots of famous stars (Robert de Niro's neck, Julia Roberts' teeth, the hands of Leonardo di Caprio) and play them for others to guess.

BOX 34   Feet

a foot caught in a railway track (*Fried Green Tomatoes*)
the dangling feet of a hanged man or woman (*Michael Collins, Gladiator*)
the tramping feet of prisoners and warders (*Blues Brothers*)
a foot putting a record on the gramophone (*My Left Foot*)
a deer's feet stepping delicately across a railway line (*Stand by Me*)

Book and film

Aim:	to highlight the differences between the book and film
Level:	intermediate
Material:	parallel scenes from book and drama film
Preparation:	Find a matching book and film scene.

Procedure

1 Before looking at the book or film, give students the list in Box 35 and ask them to tick the things they think films and books handle particularly well.

2 Read and view the parallel scenes; students pick out the elements that each scene does well.

Variation

If the class are all studying the same book, half of them can look through the book for good examples of the features on the list, while the other half can collect examples from the film. Students then come together to show each other their three best examples.

Note

Whatever can be made visible or audible appeals to film-makers, hence films tend to prioritize action, setting, objects, physical reactions, visible feelings and interactions, and play with screen composition, textures and shapes, lighting and sound. Novels are better at the wide social picture, inner feelings and shades of feeling, thought in general, poetic description, general comment and specific irony; they also have more room to develop ideas, character, interactions, themes and historical depth.

BOX 35 Film and book: What do they do well?					
	Film	*Book*		*Film*	*Book*
action	☐	☐	long-term relationships	☐	☐
atmospheric setting	☐	☐	mood	☐	☐
attitudes of director/ writer	☐	☐	movement	☐	☐
character	☐	☐	physical appearance	☐	☐
characteristic behaviour	☐	☐	physical sensations	☐	☐
colour	☐	☐	realistic setting	☐	☐
facial expression	☐	☐	social/historical background	☐	☐
feelings (deep, superficial, hidden)	☐	☐	sound	☐	☐
interaction	☐	☐	textures and shapes	☐	☐
lighting	☐	☐	thoughts/ideas	☐	☐

Case study

Aim:	analysing and discussing a case study
Level:	intermediate
Rationale:	Case study materials must be 'raw' (unanalysed): news and soap operas are the nearest thing.
Material:	news stories dealing with students' own expertise or interest (e.g. a deadly computer virus); soap opera plot lines about issues of general concern (e.g. a case of child abuse)
Preparation:	Find (or get students to find) a suitable ongoing story (news or soap).

Procedure

1 Students gather supporting information about the story from various sources, e.g. websites, organizations, encyclopaedias.
2 Together, summarize the story as it unfolds (as for **Follow the news**).
3 Distribute other information as it is found; ask for volunteers to select and present significant points from each source.
4 Follow the simplified case study approach in Box 36, orally or in writing.

Variation

For steps 5 and 6 in Box 36, students adopt the roles of the players and respond to the questions in **Decisions**.

BOX 36   A simple case study approach

1 Describe the background to the situation briefly, bringing out the significant factors.
2 Explain the latest developments.
3 List and describe the players, their interests and priorities, their relationships, their strengths and weaknesses if known (use **Character network**).
4 Describe the immediate or main problem and identify its causes.
5 List and describe the options for action and evaluate them.
6 Recommend a course of action for one or more of the players.

Casting couch 1

Aim:	interpreting and describing character as a lead-in to viewing the film
Level:	intermediate
Material:	film and book
Preparation:	Find an early film scene which introduces the character(s).

Procedure

1 After reading the book or part of it, students' homework is to hunt for photos in magazines/newspapers which seem to fit particular characters (see Box 37 for an example).

2 Students display their pictures to the class and say why they chose them (e.g. *He looks old and ruthless*). Push them to explain their choices with reference to the book (e.g. *How do you know this character is ruthless?*).

3 If there is more than one candidate for any of the roles, the class makes their casting choice.

4 View the selected scene and compare the characters' appearance with the class's chosen pictures.

BOX 37   Candidates for the role of Claudius (*Hamlet*)

Casting couch 2

Aim:	a lead-in to viewing; describing physical appearance
Level:	lower-intermediate
Material:	film and book
Preparation:	Find passages in the book which describe the main characters physically, and the scene(s) in the film which introduce(s) these main characters.

Procedure

1 Before viewing any of the film, give students the book passages. Ask them to gather evidence about the characters' appearance on a check-list (see Box 38 for an example).
2 Students view the selected film scene(s), check how the characters match the book's description and add any striking new (film) features to the table with appropriate descriptive vocabulary.

Variation

If there is no description of physical appearance in the book, students imagine the character's appearance before viewing, selecting just a few features from the checklist.

Note

There may be only a few points to fill in (e.g. in Chapter 1 of *Great Expectations* Dickens describes Joe Gargery as strong, with blue un-decided eyes and fair curly hair), but it's the search that counts!

BOX 38	How they look	
Name	....	....
Age	....	....
Height	....	....
Build	....	....
Arms and legs	....	....
Posture	....	....
Face	....	....
Skin	....	....
Eyes	....	....
Nose	....	....
Mouth	....	....
Ears	....	....
Head	....	....
Hair	....	....
Expression	....	....
Voice	....	....
Clothes	....	....

Celebrity interview

Aim: oral practice; interviewing techniques
Level: lower-intermediate
Material: interviews with well-known people (as models)

Procedure

1 Propose that students do their own 'celebrity interviews' with each other.
2 Discuss what goes into a celebrity interview (see the questions in Box 39).
3 View interviews (or excerpts) to illuminate these questions.
4 Explain that interviewers do background research and 'pre-interviewing' so they already know what questions to ask and most of the answers.
5 Students pre-interview each other in pairs, decide what to focus on (i.e. what they are 'famous' for), select the three most interesting main questions and decide what information to give in the introduction.
6 With small classes, run the interviews one-to-one in front of the class, as if on TV, one per lesson. If the class is large, divide it into three groups and circulate, or get students to record/film their interviews one-to-one outside the class. Give a time limit for the interviews.

Variation

Interviewees 'become' a famous person (dead, alive or fictitious), research the background, then prepare and run the interview in the same way.

Follow-up

Write up the interview with **Interview article**.

BOX 39   What goes into a celebrity interview?

- How does the host introduce his guest? (giving information about him/her)
- Is the interview just a talk-through biography? (no)
- What does it focus on? (e.g. formative influences, interesting experiences, emotions and attitudes, achievements, current activities, future plans)
- What are the main questions? Are there follow-up questions?
- How does the interviewer show interest? (e.g. smiles, nods, makes encouraging noises)
- How do we get background information? (e.g. in the introduction and the questions)
- How does the host sign off?
- How do you think the interviewer prepares for the interview?

Changes

Aim:	close reading and listening comprehension
Level:	lower-intermediate
Material:	parallel scenes from book and drama film
Preparation:	Choose short fairly close parallel scenes with a mixture of action, dialogue and description.

Procedure

1 Students read the book scene twice (to be really thorough do **Reading aloud**).

2 Students view the scene from the film, and then go back to the text and tick (✓) details which correspond, cross (✗) details which are missing from the film, and query (?) points they're not sure about (see Box 40 for an example).

3 View and read again with a view to discussing possible reasons for the changes (e.g. simplicity, time, cost, the visual medium).

Variations

1 Half the class views the scene for homework, the other half reads it. Each student prepares ten questions on points of detail (e.g. *What colour is her hair? What floor are they on?*). In class they meet in pairs to swap questions and finally they read/view the other version. Alternatively, they tell each other the story and try to find one difference, one omission and one addition for each version.

2 *Dialogue differences* Students view the film scene several times, concentrating on the dialogue, then read the book version. They underline dialogue they heard, write in any changes they remember, view again to check, then discuss reasons for the changes.

BOX 40   *Accidental Hero* – book and film
The film script

On the roof of a high office block, Gale Gayley is interviewing Mr Broadman, filmed by Chucky.

Broadman: Well, to be honest, it doesn't make a lot of sense to me either, Ms Gayley. Things seem to be on the upswing, our differences with the SEC have been favorably resolved. In a business sense I think we've turned the corner.

The book
✓ = same in the film   ✗ = not in film   ? = not sure

They were outside the building (✓) in which Broadman had his brokerage offices. The brisk November wind ruffled Gale's auburn hair (✓) and lovingly stroked (✗) the lapels of Broadman's four-thousand-dollar custom-made Savile Row suit (?). Behind Gale (✓), Chucky, the young hot-dog Channel Four News cameraman, kept the videotape rolling on his camcorder (✓). Only twenty-five (?), Chucky was sharp, fast, and a genius behind the lens, and once Gale had worked with him, she wouldn't work with anyone else.

'But it really makes no sense, Mr Broadman,' (✗) said Gale, holding her mike out (✗) for the businessman's reply.

Broadman smiled a smile of rare sweetness (✗) ... 'To be honest, I can't make sense of it either, Ms Gayley.' Broadman spoke frankly, as though he had nothing to hide, looking directly into Chucky's lens (✓). 'Things seem to be on the upswing, our differences with the Securities and Exchange Commission have been favorably resolved. In a business sense I believe we have turned the corner.'(✓)

Accidental Hero by Leonore Fleischer, based on a screenplay by David Webb Peoples

Character network
Aim:	establishing the relationships between character/players; vocabulary of relationships and attitudes
Level:	lower-intermediate
Material:	any film/programme where the characters/players and their relationships are important

Procedure
For drama
1 After viewing the first 15–20 minutes of the film, set out the names of the main characters in a circle on the board and get students to copy the circle. Ask them to indicate the material relationships between the characters by drawing lines from one character to another and labelling the lines (see Box 41 for an example). Discuss the exact wording and grammar of the labels. If students disagree, do not give 'right answers' but re-view to clear up uncertainties.
2 Do a second network in the same way for psychological relationships.
3 After viewing the whole film, go back to the diagram and discuss how the relationships (or perceptions of them) have changed.

For non-fiction

1 Follow the same procedure. The 'players' may be groups or institutions as well as individuals (e.g. the Church, Cuba, the Union): write them in capitals and their representatives in lower case.

2 After re-viewing, students summarize the situation by saying what each player has, wants, fears, and what outcomes are likely. If they wish, students can take on the roles of the players to do this.

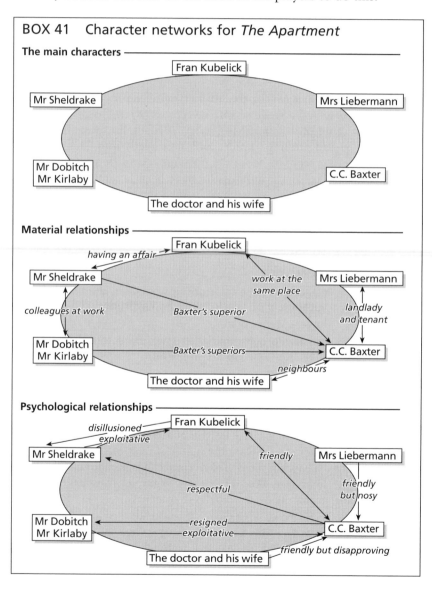

BOX 41   Character networks for *The Apartment*

The main characters

- Fran Kubelick
- Mr Sheldrake
- Mrs Liebermann
- Mr Dobitch / Mr Kirlaby
- C.C. Baxter
- The doctor and his wife

Material relationships

Fran Kubelick — *having an affair* → Mr Sheldrake

Mrs Liebermann — *work at the same place*

colleagues at work

Baxter's superior

landlady and tenant

Mr Dobitch / Mr Kirlaby — *Baxter's superiors* — C.C. Baxter

The doctor and his wife — *neighbours* — C.C. Baxter

Psychological relationships

Fran Kubelick — *disillusioned* / *exploitative* → Mr Sheldrake

friendly — Mrs Liebermann

respectful

friendly but nosy

Mr Dobitch / Mr Kirlaby — *resigned* / *exploitative* — C.C. Baxter

The doctor and his wife — *friendly but disapproving* — C.C. Baxter

Chases

Aim: oral narrative and present simple verbs; predicting events; temporal conjunctions

Level: intermediate

Material: drama film: chase sequences which clearly identify pursuer and pursued

Preparation: Prepare lists of the main people in the chase, their actions, the things involved and the settings (see Box 42 for an example).

Procedure

1 Give out or write up the lists. Discuss the vocabulary.
2 Ask students to speculate on possible connections between actions and things (e.g. *lock* the *cupboard* with the *key*).
3 Explain the situation and ask them to guess who does what to whom. Correct dependent structures of verbs (this is important for step 4).
4 Play the clip, then recap on who does what to whom with what and where, ticking off the elements on the lists. This will thoroughly exercise third-person present tense verb forms, singular and plural. View again, getting students to report pairs of events joined by *while* or *when*, and to say what happens before and after what.

Variations

1 If you are doing a film with a chase, use the same procedure as a prediction activity.
2 Advanced students can deliver a prepared account in class, as in **Seen it before** Variation 2, before the whole class views the scene.

Note

Related activities are **Plan a chase, Runabout**.

BOX 42   The chase from *A Fish Called Wanda*

People	*Actions*
the lawyer (Archie)	check in
the woman (Wanda)	go on board (something)
the stammerer (Ken)	shoot (someone)
the American (Otto)	lock (someone) up
an innocent traveller	throw (something) away
a cleaner	fall down (something)
	get stuck in (something)
	roll over (someone/something)
	drive (something)
	steal (something)

Things	*Places*
a steam-roller	a check-in
wet concrete	the tarmac
a gun	the plane
a barrel of water	
a cupboard	
a key	
the bag with the diamonds	
a boarding pass	
a luggage chute	
a cosh	

The opening situation

At the beginning of the chase Otto is taking Wanda to the airport. They are planning to fly to Rio with the stolen diamonds. Otto has a gun. They are pursued by Archie (who is in love with Wanda) and Ken (who hates Otto because he killed his pet fish). Otto and Wanda arrive at the airport a little before Archie and Ken ... Can

Choose your words

Aim:	developing the habit of noticing useful language items
Level:	elementary
Rationale:	Conscientious students who want to extend their vocabulary are often quite indiscriminate, selecting rare or specialized items rather than high-utility expressions, and learning lists of words by heart. They also neglect expressions which they understand but don't use themselves – some of the most valuable items for extending active vocabulary. This activity re-orients students to more discriminating 'noticing' in this respect and should be done regularly to develop the habit.
Material:	clips with useful language

Procedure

1 Play a sequence which is rich in useful language and get students to record five expressions which they think they could use themselves. Emphasize that they should not concentrate only on new, unknown or rare words but go for high-utility expressions which they *Don't Use but Could Use* (give the acronym DUCU).

2 Discuss the selected expressions and agree on what is most usable. Students record the selected items under the title of the scene.

Follow-up
Students review the selected vocabulary by putting it back in the context of the scene, saying who used it and about what. This reinforces meaning and use as well as form.

Note
Other activities for 'active noticing' are **Interactive language**, **Questions**, **Tenses** and **Wordhunt**.

Climax

Aim:	reviewing the overall plot structure
Level:	lower-intermediate
Material:	drama films; film and book

Procedure

1 After viewing the film (or after reading the book and before viewing the whole film), identify the main crisis/climax of the plot, where everything comes to a head (usually near the end), and view the film scene of the crisis.
2 Write the main event at the top of the board in a circle.
3 With students, work out what events lead directly to the crisis and arrange them in separate circles below the first circle, with arrows to show the cause-and-effect connections (see Box 43 for an example). Use the present tense.
4 For each circle, ask *Why?*, *How?* or *How come?* This will lead to the other events and factors which have contributed to the final crisis.
5 Go on asking *Why?*, *How?* or *How come?* and adding circles until you have a complete cause-and-effect map of the plot.

Note
This activity takes at least an hour, and will need discussion and revision to arrive at a satisfactory picture. It also needs space: if you have only a small board, get students to copy the first part onto a large sheet of paper, to be pinned up while work continues on the board.

BOX 43   The climax in *Howard's End*

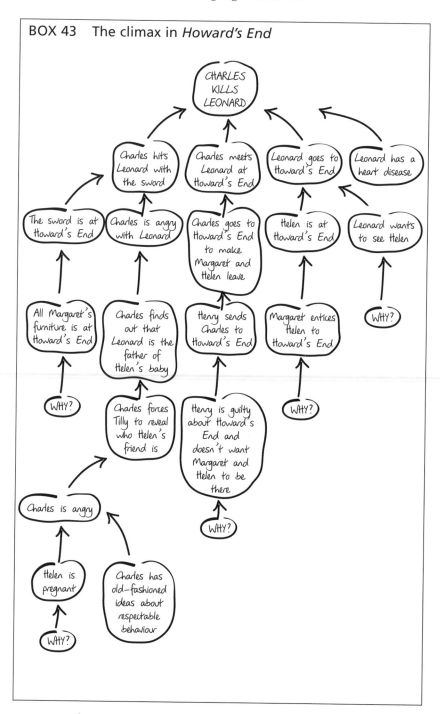

Comment

Aim: comprehension; oral production (question and answer); a sense of news values

Level: intermediate

Material: comprehensible news items, some with 'quotations' from interviewees, and some without

Procedure

1 Tell students they are going to do some location interviews, like TV news reporters.

2 Play one or two news items; note the length of the 'quotations' from interviewees (ten seconds or less) and how they are introduced; and discuss who is interviewed and why (experts, witnesses, victims, participants, perpetrators, VIPs, spokespersons).

3 Play an interesting news item which has no interview quotations. Discuss who might be interviewed, what questions they would be asked and what they might say.

4 Pairs/groups prepare brief interviews and perform them for the class.

5 The class select three brief quotations from the interviews to include in the news item and decide where to fit them in. (If it is possible to record the interviews, this makes a good excuse for replaying them and getting comments on the language.)

Note

This is a simple version of **Interview**, tagged to an existing news item.

Commentary/Copywriter

Aim: writing and speaking (voice-over commentary); a lead-in to a programme or part of one; a taste of advertising copywriting

Level: elementary

Material: short non-fiction sequences (e.g. from documentaries and ads) with images which are suitable for a voice-over commentary – either with self-evident meaning (for structured writing), or enigmatic, with room for interpretation (for creative writing)

Preparation: Choose the sequence according to the level and interests of the class and the language to be generated, e.g. a flow diagram for a process description, a how-to demonstration for the simple present, a cross-cutting sequence for comparisons, a commercial for description and persuasion, a

145

thematic sequence for an area of vocabulary (see **Themes**). View the sequence without sound in advance to make sure the visuals are suitably unambiguous (or ambiguous). (N.B. Ads in incomprehensible languages are good, since they can be viewed with all the sound effects.)

Procedure

1 View without sound, discuss what the sequence is about and invite individuals/groups to try writing the voice-over commentary. Note the time the sequence takes and suggest a word limit (estimate three words per second).
2 Students read out their finished commentaries along with the (soundless) clip and the class selects the most interesting.
3 Play the original with sound for comparison.

Variation

Advanced students may enjoy producing a parody of a particularly corny ad. This is highly motivating but takes a lot of time and is best done for homework and presented in class.

Note

Commentaries can be anything from three words to a hundred and can be done at any level. Other commentary exercises are **Fashion parade**, **Fights** Follow-up and **News script**.

Completions

Aim:	building sentences with adverbial extensions
Level:	elementary
Material:	comic sketches which depend on overturning normal expectations
Preparation:	Prepare by formulating a sentence (related to the sketch) which expresses what people *normally do*, e.g. if the sketch shows Mr Bean getting dressed in his car while driving to work, the norm is *People get dressed at home in the morning to go to work.* If it shows John Belushi, dressed as a samurai, serving food by slicing it in the air with his sword, the norm is *People prepare food in delicatessens to serve to customers.*

What?	Where?	When?	Why?
People get dressed	at home	in the morning	to go to work
People prepare food	in delicatessens		to serve to customers

146

Procedure

1 Tell students they will see a sketch where an ordinary action is done a little differently from normal, but they have to start by guessing what the *normal* action is. Write up *What? Where? When? Why?* on the board, give the first part of the sentence (e.g. *People get dressed ...*) and invite guesses for the next part. Approve all good guesses but write up only the correct ones.

2 Once students have guessed right (give clues if necessary), move on to the next part of the sentence. Indicate, by pointing, that students should repeat the whole sentence every time they make a new guess.

3 Once you have elicited the 'normal' target sentence, show the clip and formulate a final sentence to describe what actually happens and how.

Cross-cutting

Aim: close focus after viewing a whole film; to prompt descriptions of own lifestyle

Level: elementary

Material: sequences which cut rapidly between two scenes (see Box 44 for examples).

Procedure

1 Explain the technique of cross-cutting and ask students if they can think of examples and reasons for using this technique.

2 Show the cross-cut scene and discuss these questions:

- *What's happening in the different actions?*
- *Are they converging or separate? (i.e. Are the two scenes going to meet or not?)*
- *Is the cutting fast or slow? (fast is one or two seconds between cuts; slow is five seconds or more)*
- *Are the soundtracks very different? How?*
- *What's the difference between the two actions?*
- *What's the connection between them?*
- *Why has the director cross-cut them? What is he/she showing us?*

Follow-up

Students cross-cut a scene with a parallel scene from their own lives. Use any short scene which contrasts with your students' lives (e.g. a Klingon wedding, work in the mines). Work together on dividing up this scene; students then write their own scenes, dividing them into 'bites' to match the phases of the original scene.

BOX 44 Cross-cut scenes	
For contrasting lifestyles	The main characters go to bed in strikingly different styles (*A Fish Called Wanda, Frankie and Johnnie*).
For dramatic/ironic contrast	A series of assassinations is cross-cut with a scene of love, culture, normal life (*The Godfather, Michael Collins, Elizabeth*) – now a cinema cliché.
To speed up the action	The camera cuts between pursuer/ pursued or predator/prey as the chase comes to a climax (*The Wrong Trousers*, wildlife documentary *Predators*).
For advancing danger	A train advances inexorably as boys try to escape it (*Fried Green Tomatoes, Stand By Me*).
To associate a product with a lifestyle	The camera cuts between a chocolate bar being unwrapped/eaten, and a girl eying up a boy as they prepare to water ski (TV commercial).

Culture

Aim:	focusing on everyday language and cultural differences
Level:	lower-intermediate
Material:	soap operas and programmes about everyday life

Procedure

1   After viewing three or four episodes of a soap, choose one aspect of the culture (e.g. family, food, entertainment and leisure, personal relationships, work, homes, speech, dress, traditions, education) and ask students to identify three or four things which are obviously different from their culture (e.g. *they eat a lot of chips; they don't have family meals*). They should give each thing they list a rating (e.g. +2 = *I like this very much*; 0 = *I am indifferent to it*; –2 = *I really don't like this*) and explain why.

2   Students (individually or in groups) choose another aspect of the soap culture which interests them, work on it independently in the same way and then present their conclusions to the class.

Daily life

Aim: talking about aspects of daily life; present simple
                 tense
Level: elementary
Material: drama clips and comedy sketches
Preparation: Find clips which illustrate daily activities you want to
                 focus on (e.g. getting up, shopping, driving a car,
                 cooking, looking after babies, getting taxis, using
                 computers, catching trains or planes, etc.)

Procedure

The procedure will differ depending on whether you want to focus on the process itself, on cultural or individual differences, on the words spoken, or on the problems.

1 Together with students, draw up a simple flow diagram of a normal routine, e.g. the process of getting up and going out:

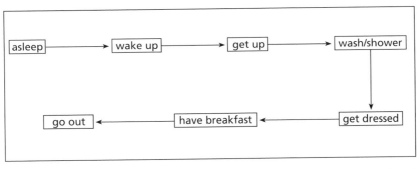

2 Discuss whatever aspect of this routine you want to focus on (cultural differences, dialogue, the difference from students' own lives, problems), using one of the Variations below.
3 View the film sequence and discuss what makes it different from the norm and from our own experiences. What aspects of character and circumstance does the sequence reveal?

Variations

1 *Culture* (if the cultural differences are interesting) Discuss any cultural differences in the process (e.g. in some countries people go out to have breakfast), and relate them to the flow diagram.
2 *Words* (if the dialogue is interesting) Discuss what is said (if anything) at each stage. Role play the scene.
3 *Conditions* (to compare the film with the norm) Ask students to think of the conditions for each stage of the process (or just one stage), e.g.

what are all the possible answers to the questions in the diagram below? This will also prepare vocabulary for Variation 4 or step 3.

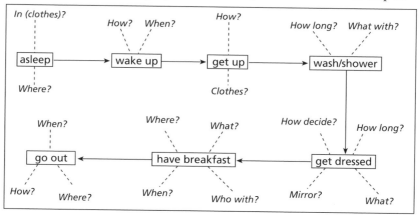

4 *Personalization* (to make comparisons between students and film characters) Personalize the process: students tell a partner how *they* do it (in response to the questions about conditions in Variation 3), and how this reflects their character and circumstances. The class report back on anything interesting they've discovered about each other.

5 *Problem* (if the clip highlights problems in the process) Focus on one or more parts of the process and discuss the possible problems, the possible solutions and the words that come up (see below). Role play the appropriate situation.

Problems	*Solutions*	*Words*
can't wake up	alarm clock	(grunt)
	mother	
wake up in a strange place	look around	Where am I?
oversleep/wake up too late	hurry	Oh goodness!
	give up and go	Look at the time!
	back to sleep	

6 For comedy sketches, follow the same procedure. Discuss the normal process (e.g. cooking and serving spaghetti, making a grant application, getting up and dressed). Warn students to expect something a little different from the norm, then play the sketch and discuss the differences. Extend by getting students to think of other wild variations, and to prepare and present sketch ideas.

Follow-up

Extend any problem situation by getting students to build the problem into different sorts of film genre (see Box 45 for an example).

Notes

– This is a powerful and useful activity and easy to do. Don't be put off by its apparent complexity – you would normally only do two or three parts.
– It's usually quite easy to find a written fiction scene representing the same area of life, with its normal process, script, conditions and problems, to supplement the film scene.

BOX 45   Opening a door

• How do you normally open a door? Describe the process.
• What could go wrong? (e.g. It could be locked, jammed, held tight outside, barricaded, electrified; you could have the wrong key; your key could break in the lock; your hand could be paralysed/frozen; the door could be a fake or a virtual illusion). Think of some solutions in each case.
• View the clip from *The Pink Panther* where the door handle comes off in Inspector Clouseau's hand (Sketch 2, Box 14) (or any other scene with a door problem). What's the effect?
• Choose a film genre (e.g. a horror movie, a love story, a chase, a children's story, a ghost story, an action movie) or a specific film and think of what kind of 'door problem' it might have. Create the scene and write it up in a group, or prepare to act it out.
• (Optional) For inspiration read about 'door problems' in your chosen genre (e.g. for children's stories: the door into the garden in *Alice in Wonderland*; the story of Bluebeard; the story of the Three Little Pigs; the doors into mountains in *Lord of the Rings* and *Ali Baba*).

Decisions

Aim: predicting and recapping
Level: lower-intermediate
Material: TV drama series; work-based drama where important decisions are taken during the action

Procedure

1 Stop the video just before the decision is taken. Students identify the decision-maker(s) and adopt his/her/their position(s), then discuss the questions in Box 46

2 View to see if the decision matches the predictions, and if not, why not.

Variation

The same series of questions can serve as the basis of a written report justifying a decision.

Note

This is the fiction version of **Case study**.

BOX 46 Decisions	
Situation	What's the problem?
Causes	How did we get into this situation?
Significant factors	What are the important things we have to take into account?
Choices	What are our possible lines of action?
Consequences	What are the possible outcomes in each case?
Rules	Are there any rules? What happens if we ignore them?
Character	What kind of person are we? Noble/nasty? Impulsive/cautious? Brave/cowardly? Cunning/straightforward?
Decision	What are we going to do?

Describe an ad

Aim: written description and evaluation of TV ads
Level: lower-intermediate
Material: TV commercials

Procedure

1 Tell students that they are going to select a TV ad, study it and describe it (they may use ads in other languages, but should supply a translation). Give them the outline in Box 47 – higher levels should cover *both* columns. Do one or two descriptions together in class as models (or give the IKEA or Delta Airlines descriptions as examples).
2 Students write their own description for homework.

BOX 47   Describing TV commercials

Basic description for LI levels	Add-on elements for higher levels
• Give the name of the product and say what it is.	• Describe the general sales approach of the ad – its angle and its market.
• Say what kind of ad it is: dramatic, atmospheric, comic, or a mixture.	• Say what the explicit and implicit messages are.
• Say what the ad tells us about the product (what it is, what it has, what it does).	• Bring out the atmosphere, mood and tone of voice, and show how the messages are conveyed. Comment on language, wordplay, visual devices and level of hype.
• Describe the action: what we see and what we hear (use the present tense).	
• Say how the ad concludes and give the final slogan if there is one.	• Evaluate the ad for originality, persuasiveness, honesty, memorability and attractiveness.

IKEA (lower-intermediate)

This is an advertisement for a big furniture manufacturer, IKEA. It's a comic ad, which uses visual tricks and surprise. It doesn't tell us anything about the products, it only tells us that we need them. We see the figure of a man against a blank white background. He is facing us. In silence he walks forward and presses his face against the screen. His nose becomes a blob. His eyes go right and left, as if he is looking into our sitting-room. After some seconds he steps back. 'You need some new furniture!' he shouts. The camera cuts, and a hand holds out the IKEA catalogue.

Delta Airlines (advanced): a description and evaluation

The ad is aimed at business people. It tries to give an impression of space, comfort and quiet, freedom to work and enjoy yourself and impeccable personal service, while at the same time highlighting specific facilities offered by the airline. The ad is very atmospheric. It starts with slow relaxing music, showing a long light space. An angelic white figure floats down and silently places a cup by a beautiful woman working at her laptop. No other passenger is visible. The hypnotic music continues; the same figure bends to whisper to a businessman absorbed in a video and drinking champagne. He smiles briefly and returns to his viewing. A soothing voice says, 'On Delta's business class we know how to treat you as an individual ....' The two passengers appear briefly again, with the captions *Laptop power supply* and *Individual videos*. The voice boasts, 'That's why we fly more individuals worldwide than any other airline.' We cut to a picture of the globe against the stars. The voice concludes 'Delta Airlines: on top of the world' and the words appear on the screen. The caption means that the airline flies over the world's surface, but it also suggests that it is better than the competition (the rest of the world), and also means *very happy*, which is how the passengers are supposed to feel.

Personal comment: this ad is a little hard to believe – I have never been on an aircraft with so much space and quiet.

Describing real interaction

Aim: describing verbal interaction

Level: intermediate

Material: interviews and talk shows with interesting personal interactions

Procedure

After viewing the sequence, talk through the questions in Box 48, then view again to confirm and extend.

Follow-up

Students write up a short description of the programme or part of it for homework, or choose their own programme to describe in the same way. Attach written descriptions to the video box or file them where they can be read by other students.

BOX 48   Describing real interaction
(interviews and talk shows)

1   What is the name of the show? Who are the participants? Why were they chosen? What makes it interesting?

---

2 What is its main purpose?
   • *Social/showbiz* – aims to establish rapport, draw people out, reveal their interests and personalities, get some interesting stories (often deals almost entirely with media personalities)
   • *Expert* – aims to get information and opinions from experts or people with relevant experience
   • *Political* – aims to hear what important people have to say
   • *Discursive* – aims to air an issue, discuss the pros and cons, hear the present state of play
   • *Sensational* – aims to stir up strong reactions between participants
3 Describe the participants briefly: dress, appearance, speech style, character. What do you learn from their clothes? Are there some strongly contrasting personalities? Which is the most/least dominant? Do they have any interesting ways of speaking? (**Describing speech style**)
4 What are their general attitudes to each other? (e.g. flattering, friendly, encouraging, neutral, wary, nervous, distant, hostile) (Do a psychological **Character network**.)
5 Pick out the most interesting interaction and describe it. What feelings are evident? What are the people trying to do? What's the outcome? (**What's going on?**)

Describing speech style

Aim: describing ways of speaking and imitating them
Level: intermediate
Material: short sequences showing very different speaking styles, e.g. Woody Allen, a racing commentator, the Borg in *Star Trek*

Procedure

1 Review the vocabulary in Box 49 then view one clip and ask students to choose appropriate adjectives for the speech style. Discuss other vocabulary needed to describe gesture and expression.
2 Students select one utterance for imitation and try it out. Discuss why the speaker speaks like this (consider topic, format, context, purpose, audience, mood and personality). Describe the style briefly (see Box 49 for examples).
3 Do another utterance and compare.

Variation

Start by playing the sequence with sound only and ask students to guess the speakers.

Follow-ups

1 Students find other striking speech styles on video, describe them to the class, play them with sound only and ask the class to guess the speakers; or students can write up a description independently (this is difficult; advise them to use dictionaries carefully).

2 Students invent a love scene/interview/shopping dialogue between two of the characters.

BOX 49   Speech styles

fast	slow	articulate	inarticulate	wordy	terse
emotional	cool/cold	emphatic	low-key	colourful	plain
loud	soft	low	high	clipped	drawling
spontaneous	planned	expressive	flat/monotonous	clear	confused
chatty	formal	energetic	calm/laid back	fluent	hesitant

The Bug in *Men in Black* speaks very loudly and violently, but he is inarticulate because he is a monster pretending to be human and doesn't know how to form the words.

Martin Luther King is very fluent and emphatic and uses colourful language. He is making a speech but it seems spontaneous. He feels deeply about injustice and so does his audience, so it is very emotional.

Diary

Aim: writing; recapping action
Level: lower-intermediate
Material: drama which has a feeling for a day's time span, e.g. soap operas, drama series

Procedure

When students know the characters quite well, ask them to pick one and to write his/her diary for that day: an account of the events and his/her feelings about them, comments and reflections. Remind them to use the past tense for narrating the day's events, but the present and the present perfect for reflecting on the current situation.

Dossier

Aim: reviewing character or action; everyday vocabulary; question formation

Level: lower-intermediate

Material: drama films; soap operas; parallel book and film scenes

Procedure

1 After viewing, choose one of the characters and write on the board any details the class can remember on every aspect of his/her life, from where she buys her shoes to the name of his cat or the make of her car, using the headings *history, domestic situation, looks, lifestyle, virtues and vices, habits, hang-ups, pastimes, love life, work and career, prospects, hopes and fears.*

2 Students then choose their own character (one each, or one per group), create a similar dossier and write it up or report orally. Remind them to use the present tense.

Variations

1 *Quiz* Students devise ten questions about the character as a quiz for other viewers, providing a key on a separate page. The questions must be detailed and answerable (points of fact, not opinion), require short answers, and be grammatically correct.

2 *To recap the beginning of a film* Students select one main character each, or one per group, and write down all they know about him/her, one fact per line. They should include obvious things like age, job, height, appearance, as well as more complicated information. If not sure they should write questions or *I think / She seems / He could be.* Students compare notes, then view the introduction again and extend their lists.

3 *For soap operas* To orient themselves when they first enter the scenario, students re-view the first episode and make lists of *Who* (the people), *Where* (places) and *What* (organizations, major activities), with the important facts about each (divide the work between three students). Later, after viewing other episodes, they select three people, organizations or places and collect the essential information about them on index cards. These can be updated into a mini-archive to brief students starting on the soap, and can form a basis for quizzes and scrapbook contributions (**Soap chronicles**).

Dress

Aim: reinforcing the verbs related to clothes and dressing, which are easily confused

Level: elementary

Material: clips of people wearing clothes and getting into and out of them (these must be suitable for students' cultural background)

Procedure

1 After teaching clothing vocabulary, check that students can handle the related verbs (select from *have on, wear, put on, take off, try on, change/get changed, dress up, do up, undo, get (un)dressed*; and also *get out of, get into, pull on, dress, get something on/off*).

2 Show the clips. Students select appropriate terms to describe the action, checking the verbs off the list. The more clips they do, the better they get!

Effects

Aim: turning a book scene into film, deciding on lighting/sound effects (this can serve as part of the *Make the movie project*, page 29, following scripting and setting the scene).

Level: lower-intermediate

Material: parallel scenes from book and drama film

Preparation: Choose a book scene with plenty of tension or atmosphere which has a parallel scene in the film. Photocopy the book version.

Procedure

1 Tell students they are going to play film director. Read the book scene together, visualizing the action and setting (for in-depth treatment do **Reading aloud** and **Set the scene**).

2 In groups, students decide on how they would shoot the scene, responding to the questions in Box 50 and writing their suggestions onto the photocopy.

3 Groups explain their plans to the class and finally view the original scene and compare.

BOX 50   Effects

1 What general atmosphere do you want to create?
2 What moments do you want to emphasize?
3 How do you want the viewers to feel about the characters and actions?
4 How do you aim to achieve these effects?
   • *Lighting* Main lighting? Any big lighting changes?
   • *Camerawork* Kind of shots? e.g.:
     – panning shots (the camera swings round the scene)
     – tracking shots (the camera runs alongside a moving person/thing)
     – cover shots showing the whole scene from a distance
     – mid shots
     – close-ups
     – zooms (the camera moves in from a distance)
     – fade out (the image dissolves slowly)
     Any strange angles or shots? e.g. from below, from above, very close up, wobbly tracking
     Any special effects? e.g. slow motion, speeding up, coloured filters, superimposed images
   • *Sound*
     – Background sounds and sound effects?
     – Music – what and when?
     – Any big changes in volume?

Enigmas

Aim:	naming sports; speculating about a situation; 'present situation' tenses
Level:	elementary
Material:	very short clips of intriguing moments where it's not clear what is going on (frequent in sports programmes) (see Box 51 for examples)

Procedure

Play the 'enigmatic moment' and ask students to say what sport they think it is and why; what's happening; what they think has happened and is about to happen – and how they know. Establish the *present* context very firmly so as to get the right array of verb forms (**Situation report**). Finally play the whole clip to illuminate the moment.

Variation

Students find their own enigmatic clips and present them in the same way.

Note

A speculative non-fiction version of **Before and after**.

<table>
<tr><td colspan="3">

BOX 51   Enigmas
</td></tr>
<tr><td>*Clip*</td><td>*Sport*</td><td>*What's happened / about to happen?*</td></tr>
<tr><td>A small helmeted figure with drooping arms and hanging head zigzags confusedly into shimmering blue dust, a picture of despair and disorientation.</td><td>motor cross</td><td>He's just crashed his bike.</td></tr>
<tr><td>A man in a bow tie and black waistcoat sits on a chair surrounded by spectators, smiling to himself.</td><td>snooker</td><td>He's just missed an easy shot and lost his turn. The smile is embarrassment.</td></tr>
<tr><td>A man in shorts and vest rocks back and forth on his feet.</td><td>high jump</td><td>He's just about to do the high jump.</td></tr>
<tr><td>Crowds are seated in tiers around a large grassy area.</td><td>cricket</td><td>The game is about to begin.</td></tr>
</table>

Experts

Aim:	talking about an area of expertise; specialist vocabulary
Level:	lower-intermediate
Material:	short sequences on subjects learners know well (sports, business, medicine, their country's political situation, etc.)
Preparation:	Find out what your students are experts on and look out for sequences on suitable subjects, or ask students to do so. News items and match highlights are a good length.

Procedure

1 'Experts' prepare by viewing the item outside class. They collect key vocabulary, check pronunciation from a dictionary if necessary and decide what background information is needed.

2 In class, students teach the vocabulary, explain the situation, show the sequence (with or without sound) and answer questions, e.g. *What is a merger? Where is Azerbaijan?*

Variation

For sports Each 'expert' selects, shows and explains one very short sequence which illustrates an important rule, technique or game phenomenon (e.g. a try, hitting a ball for six, the scoring in tennis). Each also prepares three comprehension questions on the clip: the teacher selects one from each set and uses them, together with the clips, as a final test for the whole class.

Eye on the object

Aim:	reviewing action; practising passives
Level:	elementary
Rationale:	Objects are often important in film drama (famously, the handbag in *The Importance of Being Ernest* or the sled 'Rosebud' in *Citizen Kane*).
Material:	any drama

Procedure

After viewing the film or part of it, students list the significant objects, say what people feel about them, what happens to them and why they are important.

Variation

In drama with a work setting the objects are often documents; students recall what documents have played a role, say what they are called (e.g. scrap paper, reports, memos, IDs, scale plans, betting slips), what form they take or what they are made of (paper/electronic), their origin, their function, who they are addressed to, what they say and why they are important in the action.

Famous films

Aim:	a structured discussion about famous films; relative clauses
Level:	lower-intermediate
Material:	none

Procedure

1 Pre-teach some vocabulary for talking about films as in Box 52.
2 In groups, students think of famous films about given topics, e.g. the future, a war, nuclear war, a blind man, the south of the USA, space travel, aliens, animals, Africa, a fish, native Americans, a natural disaster, cross-dressing. Build up a list of film titles on the board.
3 Each group thinks of another famous film and describes it like this: *I'm thinking of a film in which someone is drowned / a film which ... / a film where ...* Others guess the film and add more information e.g. *It stars Harrison Ford / It's set in Cuba.* Add these films to the list on the board.
4 Students nominate their top three films from the list, giving reasons, and then vote.

Follow-up

Go on to film criticism (**Oscar**) or describing a **Favourite scene**.

BOX 52   Film vocabulary

X plays Y / X plays (the part of) ... It's a(n) ...	satire
The film stars X and Y.	horror film
X stars as ...	love story
The characters ...	romantic comedy
The director ...	cartoon
It's set in ...	animated film
It's directed by ...	sci-fi film
It's based on ...	disaster movie
It's about ...	detective story
	issue movie

Famous people

Aim: a lead-in to improve viewing comprehension
Level: lower-intermediate
Material: biographical and history films; celebrity interviews
Preparation: If possible, find and copy a short encyclopaedia or Internet article about the famous person/people in the film; current celebrities often have a website with biographical information.

Procedure

1 Before viewing, students say what they know about the famous person/people represented. (If they say they know nothing, push them to state the obvious by making easily contradicted statements e.g. *So Abraham Lincoln was Australian? And he died peacefully in his bed?*). Leave gaps in knowledge unfilled, then hand out the biographical information for students to read.

2 *For celebrity interviews* Discuss what questions students would ask the celebrity if they were the interviewers, write them up, then view; check through them again at the end.

For films Discuss who are the main players (including groups/ institutions) (do a **Character network**); what events will appear in the film; and at what point the story will begin. Re-visit the written material while viewing and get students to underline any events and people they see in the film.

Variation

To focus on working lives, get students, before viewing, to fill in (as far as possible) a questionnaire about the protagonist:
• What job/work did/does he/she do? How did it start?
• What was new about what he/she did?
• What problems did he/she have with work?
• Did he/she fail or was he/she successful? Why?
• How did he/she react to success/failure?

After viewing, the questions can be used to structure written homework.

Follow-up

Do **Celebrity interview**, **Interview article** or **Turning points**.

Fashion parade

Aim: clothing vocabulary (see also **Dress**); word-order with adjectives; a lead-in to a talk show

Level: elementary

Material: 'dress' clips of people in clearly defined or striking clothes and costumes – even very short clips if you have slow motion (fashion parade clips are useful for modelling the commentary)

Procedure

1 Explain that an *outfit* is all the clothing that someone wears for a particular occasion, usually with an overall style or coordinated in some

way (introduce the word *matching*). Students are going to describe outfits as in a fashion parade.

2　If you have a fashion parade clip as well, play it as a model; if not, ask students to recall what fashion parade commentary does: names the model (*Sandra is wearing* ...); describes the clothing and its purpose (*sportswear, a tennis outfit*); gives details of colour, material and style of the items (*a short white cotton tennis dress with a flared skirt*); and comments on beauty/utility/interest (*comfortable but a bit dated*).

3　Play the 'dress' clips with sound off; students choose a clip and prepare a commentary.

4　Students read out their commentary along with the clip.

Variations

1　*To lead in to a talk show* Play the first few minutes without sound and ask students to study the guests' appearance and to try to identify role and personality by describing their style of dress (casual, exotic, formal, sporty, sloppy) and saying what type of person they look like (a businessman, a student, an artist).

2　*Picture dictation* For outrageous costumes, individuals or groups view a clip outside class, prepare a description and get the English checked. In class they read out the description while the class tries to draw the costume. Finally, view the original.

Follow-ups

1　Students pair off as models and commentators and organize a fashion parade in class. Filming it adds intense motivation.

2　Students design an outfit for homework, with a rough sketch and a written description.

3　Students choose their own 'fashion plate' from a magazine, newspaper or TV and describe it in speech or writing.

Note

This is a specialized version of **Commentary/Copywriter**.

Favourite scene

Aim:	narrating in the present; describing a scene
Level:	elementary
Material:	none
Preparation:	Find descriptions of favourite film scenes: prepare to describe your own, get colleagues to record theirs on tape or in writing, or use the example in Box 53.

Procedure

1 Give students the descriptions of favourite film scenes and ask if they would enjoy these scenes themselves. Ask them to notice the tenses used.
2 Students decide on their own favourite film scene and prepare to describe it (to jog their memories you can also do **Famous films** steps 2 and 3).
3 Students form groups of three or four and relate their scenes to each other as vividly as possible; others guess how the story develops.

Variations

1 Students conceal identifying details in their description and others guess the film.
2 Volunteers describe stunt scenes from well-known films for others to guess the hero.

Follow-up

Students write up their accounts, get them corrected and pin them up.

BOX 53   Sally's favourite scene

Well, my favourite film sequence is the opening part of *The Night of the Living Dead*, which is a horror film by Romero. It's a black and white film, and at the beginning you have this brother and sister who arrive by car at this country cemetery which is very isolated, deserted, and they're going to put flowers on their parents' grave. And they walk to the grave and put the flowers on the grave, and then the brother starts to tease his sister, and he's trying to frighten her; he says, 'I'm coming to get you! I'm coming to get you!' And she says, 'Oooh! Stop it! Stop it!' and she runs off sort of giggling and screaming, off to the side of the cemetery, slap bang into this kind of lurching shambling THING which comes out of the forest and – *eats* her up. And that's the end of the scene.

Feeling flow

Aim:	describing feelings in crucial scenes and events
Level:	elementary
Material:	drama; sports sequences
Preparation:	Select a sequence where the feelings are very clear.

Procedure

View, and ask students to draw a graph of the scene reflecting one character's (or group's) feelings. Together, label the graph with the events and feelings in the scene and then explain how the character feels during the scene and why (see Box 54 for an example).

Follow-up

Students draw a graph which represents their ups and downs over the last year and write it up or talk it through, saying what happened and how they felt. Sports addicts can draw a graph of a match they attended, then explain it.

Variation

Do the Follow-up as a lead-in instead.

Note

This activity can be included in the mini-project *Describing interaction* (see page 52).

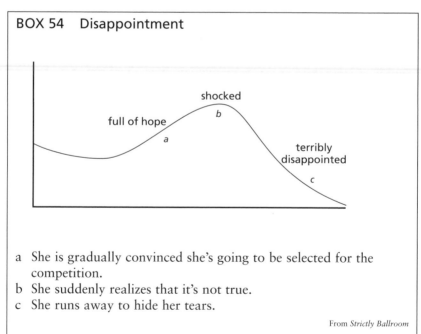

BOX 54   Disappointment

a   She is gradually convinced she's going to be selected for the competition.
b   She suddenly realizes that it's not true.
c   She runs away to hide her tears.

From *Strictly Ballroom*

Fights

Aim:	talking about conflict; (for drama) discussing the role of the fight in the plot
Level:	lower-intermediate
Material:	drama films containing set-piece battles, shoot-outs and punch-ups; documentaries about political, legal and military conflicts; major competitive sports events; combative interviews

Procedure

1 Pre-teach the vocabulary of conflict (e.g. *victory, defeat, win, lose, beat, give in, strategies, weapons, advance, retreat, run away*, etc.).
2 Use the A questions in Box 55 as a lead-in to the fight, and the B questions after viewing to review the action, selecting the most appropriate questions. They can be discussed in pairs, in groups, or with the whole class.

Follow-up

Students divide the fight into stages, take one stage each and prepare a voice-over commentary on the action with a view to explaining the outcome (see Box 56 for an example). Replay the scene, stage by stage, with the volume down while students comment, pausing as necessary to demonstrate a point (a version of **Commentary/Copywriter**).

BOX 55   Fights

A Before the fight

- Who's going to fight and who isn't?
- Why are they going to fight?
- What are the strengths and weaknesses of each side?
- What are the odds? How would you bet? (e.g. '2 to 1 against the king')
- How will they fight? Predict/suggest strategies for both.

B After the fight

- Explain the outcome.
- Was the victory due to strength, strategy, skill, bravery, brains, luck, weapons, heroic sacrifice?
- Was the defeat due to weakness, fear, cowardice, incompetence, stupidity, bad luck, trickery, treachery?
- What was revealed about the players?
- Was the result inevitable? Why/Why not?

BOX 56   The Battle of Falkirk in *Braveheart*: commentary
(The first three stages)

1 Here we are before the battle. You can see the Scots are preparing the ground in some way (we discover later they are laying pitch on the field – they have a crafty plan). They discuss whether Robert the Bruce is coming to support them (the Bruce is politically the most important Scottish nobleman).

2 Now the two armies are drawn up. We see a mysterious black knight in a closed helmet at the side of the English king. We begin to suspect that this might be the Bruce, who has changed sides on his father's advice.

3 The battle is beginning. King Edward orders the infantry to advance (they are mostly Irish). The infantry goes forward on both sides. Here they are heading for the clash, faster and faster. Then, two metres apart, they stop and greet each other. The Irish have decided to go over to the side of the Scots. At this point everything looks good for Wallace – but it's not going to last ...

Film presentation

Aim:	talking about films
Level:	intermediate
Material:	drama films

Procedure

Individually or in small groups, students study a feature film of their own choice outside the class and prepare to present it to the rest of the class (see the instructions in Box 57). The presentation should take not more than 15 minutes and should aim to interest the audience as much as possible. If the presentation is by a group, students can share out the different tasks (introducing the film, outlining the story, presenting the illustrative scenes and evaluating the film). Give them advice on how to do the presentation (see Box 57). After the presentation, make the video available to students who want to see the whole film.

BOX 57   Film presentation
Instructions and advice for students

What to do in your presentation

• Explain the type of film, the main characters and the basic situation.

- Tell the first half of the story. Show two or three scenes from the film to illustrate the story, introducing each one by explaining the situation.
- Finish by saying whether you recommend viewing and why.

Advice for a good presentation

- Write up all the characters' names and other important names at the start.
- Introduce a little key vocabulary or essential information.
- Speak very slowly and clearly and say everything twice (in different ways).
- Back up the explanation visually (e.g. with a chart of characters, a map).
- Check frequently that your audience understands.
- To avoid embarrassing pauses, make sure you can locate the illustrative scenes quickly. Make someone responsible for having the next scene ready.
- Don't say what happens in the end – leave your audience in a state of suspense!

Floor

Aim: describing turn-taking behaviour and observing how it is expressed

Level: lower-intermediate

Rationale: If there are several participants who have the right to speak, they have to share 'the floor'. A TV host or chairperson 'manages the floor'. Students need to learn to talk about this.

Material: excerpts from talk shows and videos of meetings or discussions showing a variety of turn-taking behaviour and floor control

Procedure

1 Discuss the rules of conversation. How do people behave: when they want to speak; when they want to go on speaking; when everyone wants to speak; when they want others to speak; when they don't want to speak? How do they get, keep, give or hand over the 'floor'?

169

2 Present a selection of expressions from Box 58 – those illustrated in your selected clips and a few others – and discuss what they mean.
3 Students view the clip(s), and identify and comment on 'floor' behaviour and language.

Variation

Use **Holophrases** to focus on single expressions for floor management.

Note

When looking at speech behaviour in any discussion (**Speech acts**), add appropriate 'floor' expressions (e.g. *Someone kept interrupting someone, someone kept very quiet*).

BOX 58   Floor actions

all talk at once	interrupt	sit back
bring someone in	keep quiet	raise your hand
butt in	leap in	catch someone's eye
come in	say something	lean forward
cut someone off	shut up	raise your voice
draw someone out	speak/speak up	say something (e.g. *Can I*
not get a word in	take your turn	*come in? Don't butt in!*
hang back	talk someone down	*Let him have his say.*)
have your say	turn your head	

Fly on the wall

Aim: comprehension of the action; vocabulary of human behaviour; written narrative
Level: lower-intermediate
Material: drama films

Procedure

1 After viewing the film, students choose an important scene and (individually or in groups) try to reconstruct it from memory, as if they were an unseen witness or 'fly on the wall': who is there, what do they say, what happens?
2 Without re-viewing, students write up their account – double-spaced – then view the scene to check their recall and amend their account (or each others'). They should write the changes in the spaces between the lines or use the 'revision' function on the computer.

Variation

Students create their account orally, or take the roles and walk through the scene, trying to remember the dialogue, as in **Walkthrough.**

Note

Remind students to use the present tense for describing the action. This activity forms part of the mini-project *Describing interaction* (see page 52).

Follow the news

Aim:	news comprehension; discussion, analysis and exposition; vocabulary building; summarizing
Level:	intermediate
Material:	ongoing news stories (this activity integrates news from all sources, including television)
Preparation:	Find an ongoing news story which appeals to the majority of students. Decide the length and depth of the project and how it will be organized.

Procedure

(Stages 5, 6, 7, 9 and 11 are optional.)

1 *Explain* the project to students.
2 *Issues* Discuss why the topic is important or interesting and what questions it raises. Record these questions on a poster/flip chart.
3 *Discuss* how to divide the work of gathering the news, and how the events will be dealt with in class (e.g. groups report on the day's or week's events OR everybody reads and views all the sources).
4 *Follow the news* in more than one medium: TV, radio, newspapers, teletext, Internet.
5 *Roles* Identify the major players in the story and allocate them to individuals or groups (or let students choose). Students monitor events from their adopted points of view so as to understand the players' actions, motives and interests, and predict what they will do.
6 *Summary* Summarize the events in stages. Do this in class until students are good enough to do it on their own. At each stage add to or change the poster 'issues' and discuss the old ones.
7 *Vocabulary* Build up a vocabulary map for the subject from all sources.
8 *Background* Get volunteers to research the background (recent history, political structures, ethnic groups) with reference books or Internet sources, and to report back.

9 *Forum* Students formulate questions for the players and have a round-table question and answer session in the form of a press conference.

10 *Analysis* Go back to the poster questions, discuss them and come to some conclusions.

11 *Write-up* Write up the complete summary and the analysis.

Getting things done

Aim: directives and other language for getting things done
Level: intermediate
Material: drama series or other work-based drama
Preparation: Select sequences where a lot of action is organized.

Procedure

Once students understand the sequence well, view it again and look at the language used for organizing action. See Box 59 for an example.

Variation

Use **Speech acts** to match the acts to the words/people instead of vice versa.

BOX 59 Getting things done		
Examples Language from the video	*Give us a hand here,* *would you?* *– Sorry, I'm busy.*	*Perhaps you'd like to look* *around? Be my guest.* *– Don't mind if I do.*
WHAT ARE THEY DOING? *e.g. advising, asking, forbidding,* *commanding, giving permission,* *asking permission, urging*	asking	giving permission
WHAT'S THE RESPONSE? *e.g. protesting, putting it off,* *objecting, agreeing, refusing,* *making an excuse, hesitating*	making an excuse	accepting
HOW DIRECT ARE THEY? *e.g. very rude, direct but* *friendly, neutral, polite, very* *polite, polite but sarcastic*	fairly direct but not rude	indirect (polite irony)

Gossip

Aim: observing and practising 'talking about talk'

Level: intermediate

Material: drama clips, especially from soap operas, where people talk about other conversations; remembered interactions in interviews and talk shows

Procedure

View the sequence and ask students to:

- notice how people talk about talk (e.g. words for speech acts, attitudes and reactions, manner of speech)
- notice backshift tenses for reported speech, and any contracted unstressed forms (e.g. *He said he'd never been there; she promised she'd come*)
- if possible, reconstruct the conversation described – they may also like to script the scene, using **Scriptwriter** to help with the layout

Follow-up

Students choose a short interesting dialogue scene, think about the reactions of one of the characters and decide who the character will tell about the conversation and why. Adopting the character's point of view, they recount the conversation briefly in speech or in a letter, explaining what happened and how they felt. The basic narrative tense should be the past.

Note

This activity can stand alone or can be used in the mini-project *Describing interaction* (see page 52).

Grading

Aim: helping students choose material for independent viewing

Level: lower-intermediate

Material: most video material

Procedure

Discuss the choice of video material for independent viewing in class. Advise students to look for 'comfortable viewing' – not too easy, but not so difficult as to be discouraging. They should test-view the beginnings of videos and abandon them if they are too tough.

Lower levels After viewing a complete video, students discuss and complete the form in Box 60. Attach it to the cassette/DVD box for other viewers.

Higher levels View the first ten minutes of three or four popular films with a range of difficulty. Discuss what makes each film easy/difficult to understand, e.g.:

Speech

- There is/isn't a lot of important information in the words.
- There is/isn't a lot of speech in relation to action.
- There are/aren't a lot of pauses.
- The speech is very fast/quite slow.
- There are/aren't heavy accents and dialect words.
- The words are very clear/very difficult to hear.

Content/Action

- The actual events are easy/not very easy to understand.
- There's a lot happening/not much happening.
- The action and the speech support/don't support each other.

Students give each film a difficulty rating, and finally write a short 'difficulty report' on a self-selected film introduction, saying how difficult it is and why (see Box 61 for an example). Attach the reports to video/DVD boxes or file them; well-organized institutions can use them to contribute to a film grading system.

BOX 60 Grading (1 is low, 5 is high)			
Title: Length: Subject: Signed	Difficulty (1–5)	Weight (1–5) (= seriousness)	Emotional impact (1–5)
	Comments:		

BOX 61   *Dances With Wolves:* Difficulty report

The beginning of this film is quite easy to follow. It's obvious from the uniforms that it's the American Civil War. There's a lot of action and not many words. Many of the words are incomprehensible: they are spoken fast and indistinctly and seem to be in quite strong accents. But the words aren't very important in this part – they are mainly a commentary on the action, which is self-explanatory.

Heard and seen

Aim: close comprehension and an overview of the plot
Level: lower-intermediate
Material: drama film, especially 'true stories' and soap operas

Procedure

Students re-view the whole or part of a film to find references to plot events (see Box 62 for an example). They write down the references; say when the events take place in relation to the reference; say whether they are seen in the film and, if so, when.

Variation

After viewing, students recall what 'news' is given in the film, who gives it, where/when and what effect it has on the story (see Box 63 for an example). (Point out that *news* is uncountable and not plural.) Re-view scenes on which there is disagreement.

Note

This activity (a more elaborate version of **Matching**) needs to be modelled before students embark on long sequences or independent work.

BOX 62   References to events in *Braveheart*

Reference to event	*When?*	*Seen?*	*When seen?*
The English are advancing an army towards Stirling.	present	no	–
Wait until we've negotiated.	future	yes	soon after
They killed her to get to me.	past	yes	when Morag is executed

---

BOX 63   News in *Quiz Show*

The news	*Who gives it?*	*Where/When?*	*Significance*
The audience is tired of Herb in the quiz show	Dan Enright, the producer	in the restaurant	Charles replaces Herb on the show
The quiz show is fixed	Herb Stempel (to Goodwin)	in the hotel lobby at the lift	Dick Goodwin decides to take the case to court
Dick has hard evidence that the show is rigged	Dick Goodwin (to Dan Enright)	in the TV studio	Enright loses his job

---

Holophrases

Aim:	focusing on one-off functional expressions, e.g. *Be seeing you, Good luck, Pull the other one, I agree*
Level:	elementary
Rationale:	It's not easy to get these conversational tokens right first time: students need to observe them used in context.
Material:	interactive sequences
Preparation:	Collect clips which feature *one* useful functional expression.

Procedure

Describe the situation of the clip: e.g. *You are parting from travelling companions. They may be going into danger and you want to wish them well. What do you say?* Discuss possible alternatives, then students view and discover the expression (*Best of luck!*).

Variations

1 Collect two or three clips having expressions for the same function (e.g. parting, objecting, expressing incredulity). List the expressions and add others which are not in the clips (see Box 64 for an example). Give out or write up the list, discuss appropriate context and tone for each item, then use the film sequences as above.

2 As a preliminary to class discussion, look at expressions for agreement, disagreement, opinion, and turn-taking (see **Floor**).

BOX 64   Well-wishing

This list of functional expressions for 'well-wishing' was compiled for an advanced class (the underlined examples were illustrated in clips):

Good luck	*Break a leg*	*Sweet dreams!*
All the best	*Good health!*	*Happy birthday*
Give her my love	*Have a good day*	*Best wishes*
Enjoy yourself	*Best regards*	*With compliments*
Congratulations	*Have a nice time*	*Bless you!*

How it's done

Aim:	practising adverbs and adverbial phrases
Level:	elementary
Rationale:	Films provide evocative acting of everyday behaviour which cries out for mood adverbs.
Material:	drama clips; some sports clips
Preparation:	Collect two or three clips showing the same action (e.g. sitting down, driving a car).

Procedure

1 Review adverb formation.
2 View each clip. Students describe the action in one sentence in answer to the questions *What? How? Where? Why?* e.g. *He's sitting down very sadly on the pavement because he has nowhere to go.*
3 Students work with a partner to think of other ways of doing the same action, formulating a sentence in answer to the same questions (e.g. *She's sitting down nervously on the edge of a chair because she's doing an oral exam*). One of the pair demonstrates the action while the other describes it.

Note

The activity can contribute to the project *Describing interaction* (see page 52).

I spy

Aim:	practising basic vocabulary, prepositions of place and question forms
Level:	elementary

Preparation:	View the clip and create a blackboard quiz (e.g. *Find something beginning with P, something blue, something on top of something else, two things you use for cooking*).
Material:	any clip with a number of clearly visible ordinary objects or actions

Procedure

Give the quiz questions and play the clip. Students find the answers to the quiz, competitively if they wish. To focus on prepositions of place, ask questions about location (e.g. *Where is the mirror?*).

Variations

1 View first, exhorting students to notice as much detail as possible, then give out the quiz. Students answer as much as they can, then view again to check and complete.
2 Teach the words first (e.g. for furniture, colours), then students view to spot the things.
3 For sports actions, first identify the players (*the one with glasses, the little one*), then students view, and ask and answer questions: e.g. *Who scored the goal? Who fell down?*
4 Students prepare quizzes for each other, either in class after viewing or individually at home.

Interactive language

Aim:	focusing on interactive language
Level:	lower-intermediate
Material:	drama clips
Preparation:	Use short scenes which students already know well and which contain useful interactive language (see Box 65 for an example), e.g.:

- functional expressions
- colloquial multi-word verbs
- close colloquial collocations, including expressions with *make, do, go, get, have, take*
- expressions of doubt/certainty/opinion
- modifiers and hedges (e.g. *a bit, pretty, rather, really, sort of*)
- fillers (e.g. *um, ah, well, er, yes*)
- talk about talk (references to/reports of other talk, past, present or future)
- question tags

Procedure

1 Before viewing, study some short scripts (see Box 65 for an example) so students can get an idea of 'interactive language'. Use one scene to establish the idea, and another for students to hunt through on their own.
2 Students view a well-known scene, pick out some interactive language and say whether they use such language themselves.

Variation

Start a project collecting multi-word verbs and recalling them by context.

Follow-ups

1 Students do the same activity for homework if they have access to video.
2 Review the selected items a week later by putting them on the board and asking students to recall the context (who said it, to whom, about what).

Note

This activity should be done regularly to get practice in noticing interactive language.

BOX 65   *Home and Away*
An excerpt from the Australian soap opera

Functional expressions = *special type*.   Tags = CAPITALS
Doubt/certainty/opinion = SMALL CAPITALS   Talk about talk = **bold**
Modifiers, hedges, fillers = *italics*
Multi-word verbs and other strong collocations = underlined

(*In the kitchen, Mr Fisher's house. Shane is cooking.*)

Fisher: Well, I MUST SAY, I wish all my students were as motivated as your sister, Damien.
Damien: Oh *don't worry about it*. She'll get over it.
Shane (*proferring a spoonful of stew*): So what DO YOU THINK?
Fisher: *Mm. Ah*. Yes, that's, that's very distinctive.
Shane (*anxiously*): Ah. What's wrong with it?
Fisher: Oh nothing, *absolutely* nothing.
Shane: No, it's missing something, ISN'T IT?
Fisher: Well, *a little* extra flavour wouldn't go amiss. Some seasoning, maybe, or mixed herbs.
Shane: Oh no, there's none left. I already checked.
Fisher (*taking out some money*): Oh, *here you are*. Go and get some.

> Shane: I'll send Damien. He'll go.
>
> Damien *(indignant)*: Why me?
>
> Shane: 'Cause I'm cooking.
>
> Shane *(to Fisher)*: And, *uh*, *you won't forget to* **ring** the cleaning lady,
> WILL YOU?
>
> Fisher *(resigned)*: No, Shane, I won't forget to **ring** the cleaning
> lady.

Interview

Aim: creative speaking; interview techniques; narrative tenses
Level: lower-intermediate
Rationale: The viewpoint of the naive onlooker at world-shaking
                events is a hallowed literary convention used by Tolstoy,
                Stendhal, Voltaire (and latterly Forrest Gump!)
Material: interview sequences with people who participated in
                important events (from news items, documentaries,
                interviews, talk shows)

Procedure

At least two lessons will be required for this activity.

1 Explain that students are going to interview each other about important events as if they were there. Divide the class into interviewers
  and interviewees. Interviewees select a major historical event (e.g.
  Pompeii, the Kennedy assassination), decide on their role (player,
  onlooker) and one thing they did/saw, and record these anonymously
  on a slip of paper, which goes into a hat. Interviewers pick a slip from
  the hat – thus they know the event and the role but not who the
  interviewee is.

2 Look at some interview clips as models. First, students look for
  convincing or unexpected detail and any feelings and reactions mentioned. On second view, study questioning techniques (open questions, encouraging noises, follow-up questions), question forms and
  narrative tenses (**Questions**).

3 For homework, interviewees invent recollections (with convincing
  detail), and interviewers plan three or four main questions and check
  their grammar. Remind interviewers that they should introduce the
  interviewee and sign off at the end.

4 Run the interviews. With small classes, do them in front of the class;
  divide large classes into groups and circulate; or get students to record
  the interviews. Give a time limit.

Variation

Students are interviewed about newsworthy events they have personally been involved in.

Note

This activity is an extended version of **Comment**, with more room for the imagination.

Interview article

Aim:	writing an interview article from a TV interview; using quotations
Level:	intermediate
Material:	a short personality interview or an excerpt; an interview article
Preparation:	For input, find a short interesting TV interview; and for a model, a short interview article (about a different person) from a magazine, newspaper or TV channel website (or use the example in Box 67).

Procedure

1 Explain the idea of writing an article from a TV interview.
2 View the interview.
3 Introduce an interview article as a model. Students study the picture and title for clues about content and tone, then read it and speculate what the interview questions were.
4 Students re-read the article, looking for background information (e.g. history and career), 'foreground' information about the present situation, comments on the interviewee's character and manner, and quotations.
5 If there is time, discuss appropriate verb forms and tenses (**Tenses, Situation report**).
6 Students re-view the interview to select quotations, background and fore-ground information and discuss impressions of character and manner.
7 Give students the instructions in Box 66 and set a word limit.
8 Students try writing the article, in groups or individually.

Follow-ups

1 Students write their own article from a TV interview or from their own real interview.
2 Students interview each other in pairs, write up the interviews and produce a Class Yearbook with one page for each student (including photo). This is good for rounding off a year.

Note

The activity **Quotes** can lead in to this activity.

BOX 66   Writing an interview article
Instructions for students

Aim to write four paragraphs.

1 View the interview (or conduct your own and record it).
2 Choose the two most interesting things the person said, and the most important comment.
3 Put one of the interesting things in the **first paragraph**, with a quotation, to attract attention.
4 In the **second paragraph** introduce the person: give a little background information (history, career) and some foreground information (what's happening right now). Support with a quotation.
5 In the **third paragraph** give the person's main comment about the situation, then explain and support with a quotation. Say something about the interviewee's personality and manner.
6 **Finish with a paragraph** about the second interesting thing, with a quotation.
7 Read through the article and improve the English.
8 Try to make coherent links between the parts of the article.
9 Produce a final copy, in columns, with headline and by-line, and photograph if possible.
10 Post it up (or circulate copies) and get comments.

BOX 67   An interview article

When Helen freezes over

The wintry Warsaw weather gave Helen McCrory, star of Channel 4's dramatization of *Anna Karenina*, all the help she needed in playing Tolstoy's tragic heroine.

Helen McCrory has a tip to share with any actress wishing to become a romantic star. 'Shoot all your big scenes in sub-zero temperatures,' she advises. It appears that the tears in McCrory's eyes when she played Anna Karenina were due to the bitter cold in Warsaw, where the film was shot, just as much as to the fate of Tolstoy's tragic heroine. Running through the snow to meet your lover may be a thrilling fantasy, but there's nothing like chilblains to add a touch of genuine agony.

But the actress found herself genuinely carried away by the romance of her role. 'I've never really done a big romantic role on TV, although I've done them in the theatre,' says McCrory, who made her name as a classical actress with the Royal National Theatre and the Royal Shakespeare Company. 'Playing a woman like Anna, with all the fantasy of a film set at your disposal, was just spellbinding,' she says. 'Putting on a ball gown and doing scenes with fifty people waltzing and a live

orchestra, or standing at midnight on a snowy station platform miles from anywhere with wolves howling in the darkness – I was just so happy.'

McCrory, who in person is warm and witty, was a bold piece of casting for this great role, most famously played on the big screen by Greta Garbo. The result is a performance that shows the human cost of love rather than the grand gestures of doomed passion. Take away the furs and the fantasies and you are left with a woman who must choose between her child and the man she loves. 'Women are still going through exactly what Anna went through a hundred years ago,' she says. 'Divorce laws may have changed, but the central dilemma remains.'

McCrory has another tip: 'My advice to women watching *Anna Karenina* is to just sit back, have a nice glass of wine and let another woman take that train for you. Stay in the warm and save yourself an affair.'

Radio Times, 20–26 May 2000

Invisible music

Aim: describing people and settings; a lead-in to films

Level: elementary

Material: music sequences where the visual scene is fairly predictable or comically unpredictable; opening film sequences with evocative music

Procedure

1 Play the clip two or three times with sound only.
2 Students discuss some or all of the questions below. Select the most appropriate ones: you may want to concentrate on the production of the music, its setting or the images it evokes.

- What kind of music is this? What instruments are used?
- What's the mood of the music?
- What kind of social atmosphere do you expect?
- Where are we? What is the occasion?
- Who's playing/singing? Describe him/her/them.
- Who's listening? Describe the audience.
- What happens/What is happening?
- What images come to mind?
- Can you imagine a story?

3 Build up notes on the board, then play the clip and compare it with students' expectations.

Follow-up

Students create their own sequence of images (in speech or writing) for a given music clip.

Note

This is the music version of **Picture it**.

Issues

Aim: to stimulate discussion

Level: intermediate

Material: drama films, documentaries, news items, interviews and talk shows dealing with controversial issues; short sequences expressing a clear opinion or attitude

Procedure

For drama After viewing, students decide what questions the film raises (see Box 68 for examples), and discuss them in class. Where there are clearcut values, get students to:

a identify some obvious goodies and baddies
b find examples of their good and bad behaviour
c explain the implicit values, i.e. what is seen as good or bad
d say if they agree with them
e take the part of the baddies and try to justify their behaviour

For a simpler activity, do only a), b) and e).

For programmes about real life Identify the main question(s) before starting. Ask students to formulate their personal position privately and to write it down. Circulate, checking the language. After viewing, students reveal where their sympathies lie. Then they view again taking notes on the arguments of the other side and thinking how to respond to them. Group students into parties and get each to state its case, producing evidence and arguments.

For short sequences Use a short 'quotation' (a brief clip from an interview) to launch a discussion. View it for word-for-word comprehension, then ask students to decide, phrase by phrase, if they agree with it.

BOX 68   Issues

Film/Programme		*Question/Issue*
Drama film *Sliding Doors*	–	Are relationships predestined?
News item on a euthanasia referendum	–	Who is entitled to make the rules?
Interview with maverick eco-economist	–	Are we worrying too much about the environment?
Sequence from *Big Brother*	–	Which of these people would you vote out?

Jumbled statements

Aim:	recapping part of a film; action vocabulary
Level:	lower-intermediate
Material:	drama of any kind

Procedure

1 While viewing, write up a set of statements about the action on the board (or students write one each while they view; then put them all on the board), e.g.:

The priest pulled the girl away.
A man fell off the roof.
The pigeon flew up to the roof.
The boss sent the man away.
Charlie counted the money.

From *On the Waterfront.*

2 Students discuss and expand each statement (*Who? When? Why?*), then try to sequence them correctly.

3 View again for students to get more detail and check the sequencing.

Variation

Utterances While viewing, each student writes down one thing that some-one says (or the teacher can write down several). After viewing, students/teacher write up all the utterances, then decide who said them, to whom, what about, when, where, why and in what manner. Students arrange them in chronological order and re-view to check their impressions. Students can also create a quiz for others by selecting a number of utter-ances and recording the correct answers (who, when, etc.) separately.

Labelling and linking

Aim:	a lead-in or recap; identifying topics, discourse links and discourse functions
Level:	intermediate
Rationale:	Most documentary texts divide into 'paragraphs' just like written articles (see Box 69 for an example), hence some paragraph-based reading activities can be extended to documentary video. Links between sections may be verbal or visual or both. Long interviews and talk shows tend to divide into topics established by the host's main questions.
Material:	documentary films; interviews or talk shows with clear sections
Preparation:	View the video, identify the separate sections, the topics they deal with, and how they are linked, and think of a suitable title or 'label' for each section.

Procedure

Use a different procedure according to your purpose.

To lead in Write up your section labels randomly and ask students to speculate on a logical order. While viewing, students tick sections they recognize, and afterwards review the order.

To recap After viewing, give or elicit the labels in the right order, then view again for students to identify where each new section starts. Or present the topics as headings, ask students to remember what they can about each and view again to collect more information.

To focus on discourse links After a first view, students re-view, identify points where the topic changes and say how the change is signalled. Get students to think of suitable labels for the sections they have identified.

To focus on discourse function After viewing, students recall some striking images and say what their function was in the whole (e.g. to illustrate, to explain, to provide a contrast, to introduce a person).

Follow-up

Students plan a mini-documentary for any subject they are experts on: nightlife in the city, memories of school, exam pressure, popular footwear. They think of three or four topics they want to cover and decide where to go, who to interview and what questions to ask.

BOX 69   Labels
for the first sections of a documentary about the history of the UN

Main claim of the documentary series
The fate of three UN employees
Early euphoria and idealism
The choice of the first Secretary-General
The character of the first Secretary-General
Background to the witchhunt
The witchhunt

Lead-in

Aim:	anticipating the whole by focusing on the first few minutes
Level:	lower-intermediate
Rationale:	In drama films the opening sequence sets the scene, mood and themes; in documentaries it includes the 'hook' or 'teaser', the proclamation of the main concern, and the announcement of what the programme intends to do.
Material:	the opening credits in drama films; the opening sequence of documentaries; book and film

Procedure

For drama film View the credits and ask students to recall the main images, identify the type of music and sounds, then discuss what kind of action, mood or theme they suggest. If the film opens with evocative music, do **Invisible music** with selected questions.

For book and film Consult students about ways into (for example) a Western (lone cactus, cowboy hat and spurs, shoot-out, man slowly approaching on horse) and what each does (e.g. sets the scene, symbolizes the themes, acts as a flash back, initiates the action, establishes a character). Ask students to suggest suitable images to introduce the film of the book they are studying, describe them in writing, read them out and explain them. Finally, play the opening sequence of the film and discuss which aspects of the story it highlights.

For documentaries Introduce the subject, look at key vocabulary, then play the first few minutes two or three times. Students discuss the questions in Box 70. Alternatively, play the opening sequence without sound and discuss what the pictures demonstrate (see Box 71 for an example); then view again with sound and ask students to spell out the messages of the pictures.

Note

For news, see **News leads.**

BOX 70 Documentary lead-ins		
Question	*Answer*	*How do you know?* (pictures, sounds, words, music?)
What is it about exactly?	....	....
Is it going to be sad/comic/ shocking/dramatic/serious?	....	....
What is its main question/point? (write it down)	....	....
What is it going to do? (e.g. tell a story/expose/describe/ explain/discuss pros and cons?)	....	....
What are we likely to see?	....	....
Who are we likely to hear from?	....	....
Does it interest you? Why/ Why not?	....	....

BOX 71   Born a girl

The introductory images of a development documentary about education of girls in Zambia. On the right is the meaning given to the images by the commentary.

The pictures	*What the pictures are saying*
Ringing the bell for school in the morning	The programme is about education.
Children running to school with packs on their backs	It's the start of the school day.
The school in the distance	
Other children coming to school (all boys)	
Children lining up to go into school (mostly boys)	More boys than girls go to school.
Cattle in the fields	The traditional occupation here
Close-up on cow grazing	is cattle-raising.
Cattle again	
A young boy driving an oxcart across the field of the camera	Boys are brought up to dominate.
A young girl carrying a baby on her back	Girls are brought up to serve.

Learning English with films

Aim:	awareness of how to get the best out of film viewing
Level:	lower-intermediate
Rationale:	If students are capable of independent film viewing and have access to English-language video, take time to discuss the value of film viewing, practical problems and the best approaches.
Material:	none
Preparation:	Read through the discussion questions in Box 72 and assemble your own thoughts. You'll find some ideas in the *Introduction* and on pages 12–17.

Procedure

Discuss the questions in the box with students. Allow plenty of scope for them to talk about their own experience – they can usually give each other valuable information and advice.

BOX 72   Learning English with films

1 Do you think films and TV programmes are good for learning languages? If so, why?
2 Where can you get videos and DVDs?
3 What are the problems with using them for learning languages?
4 What are the advantages of DVDs?
5 What kind of films/programmes would you say are too difficult? What makes them difficult/easy?
6 Is it a good idea to watch very difficult video material?
7 Would you recommend seeing the film/programme dubbed into/subtitled in your own language before seeing it in English?
8 Would you recommend watching a film in your own language with English subtitles? Why/Why not?
9 Are English subtitles on English films/programmes a good idea?
10 If you have an English film/programme, what can you do to help you understand it?
11 Apart from watching the film/programme straight through, is there anything else you can do to appreciate it better?

Letters to the editor

Aim: leading in to and following up a controversial programme; inference reading; expressing opinions in writing and speech

Level: intermediate

Material: controversial TV programmes and letters about them to TV magazines/websites

Preparation: Find letters written to a TV magazine about a controversial programme (or use the examples in Box 73). If you have time, write your own (anonymous) inflammatory letter about the programme you plan to use.

Procedure

1 Before viewing the programme, give students viewers' letters about another programme to read. Get them to: infer what they can about the programme (what kind of programme? who was involved? what happened?); and say on what grounds it was praised or criticized.
2 After viewing, discuss the programme and ask students what they would like to say to the TV channel that aired it. Read out your own letter if you have written one.
3 Students write a short letter to the editor, as groups or individuals, expressing their views, anonymously.

4 Correct the English. Number the letters, display them on a real (or virtual) bulletin board, and give students the opportunity to comment and reply.

Variation

Use the inference reading activity with newspaper criticisms about TV programmes.

BOX 73   Letters to the editor

BLACK SHEEP CASTS A SHADOW OVER *CASTAWAY*

What was the selection committee for *Castaway* thinking about, to allow so many misfits through the net? And the sloppy management was unforgivable that allowed personal belongings to be lost at sea and failed to put up accommodation in time. Or were all these mistakes deliberate? After all, they made for great television!

(Name & address)

After watching the latest updates of *Castaway*, my mind wandered back to the selection team and in particular the team psychologist. I have no training as a psychologist, but I am a trained nurse and, right from the very first televised interview with Ray Bowyer, it was unanimous in my family that he was going to be trouble.

(Name & address)

Survival it is not – the castaways have everything, including alcohol, supplied regularly by helicopter. Is it poetic licence to state that they have had 100 mph winds? Rubbish – 70 mph has been the worst this winter. Sub-zero temperatures? Surely everyone knows that the Gulf Stream floats past the back door here? *Castaway* is just a bad programme-maker's cruel joke on a gullible group of people.

(Name & address)

Congratulations to the BBC and Lion TV for the early return of *Castaway*. What a wonderful and exciting programme it was, especially the antics of rapscallion Ray Bowyer. I look forward to watching the next instalment, hopefully very soon.

(Name & address)

Adapted from *Radio Times*, May 2000.

Lifestyle

Aim: describing and comparing lifestyles; expressing preferences; practising the present simple

Level: elementary

Material: a sequence which presents a very clear picture of lifestyle (e.g. drama, ads)

Procedure

1 Introduce the word *lifestyle* and ask *What kind of lifestyle does Dracula have?* To help, suggest something easy to contradict, e.g. *Quiet but comfortable?*

2 View the clip and ask the same question about the main character in the video.

3 Extend the first impression by going through the following checklist, asking for illustrations:

- Domestic routines?
- Wealth and spending patterns?
- Dress?
- Work?
- Leisure activities and interests?
- Social life and personal relationships?
- Priorities in life; general attitudes and philosophy (if any)?

4 Ask which aspects of this lifestyle they would love or hate.

Follow-ups

1 Students compare this lifestyle with their own.

2 Students write up a lifestyle description for someone they know, giving plenty of detail.

3 Students find two very different lifestyles (e.g. ads or real life) and compare them.

Lipreading and mindreading

Aim: producing interactive language

Level: lower-intermediate

Material: short drama clips (five to six utterances) with very distinct utterances and visible reactions OR (Variation) scenes with vivid non-verbal expression

Procedure

1 Play the sequence without sound and discuss what the characters are feeling and saying.

2 Students count the utterances in the sequences and construct a dialogue. Replay the soundless scene as often as necessary and help by providing the first utterance, several key utterances or one complete side of the conversation; or (if possible) by slowing down the film to focus on the actors' mouths.

3 Students **Act along** with the actors before viewing with sound.

Variation

Where characters are clearly saying one thing and thinking another, freeze the frame and discuss the 'interior text'. Write it up on paper in 'thought bubbles' and stick them over the appropriate heads (normal paper will adhere naturally to the screen).

Note

This activity lends itself to wild fantasy, as many excellent parodies bear witness. When choosing your clips beware suggestive mouthings! This is the dialogue version of **Commentary/Copywriter**.

Long and short

Aim:	practising conjunctions *when* and *while*; contrasting simple and continuous tenses
Level:	elementary
Material:	drama scenes which combine continuous and single actions

Procedure

1 After viewing the scene, draw a line on the board. Write the continuous actions above it (with the students' help); below it, write the single actions; and next to it write *when* and *while*, e.g.:

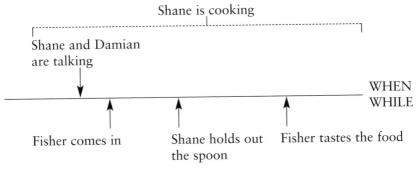

From the soap opera *Home and Away* (see page 179)

193

2 Students link actions with *when* or *while* (e.g. *While Shane is cooking, Fisher comes in. When Shane holds out the spoon, Fisher tastes the food.*)

Loves and hates

Aim: talking about character and behaviour
Level: lower-intermediate
Material: video drama, especially soap operas and drama series; interviews and talk shows

Procedure

For drama After viewing one or two episodes, students sum up their feelings about the characters. Ask them to divide a sheet of paper into four as in Box 74. In the top left box, students write the name of the two characters they like most; in the bottom left, two they really dislike. They then write one sentence on the right for each character, explaining their likes and dislikes, referring to what the characters have said and done (or just what they look like). Circulate and check their writing. Students share their opinions with their classmates and find someone who agrees with them.

For interviews, talk shows Students divide the page into four columns: in the first they list the participants; in the second they indicate their like/dislike; in the third they write an adjective for each person; and in the last they justify their judgement. Students can do this in small groups and report back, or work individually and then circulate to compare notes.

BOX 74   Loves and hates

The characters I like most:	*Why?*
1	....
2	....
The characters I dislike most:	*Why?*
1	....
2	....

Make a case

Aim: reviewing action; stimulating discussion; practising argument

Level: elementary

Rationale: Drama video is very suitable for case-making, since many scenes are designed to demonstrate something or make a point. See also **Make a case for character**.

Material: drama of any kind; shots which establish setting

Procedure

1 After or while viewing, make some obviously true or untrue statements about the story or setting (e.g. *The daughter is very rich/has no money; the police are corrupt/honest; it's winter/summer*) and get students to find evidence in the film to support or confute them.

2 At a more advanced level, make one fairly controversial wide-ranging statement (e.g. *The message of* Tootsie *is that cross-dressing can improve your character*) and get students to discuss its truth, bringing evidence on both sides and coming to a personal conclusion.

Make a case for character

Aim: recapping the introduction; describing and demonstrating character

Level: lower-intermediate

Rationale: Many early scenes in a film are set up to establish and demonstrate character.

Material: drama films; book and film; interviews and talk shows

Procedure

For drama Divide the board into three columns with the headings *characters, traits* and *evidence*. Write three of the main characters in the first column: students think of three adjectives to describe each of them – write these in the second column (it might help to suggest what they are *not* like, e.g. *Sherlock Holmes is stupid and easygoing*). Students then find the behaviour that supports their choice of adjectives – write this in the third column (students studying the book draw on both film and book). Replay to confirm and reinforce impressions.

For interviews and talk shows Present ten descriptive adjectives (e.g. *smooth, shy, articulate, assertive, sensitive, self-confident*), some of which apply to the people in the show, and discuss meanings before viewing. After viewing, students select those adjectives that fit the people in the show, referring to behaviour in the programme.

Variation

Students choose an animal for each participant and say how they resemble this animal.

Maps and journeys

Aim: comprehension: lead-in and review of action

Level: lower-intermediate

Material: any film/programme/sequence with real and recognizable geographical locations

Preparation: Find and photocopy a map of the area and reference material (encyclopaedia/Internet) describing the events or the place/area. Make a list of the places named.

Procedure

Before viewing, give students the map and the reference information/list of places and ask them to find the places on the map. In the course of viewing, go back to the map from time to time; write in information or draw in the movements of the various parties.

Variations

1 To recap drama films, students can recall and list all the main settings and create a notional map OR pick one location and tell its history in the story.

2 As a general recap, students describe the journeys made and their purposes, using these questions as prompts:

Who went where? When? How? Why? With what result?

Note

Disaster movies with known settings (e.g. *Godzilla, Independence Day*) become quite educational with this approach!

Matching

Aim: comprehension and listening strategies; recapping

Level: elementary

Material: any video clip with voice-over commentary

Procedure

Play the sequence twice. Students find where words in the commentary match pictures and write down any words directly 'illustrated' (see Box 75 for an example). Re-view without sound, pausing for students to 'label' the pictures orally as they see them.

Variations

1 Students work in pairs: one writes down the text, the other lists the images. They come together to match their accounts.
2 Give the 'illustrated' words before viewing; students infer the meaning while viewing.
3 For sports clips, advanced students can pick up references in the commentary to specific actions (see Box 76 for an example); lower levels listen for crowd reactions (*oohs*, *aahs*, clapping, booing, cheering): sports experts in the class can explain these reactions in relation to the screen actions (see **Experts**).

Note

The drama equivalent is the more elaborate **Heard and seen**. A special case of matching is **Quoting and illustrating**.

BOX 75   Matching

From the documentary *Predators*. The underlined words are clearly 'illustrated'.

Words	*Pictures*
Here in <u>the Arctic</u> it's vibrations travelling through the air that can give the game away. <u>This lemming</u> is ten centimetres under a vast security blanket of <u>snow</u>. It's unseen, seemingly protected on all sides. But in a few seconds it will be dead.	snowy wastes lemming in snow tunnel
	Huge owl descends, sinks talons into snow, grabs lemming and takes off.
<u>The great grey owl has struck</u> again. But how did it know the lemming was there?	

BOX 76   Comments on the match

These voice-over comments were visibly 'illustrated' in the play:

Made a good decision there.   *Beautifully done.*
Timed that kick perfectly.   *He looks onside to me.*
Ooh! Inches from the line!   *Great side-stepping ability there.*

Misapprehensions

Aim:	reviewing the whole plot or the action so far
Level:	lower-intermediate
Rationale:	Many conventional plots depend upon some kind of *misapprehension*: mistakes, lies, deceptions, misunderstandings. The effect is enhanced by dramatic irony, where the audience knows something that the characters don't know.
Material:	drama film of any kind

Procedure

Make a list of the misapprehensions in the plot, find their causes and effects, and get students to set out their findings in a table. If an element of dramatic irony contributes to the drama, ask *Who knows?* to bring this out, or make a break to intervene with the activity **Advice**.

Missing character

Aim:	producing interactive language; reviewing action
Level:	lower-intermediate
Material:	drama of any kind

Procedure

In the middle of the film, suspend viewing and ask students to pick out a very minor character or invent a 'missing character' who must have existed (a relative, a friend, a dogsitter, a salesman, etc.). This person is to make a surprise comeback/appearance and take on a major role. Discuss how this will happen, and plan, script or role play the scene.

Variations

1 For courtroom drama, suspend viewing in the middle of the trial when there has been enough cross-examination to provide a model. Students form pairs, invent a surprise witness (the 'missing character') for the defence or the prosecution, and take on the roles of attorney and witness. Attorneys and witnesses prepare their stories, then witnesses take the stand and are questioned first by their own attorneys, then by the opposition.

2 If there is an invisible missing character, constantly referred to but never seen, get students to reconstruct all they know about the character.

Note

Time-consuming but fun.

Missing scene

Aim:	producing interactive language; overall comprehension; creative writing
Level:	lower-intermediate
Rationale:	In all drama there are scenes which must have taken place although we don't see them.
Material:	drama film

Procedure

1 Students identify a scene which is not seen but which must have happened. They discuss where and when it took place, who was there, what was said, what was felt and what was done.
2 Students role play or script the scene, then improve the language and do it again.

Variation

Students recall an important conversation in their own lives and script it for homework. (Advanced students can do a proper script, as in **Scriptwriter**, but this takes time!)

News leads

Aim:	comprehension
Level:	lower-intermediate
Rationale:	The lead, the quotations, the graphics and the footage all make good entry points for anticipating the rest of the news item (see Box 77 for examples).
Material:	news items

Procedure

1 Lead in to the subject (e.g. by asking what students know about it).
2 Students write down the lead as a progressive dictation (**Transcript**).
3 Students divide into three groups to discuss and list expectations of what *details* will be given, what *images* will be seen, what *people* will be interviewed and what they will say.
4 View the rest of the item twice. Students check off what they see or hear, add to their lists, and report back.
5 Students view again and ask each other comprehension questions.

Variations

1 Use a 'quotation' from the news item, silent footage, or graphics, for advance speculation. Play and ask *Who is he/she? What's he/she talking about? What do you think the item is about?*

2 Reverse the process. Play two or three news items to demonstrate how the news lead sums up the item. Then play a news item without the lead and work on comprehension. In groups, students write the lead. Make sure they are using the appropriate tenses. When they have a final version, they take turns to play anchorman from the teacher's desk. Finally, play the missing lead.

Note

This activity parallels **Lead-in** (for documentaries).

BOX 77   News leads and quotations

The essential information in a news item is summarized in the 'lead', the first one or two sentences, spoken by the newsreader. The following 'location report' expands the lead and shows illustrative footage and brief 'quotations', i.e. comments from interested parties.

Newsreader: *In America a nuclear research plant is under threat from a forest fire which has swept through parts of New Mexico.* (The item moves to footage of the forest fire and a location report giving details of how it started, what is being done, what damage has been caused and what dangers still threaten. There is a comment ['quotation'] from the local police chief.)

Newsreader (spoof news item from *The Day Today*): *The Bank of England is in chaos following the discovery that the pound has been stolen.* (The newsreader then gives details of who, when, where and how, against footage of Securicor vans, a London bus, and an aerial shot of the escape car.)

A news 'quotation' (Britain's 'cancer czar' comments in a news item about a man whose cancer was not diagnosed): *We certainly do have a mountain to climb in delivering cancer services in this country – I make no secret of that. Our survival rates are not as good as they should be. We know also that patients aren't receiving the quality of care that they should be, and that's where – it's my task to put that right.*

News script

Aim: controlled writing and editing; reading aloud: a first attempt at a news style (students prepare a voice-over script to accompany a piece of news footage)

Level: intermediate

Material: news items

Preparation: Find two or three short news items of general interest, with clear short leads and short illuminating footage and select one for students to script (see Box 77 for examples).

Procedure

1 Discuss the relationship between the news lead and the location report (see Box 77), looking at one or two sample items as models. Tell students they will be writing their own location report.
2 Introduce the chosen news item, play the lead and get students to transcribe it.
3 Play the footage silently and discuss the possible content of the location report.
4 Students write the location report in groups. Work out the time they have to fill and the number of words (about three per second).
5 Students read their reports aloud against the silent video, trying to fit them to the shots. (It is difficult to finish at the right moment, and creates some competitive fervour.)
6 Finally, view the original item with sound.

Variations

1 Advanced students can try to achieve a real news style. When studying the models ask:
   • Formal, neutral or informal?
   • Long or short sentences?
   • Do the words describe the images or complement them?
   • Is there information in the report which is not in the images?
   • Are there facts and figures?
   • Are there personal opinions and reactions?

   Establish that news scripts should be in simple, clear short sentences, should not describe the pictures but complement them, should pack in relevant information and should adopt an objective stance (these are some of the BBC's principles for news writing).
2 For a more authentic product, give notes on the content of the original news item; students write up their report from the notes.
3 Students draw up a 'shot list' with timing and write the location report alongside it.
4 Use only a silent piece of cryptic footage and leave the whole news item to the students' imagination, e.g. an open landscape could be Siberia in the summer, the site of a new motorway, a nuclear test zone or a nature reserve. This can produce wonderful results!

Note

This is the news version of **Commentary/Copywriter**. (N.B. Fitting text to news footage is a considerable challenge even to professional TV news writers – don't expect too much!)

News story

Aim: turning video input into a newspaper story: comprehension, discussion and writing

Level: intermediate

Material: short TV news items; newsworthy events in drama films/documentaries; newspaper stories

Preparation: Find one or two standard short newspaper stories as models, or use the students' production in Box 78. If you are using a news item, view it and identify the lead (see Box 77).

Procedure

Start by looking at the format of a few short newspaper stories (headline, by-line, picture, length of paragraphs) and the story structure (non-chronological order, summary first paragraph, expansion in the following two or three paragraphs, direct quotations from interested parties and how these are introduced, less essential details at the end which enable the article to be cut from the bottom up).

With TV news items

1 View the news item.

2 Students write down the lead (**Transcript**).

3 Do comprehension work on the rest of the item (see page 70).

4 (Optional) Students invent other interviewees, role play phone calls (**Comment**) and pull out good quotations.

5 Discuss what the newspaper headline might be, what visual information must be converted to words, and what picture might accompany the story.

6 Students write first drafts, swap them for editing and rewriting, and finally write up the story as far as possible like a real newspaper, with columns, headlines, etc.

With input from other video

1 Do comprehension work on the video input.

2 Discuss what the story is, i.e. what will go in the first paragraph (this is often the most difficult part).

3 Decide what extra information will be needed and who will be asked for comments.

4–6 As above.

202

Note

Producing a convincing newspaper story takes a lot of practice and time and one should ask whether language learners need to learn this skill. It can, however, be very enjoyable.

BOX 78   A news story from TV drama

Chirp's Gazette

What's a "Pa-pa"?

By Silvia Frigo, Silvia Marcoccio, Ughetta Palmieri

Chirp – Yesterday a little girl started speaking an unknown language.

"Pa-pa" was the first word pronounced by Candy, twenty-month-old baby, daughter of small farmers Cri and Pee-pee, while they were having breakfast. The whole village came to have a look.

"I can't understand what she says" said her desperate father, "but she was a normal girl before that", added the mother.

Expert Mr. Owl said that "it's generation gap", but according to mayor Cheep, it's "a problem of mixing cultures", because the grandfather was Italian.

It's the first case here in Chirp, but researches revealed similar experiences in Sweden and Italy seven years ago.

Created from a three-minute film about a village where everyone speaks 'Birdish' and great excitement is created by a baby whose first words are clearly not in the local language.

One-liner

Aim:	reading comprehension; sentence stress and intonation practice
Level:	elementary
Material:	parallel scenes from book and drama film

Preparation: Find a short interesting film-and-book scene and select one expressive utterance which is used in both. Also, if possible, find examples elsewhere of single lines interestingly delivered (e.g. the famous *A handbag?* as spoken by Edith Evans in *The Importance of Being Ernest*), or delivered in different ways (make a tape recording with your colleagues).

Procedure

1 Explain that the way a single utterance is delivered depends on how the whole interaction is interpreted. Play an example if you have one.
2 Write up the selected utterance from the scene. Students read the book scene silently, discuss the interaction and the feelings involved, and then decide how the utterance should be delivered: how fast/ loud, in what manner, with what pauses, stresses, gestures and expressions – and why. Histrionic students can try it out; others can write instructions for the actor (e.g. *Sit back in the chair and say it quietly, looking at the floor*).
3 View the scene and discuss the actor's performance of the utterance.

Note

Follow up with **Quotes** to highlight utterances which have significance throughout the plot. This activity can stand alone or can form part of the *Make the movie* project (see page 29).

Organization man

Aim: overall comprehension; discussion of working relationships
Level: intermediate
Material: drama with a work setting or any setting with authority relationships (families, schools, etc.)

Procedure

1 After viewing whole or part, students draw a tree diagram (an organization chart) showing the boss, the deputy and selected subordinates, e.g.:

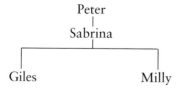

2 Give students these scales:

The boss	authoritarian – consultative – democratic – inactive
The subordinates	submissive – accommodating – independent – insubordinate
Colleagues	cooperative – competitive – indifferent

Students place the characters on these scales and find some evidence for their choice.

3 Students select a character and describe any working relationships from his/her point of view, giving examples (see Box 79 for an example). (N.B. This opens up a wide area of idiomatic vocabulary and students may need help in finding expressions.)

4 Students describe their own working environments in the same way (disguising names, if necessary).

BOX 79   Siegfried, according to James

Siegfried can be bossy, but he's also very generous. Most of the time he's all right to work with. I think I give in when necessary and stand up to him when necessary, but perhaps I'm a bit weak sometimes for the sake of peace and quiet. For example, I didn't say anything when he blamed me for the car breaking down, although it was actually his own fault.

All Creatures Great and Small, BBC TV drama series

Oscar

Aim:	talking/writing about films; critical thinking
Level:	intermediate
Material:	drama: whole films

Procedure

After viewing a film, use the checklist in Box 80 for discussion in class, prepared or unprepared. Press students to support their comments with reference to specific moments in the film, and re-view these in the light of what they say.

Variation

Students use the checklist to write a short report recommending or not recommending the film for an Oscar as best film of the year in its category. (N.B. The checklist is only an aid to thinking: students should not feel obliged to use the words or order.)

BOX 80   Oscar

Setting
Original or hackneyed? ....
Memorable or unimpressive? ....
Special effects? ....

Themes/Issues
Relevant/topical? ....
Deep or shallow? ....

Dialogue
Sharp/original or obvious/corny? ....

Acting
Convincing or wooden? ....

Action
Fast or slow? ....
Realistic or unconvincing? ....

Emotional impact
Tense or flat? ....
Hot or tepid? ....

© Cambridge University Press 2003

Other people's shoes

Aim: an overview activity; an alternative to **Turning points**
Level: intermediate
Material: biographical films, especially about ordinary people; interviews and chat shows

Procedure

1 After viewing part or whole, students recall the protagonist's main actions, reactions and achievements, e.g. *He rescues his mother by banging on the door / He learns to paint / He chats up his nurse when he's waiting to appear at the ceremony (My Left Foot).* (They should use the present tense for recounting film action.)
2 Students discuss the causes and effects of each action.
3 Students discuss these more general questions about the protagonist:

How is/was he/she different from me/us? What does/did he/she have in common with me/us?	in character/temperament/interests? in social/economic circumstances? in relationships? family? lifestyle? in general environment? country? culture?

Differences are always easier, so press students to find at least two similarities as well.

Follow-up

Students write a comparison of the protagonist with their group or with themselves, giving plenty of examples and illustrations from the film. They have a choice of titles: *He's just like us/me / She's not like us/me at all / I would/wouldn't have done the same.*

Over the top

Aim: judging the level of realism; describing normality and excess

Level: elementary

Material: any clip with the potential for hype, especially TV commercials

Procedure

After viewing the sequence, discuss how realistic it is and ask students to give it a rating:

1 = Super-realistic	*It could be true. For example, …*
2 = Fairly realistic	*It could happen, although …*
3 = Exaggerated	*It could happen, but it's unlikely because …*
4 = Fantasy/over the top	*It could never happen because …*

For all ratings students add an explanation. Help with expressions like:
X looks/doesn't look … X is too/rather/far too …
There's too much/not enough … X is unlikely/improbable …
You don't usually get/find …

Note

Related activities are listed in **Describing speech style**.

Panning

Aim: written description and comparison

Level: elementary

Material: drama clips

Preparation: Find some good panning shots of environments (e.g. a flat, a street, an office) which are different from students' own.

Procedure

View the clip, describe what is shown, and ask students to imagine that they are taking a camera around *their* flat, street, office in the same way. They are to describe what the camera sees (orally in groups or for written homework). They may also like to make comparisons with the scene in the clip.

Variation

For familiar settings (a street, apartment, bedroom, office), students make a sketch map of a similar setting they know well, label the items and then explain the picture to a partner, bringing out its personal significance. Emphasize that artistic ability is not required and demonstrate by doing your own sketch map and commentary.

Parallels

Aim: discussion; the language of comparison; oral presentations and writing

Level: intermediate

Material: history films and biographical films; news items; documentaries

Procedure

For historical and biographical films After viewing, ask students to think of parallels in their own country, past or present, and to prepare a short talk describing a comparable event/personality and making comparisons with the person or events in the film.

For current affairs, news and documentaries Ask students to compare the situation/events with those in their own country, looking for the factors that differ and explaining them. Students studying in an English-speaking country can also do a series of presentations focusing on the host country or the home country, choosing their own news items to demonstrate differences they perceive.

For well-known institutions, monuments, geographical features Use **Picture it** to arrive at a description, then ask students to describe a similar well-known feature in their own country.

Pick of the news

Aim:	comprehension and discussion of a significant current event
Level:	lower-intermediate
Material:	a TV news item selected by learners
Preparation:	Record the day's TV news and make a list of the main stories.

Procedure

1 Read students the list and ask them which story they would like to view, and why.
2 Ask them to share what they know about the situation chosen, including the obvious (e.g. where it is, how long it has been in the news). If appropriate, do a **Character network** to show relationships, and establish the geography (**Maps and journeys**).
3 Ask what questions the item raises and list them. Separate issues (e.g. *Why are the Russians and the Chechens fighting?*) from broad philosophical questions (e.g. *Why do ethnic conflicts exist?*) and simple factual ones (e.g. *Where is Chechnya?*).
4 View the item for comprehension (see page 70).
5 Discuss what light the item throws on the issues.

Variations

1 Individual students or small groups select an item, prepare it and present it in class, saying why they chose it, what they know about the situation, what questions it raises, and what the implications of this particular event are. Advise on appropriate tenses (**Situation report**).
2 If you have historic news items (e.g. the fall of the Berlin Wall, the assassination of Kennedy), play them and get students to identify them; then ask what happened and why, and why it was significant.

Picture it

Aim:	describing people, settings or aspects of settings (e.g. colour, position); raising awareness of cultural realities of place and period (Variations 2 and 3)
Level:	elementary
Material:	clips showing familiar, famous, predictable, or typical settings, people, scenes or behaviour (e.g. the White House, an English breakfast, a French farmer, an airport, a sports victory); film-and-book scenes with clear period settings and behaviour

Procedure

The general procedure is that students imagine what they will see, then view and compare expectations and reality.

1 Before viewing, tell students the situation (e.g. this is an airport scene). They then list everything they *expect* to see (e.g. check-in desks, luggage, a runway) and discuss their lists.

2 Students view the sequence and check off the items, then say: what was on the list but not in the film; what was in the film but not on the list; how what they saw differed from their expectations.

Variations

1 To reinforce vocabulary, after viewing students draw a sketch map to show the position of some things they saw, and label them, or say what things the actors touched, how and why.

2 For stereotypes or famous places, prepare by asking questions about details, e.g. *It's an English lord – Is he tall or short? Fat or thin? What's his nose like? What's he carrying? How does he walk?* Then show the clip and compare expectations with reality.

3 For films of books with strong period/cultural settings, pick short sequences illustrating characteristic settings or behaviour of the era and devise some detailed questions (see Box 81 for examples). Introduce the scene to the students, give them the questions and ask them to speculate on the answers, drawing on their knowledge of the book and the period. Then view. Students can prepare a scene in the same way for the rest of the group.

4 A victory scene is a good way to introduce a sports project. Ask students what happens in scenes of sports victory. What do winners, losers and supporters do? Draw up a list, e.g.:

winners	hug each other, clap each other on the back, shake their fists, jump on each other, clap their hands, grin, shout, shake hands with the losers, hold up the trophy, carry each other on their shoulders
losers	sit down on the ground, put their heads in their hands, just stand there
supporters	cheer, clap, wave flags, jump up and down

Play the scene, describe the behaviour and add to the lists.

BOX 81   Ernest and Elsinore

ERNEST

Introduction: *Ernest is going to visit his friend Algie in London. He is planning to propose marriage to Gwendolen so he is looking very elegant.*

The Importance of Being Ernest by Oscar Wilde

210

Guess:
- What kind of transport do you think he takes?
- How many wheels does it have?
- Where is the driver?
- How does Ernest tell him to stop?
- What is Ernest wearing around his neck? On his hands?
- What else is he wearing? What colour is it?
- What is he carrying?

ELSINORE

Introduction: *We're going to see the king's court at Elsinore.*

Hamlet by William Shakespeare

Guess:
- The king is drinking wine – out of what?
- What kind of seats do you think they are sitting on?
- What are their shoes made of?
- Is there any kind of covering on the floor?
- A letter arrives for the king – what does it look like?

Place and period

Aim:	learning and talking about a setting or period, and about changes between then and now
Level:	elementary
Material:	drama: films and series with carefully created professional or period settings (e.g. *Howard's End, Gandhi, Upstairs Downstairs*); clips from old movies which can be compared with the present; clips showing old and new forms of familiar things (e.g. trains, computers, telephones, production lines, cigarette lighters, sportswear, bathing habits)

Procedure

With drama films Students treat the film as a documentary and study it in depth to see what can be learnt about (for example) Washington, lawcourts, American homes in the forties, eighteenth-century dress, etc. (see Box 82 for an example). They may all contribute information on the same aspect, or each student take one. They can round off the activity by preparing a detailed quiz for the other members of the group.

With archive footage or old movies Play the clip and ask *What's changed?* (or ask the question first and then show the clip). Together build up a paragraph with the following verb forms:

Past	*used to be/have/do*
Present	*have changed; have become*
	are/aren't; do/don't ... any more
Future	*will probably get/become/be; aren't likely to ...*

Follow-up

Students find their own example of change and write a similar paragraph, using the tenses in **Situation report**. They may search films and documentaries and/or quiz their grandparents.

BOX 82   Edwardian kitchens

Kitchens were very different. They were usually in the bottom of the house and they had gaslight. The food was sent up to the family in a hand-operated lift. The stoves were enormous and so were the kitchen tables, which had to be scrubbed every day. The kitchen staff all wore long dresses with aprons and caps and there was a strong social hierarchy, with the cook at the top and the scullery maid at the bottom. They had to do everything by hand as there was no electrical equipment, and everything had to be prepared fresh because there was no frozen food and no cans, so they went shopping every day.

(Information gathered from the BBC drama series *The Duchess of Duke Street*)

Plan a chase

Aim:	producing narrative; present tenses; time conjunctions; prepositions of place and movement
Level:	lower-intermediate
Material:	chase sequences
Preparation:	Find a few classic chase scenes (e.g. *Blues Brothers, The Third Man*).

Procedure

1 Tell students they are going to invent their own chase scene but first you'll look at some to get an idea of what to do. View one or two chase scenes and discuss the following questions:

- *Who's chasing whom?* How many pursuers and how many pursued?
- *Why?*
- *Where?* Is it different from other chase scenes? If inside, where? (underground, rooftop, cellars, sewers, up and down stairs). What kind of building? (a flat/warehouse/power station/public library). If outside, city or country? What terrain? (hills, mountains, fields,

rivers, side streets, cemetery, football ground, racing stadium).

- *When?* e.g. night/day/evening/morning?
- *How and how fast?* e.g. foot, bus, car, tractor, lift, escalator, aeroplane, camel, helicopter, sailing ship, speedboat, horse, elephant, wheelbarrow – is it something new?
- *What with?* Any weapons or equipment? Any special clothes?
- *Who else?* Are there other people? What are they doing? (e.g. shopping, sightseeing, having a demo, the rush hour). Is there a dramatic contrast?
- *What result?* Are they caught or do they get away?

2 Give students a copy of the questions and ask them to work out their own chase in groups. Suggest they divide it into three or four phases, and heighten the drama with a narrow escape and some tricks. They should use the present tense. Circulate to advise on the language.

3 Students read their chases out and/or do a **Walkthrough** with commentary.

Variation

To practise specific vocabulary (e.g. sports, air travel), specify that the chase must be located in a sports centre, an airport, etc.

Follow-up

Students revise and write up their chases for homework.

Note

This activity can be preceded by **Chases** or **Runabout**.

Plot idea 1

Aim:	planning a film; talking about films; raising awareness of film structure (at least two lessons)
Level:	lower-intermediate
Material:	none

Procedure

1 Tell students they are going to invent a plot idea for a film. The one they judge best will get the sponsor's (notional) funding.

2 Students read through the film formulas in Box 83 and add examples from their own experience. They decide what kind of film they want to create and whether they will work individually or in groups.

3 Students choose a category for their film (see Box 84). (You can have most kinds of plot in most categories – they've even made a musical

about the Mafia!) Again, students should extend the examples from their own experience.

4 Students decide on:

- the setting (country? city/town/countryside? where exactly? when?)
- the central characters (not more than four): names, ages, nationalities, jobs, faces, and one or two interests/obsessions/habits
- the opening situation, how the characters meet and how we meet them
- what the crisis/climax will be (near the end of the story)
- a complication to prolong the plot

5 Students make notes and then write up their plot idea (using the present tense) in not more than 200 words. It is edited by the teacher or other students, then posted or read out. The class decides which plot idea will get the sponsor's funding.

BOX 83	Film formulas	
Plot type	*Description*	*Example*
Search	Someone sets out to find something (a person, a thing, the truth). After many adventures he/she tracks it down.	*The Truman Show* *Missing*
Crime	A crime is committed and one or more people work to unravel the mystery of who did it.	*Mississippi Burning* *Suspect*
Battle	The goodies are fighting the baddies. In the process the hero/heroine's courage is tested and the cowards/traitors are revealed.	*Rambo* *Star Wars*
Picaresque	The innocent hero/heroine wanders through the world, meeting adventures and revealing the nature of society.	*Forrest Gump* *Thelma and Louise*
Hunt	The hero/antihero is hunted by baddies/goodies. Ends in confrontation/capture.	*A Perfect World* *The Fugitive*
Disaster	Natural or man-made disaster overtakes a group of people. They react, interact and develop until the crisis is over.	*Titanic* *Lethal Virus*
Love story	Boy meets girl but something stands in their way. In the end they are finally united.	*You've got Mail* *Beauty and the Beast*

Trial of strength	Someone with a special capacity, interest, disability or commitment is put to the test and proves his/her worth.	*Scent of a Woman* *Children of a* *Lesser God*
Epic/ Chronicle	Set in a significant historical period, with spectacular action, the film interweaves several people's stories and shows how they affect and are influenced by their times.	*Gone with the* *Wind* *Braveheart*
Enterprise	People come together to accomplish a project.	*Blues Brothers* *Topkapi* *Wag the Dog*
Small town	A fairly enclosed community is disturbed by the arrival of a new element.	*Dead Poet's Society* *What's Eating* *Gilbert Grape?*

BOX 84 Film categories

Sci fi	Almost anything (usually some kind of adventure) happens, but in a futuristic world.	*Close Encounters* *ET*
Comedy/ Tragedy	Meant to make you laugh or cry. Tragi-comedies do both.	Comedy: *Tootsie* Tragedy: *Othello*
Musical	Almost any kind of plot, but with musical background and setpieces, singing and dancing.	*Saturday Night* *Fever* *Blues Brothers*
Realistic/ Fantastic	Realism is about the treatment more than the likelihood of events (ridiculous plots may have realistic treatment). 'Magic realism' mixes realistic and fantastic.	Realistic: *Short Cuts* Fantastic: *Lord of* *the Rings*
Horror	Normal life is disrupted by elements of the supernatural or grotesque.	*Dracula* *The Fly*
Thriller	Much the same as crime, but involving suspense and sometimes horror as well.	*The Usual Suspects* *Speed*
Parody	Any standard plot line or category sent up by comic exaggeration. 'Noir' is 'black' parody.	*Indiana Jones and* *the Last Crusade;* *Men in Black*

Children's	The main protagonists are children or animals, and the themes and treatment are suitable for children. *Babe* *Harry Potter*

Plot idea 2

Aim: discussion and writing; a lead-in to viewing the whole film

Level: lower-intermediate

Material: one stimulating scene or sequence

Preparation: Make sure the scene will be unknown to students (use an old movie).

Procedure

1 Explain that you are going to invent the film starting from one scene only. Play the scene twice, say where it comes in the film (halfway through? near the beginning?) then ask:
   - Where are they?
   - Who are they?
   - What is their relationship?
   - What are they doing? Why?
   - What/Who are they talking about?
   - What came before?
   - What will come next?
   - What other messages are coming across?
2 In groups, or as a class, students draw up an outline of a plot which includes the scene viewed.

Variations

1 Give a clip of a setting and another of some people (non-fiction clips are better) and hand over to students to develop.
2 Give a dramatic ending or opening; students reconstruct the plot backwards or forwards.

Follow-up

Show the original film – or talk through the plot, illustrating with a few video scenes.

Preview

Aim: writing a preview for other viewers; a follow-up to
                viewing the programme
Level: intermediate
Material: documentaries or interviews; written previews from TV
                magazines or websites
Preparation: Find some programme previews or use those in Box 85.

Procedure

1 After viewing a documentary, suggest that students write a preview
  for other viewers. Give out examples of documentary previews and
  ask the questions in Box 85 (if you have several previews, divide them
  among students and get them to ask each other the questions).
2 Together, write a preview for the programme you have viewed, which
  gives an idea of its content, mood, attitude and quality. Attach it to
  the cassette box for others to read.

Variation

Students write a preview for documentaries of their own choice, or
introduce the programme in class, giving an outline of the content
and whetting the appetite by showing one or two sequences.

Note

This matches the anticipation activity **Lead-in** for documentaries.

Problem

Aim: talking about problems; handling questions;
                questioning techniques
Level: lower-intermediate
Rationale: Much advice-giving fails because the adviser doesn't
                explore, listen, check, or think creatively. It can be
                improved with 'counselling' techniques, which also
                extend the language.
Material: any sequence where a practical problem is discussed,
                e.g. in consumer programmes, health programmes,
                talk shows (the video adds authenticity and gives a
                model)

Procedure

1 Explain that you are going to practise giving advice about practical
  problems.

BOX 85   Programme previews

ENGLAND'S OTHER ELIZABETH
9.30 pm BBC1

Recently made Dame of the British Empire, Elizabeth Taylor is still a class act. Although she has made more than 70 films and won two Oscars, it is for her seven marriages, her diamonds and her illnesses that she is remembered. In her first full-length interview on British TV for ten years, she sets that record straight. With extra testimony from friends Shirley MacLaine, Rod Steiger and Angela Lansbury, she talks about her childhood, the business of acting, Mike Todd and Richard Burton, and her Aids foundation, to which she is passionately committed. Generously peppered with clips this is a performance worthy of the last of the old Hollywood royalty. *FL*

THE NATURAL WORLD
8.30 pm BBC2

Australia can kill you. The most venomous continent in the world has flora and fauna that have myriad ways of taking your life. Not that it is intentional, it is just a freak of nature that the way it defends or feeds itself has a fatal effect on humans. This film lovingly portrays the kinds of life that use poison and asks why that particular continent is so full of it. On land and sea there are snakes, spiders, plants, an octopus and even a mammal (the duck-billed platypus) that are toxic. And, just in case you don't get the full picture, the makers have provided reconstructions of some accidental encounters between animals and humans. *FL*

TRUE STORIES: RAISING *ALEXANDER*
9.00 pm C4

Alexander was a happy, smiley responsive baby just like so many others. But at two he 'shut down', becoming totally self-absorbed while suffering alarming tantrums. Alexander was diagnosed autistic, a condition for which there is no cure but which, his parents hoped, could be helped with a radical new therapy. The cameras followed Alexander and his family over several years and, while scenes of a youngster screaming and crying are always distressing, the overall mood of the film is tremendously positive. One's heart goes out to Alexander's parents, who have suffered enormously just to get their son to behave in a way that most parents take for granted. *JR*

Radio Times, 20–26 May 2000

QUESTIONS

- What is each programme about – exactly?
- What is its special appeal? (e.g. horror, human interest, mystery, drama, exotic location)
- What is its main question/point?
- What does it do? (e.g. describe, investigate, explain, put an issue/person in the spotlight)
- What special images/people does the preview mention?
- Which programmes would you like to see?

2 Introduce the 'problem' sequence and view, pausing at suitable moments to check comprehension, sum up the situation, think of questions to ask and suggest solutions. Also look at the tenses used (see **Situation report**).

3 Ask students to think of a real *practical* problem they have at the moment (give your own example). It shouldn't be psychological, emotional or very private! Students write a brief description of their problem (maximum 100 words); circulate to correct the language.

4 Explain that to give good advice you need to find out about the problem in detail, check you've understood it and offer more than one solution. Outline an approach (see Box 86). Do a model interview with one student about his/her problem.

5 Distribute the written problems; students read, and think about what questions to ask.

6 Organize the 'advice' sessions. They can be done: one-to-one in front of the class, if it is a small one, and with or without audience participation; in groups of four, each taking it in turn to be the 'client'; one-to-one recorded outside the class; by letter, as written homework; or by e-mail, with the teacher logging on to check the language.

Follow-ups

1 Students vote on the most interesting exchanges and publish them in an 'Agony Aunt' column.

2 Return to the original sequence (or another) and evaluate the quality of the advice.

Note

This is a personalized interactive version of **Case study**.

BOX 86   Advising

Instructions

1 Read or listen to the description of the problem.

2 Question the client to clarify the problem; try to find out who's involved, what the important factors are, what solutions have already been tried.

3 Sum up the situation as you see it, and ask the client if you've got it right.

4 Propose at least three different solutions.

5 Ask the client to comment on the proposed solutions.

Programme proposal

Aim: writing a programme proposal; a follow-up to viewing a documentary

Level: lower-intermediate

Material: documentaries about travel, famous places, famous people or famous events

Procedure

1 Explain the idea of the programme competition (Box 87 can be adapted for famous places, famous people or famous events).
2 Discuss what should go into the proposal (e.g. the main theme, how many locations, who will be interviewed, how many people will be involved).
3 Students produce proposals individually or in groups, display or circulate them and decide which one will win the award.

BOX 87   Travel competition

TIME IS TIGHT! Get your entry in for the Journey of a Lifetime scheme, awarded by the National Geographical Society. The best proposal will be given financial backing and the winners will receive television training and a camera crew to make a documentary about their travels. The closing date is 31 May. For details see the BBC website ...

Adapted from a BBC competition advertised
in the *Radio Times*, 20–26 May 2000

Puff

Aim: a summary overview

Level: lower-intermediate

Material: drama films; film and book

Preparation: Find or prepare some examples of the short 'puffs' or 'blurbs' which are found on film posters, video sleeves or pre-release publicity trailers on TV. e.g.:
A young man obsessed with youth and beauty, a talismanic cat which gives you your heart's desire and a picture that tells the truth – forever (Dorian Grey)

Procedure

After viewing the film, show students the model puffs, and get them to write their own blurb for putting on the video box. They should list the dramatic situations which feature in the plot and group-write them into a short tantalizing description. Give a word limit.

Variation

Students write puffs for films of their own choice, get them corrected by the teacher and read them out (or pin them up) for others to guess.

Note

Serious lovers of literature may feel that puffs trivialize the story – and they'd be right! But it's a nice activity and good for summary skills.

Purrs and slurs

Aim: identifying 'loaded language' with negative and positive connotations

Level: lower-intermediate

Material: any sequence with clear emotional or dogmatic bias (e.g. speeches, ads, aggressive interview questions, strong opinions)

Procedure

1 Introduce students to the idea of 'loaded language' by giving examples of word pairs they know (e.g. *slim/thin, bossy/assertive, dictator/ father of the people, smelly/perfumed, terrorist/freedom fighter*). Ask if they are neutral, positive or negative.
2 View the sequence and write up vocabulary items which have a definite 'loading'.
3 After viewing, students separate the items into positive or negative, play again to confirm their judgement, then discuss the meaning of the expressions.

Variations

1 Students pick out the loaded language themselves.
2 (Advanced) Students reformulate utterances in neutral language, as far as possible.

Note

Related activities are listed in **Describing speech style**.

Puzzle

Aim: to stimulate questioning and speculation: a ten-minute lesson filler

Level: elementary

Material: visual comedy sketches

Procedure

1 Before viewing, present the heart of the joke to students as a puzzle, e.g. 1 and 4 in Box 14: a man eats a bootlace; a man drives with his feet.
2 Students ask questions and speculate what happens, how and why. Don't give away the answer, but write up the best suggestions.
3 Show the sketch.

Follow-up

Students think of other things one could do with a bootlace, or other ways of driving a car, etc. and the circumstances in which they might occur.

Question types

Aim:	appreciating the functional value of question forms
Level:	lower-intermediate
Material:	short sequences from interviews or talk shows illustrating different question types (see Box 88)
Preparation:	Select one interesting question from the sequence and write it down. Add your own variations of the same question, including the most basic form (see Box 88).

Procedure

1 Give students the list of question variants. Ask which are most direct, polite, challenging, encouraging or neutral, and how they would feel about answering them. Put students in pairs to try them out.
2 Show the sequence; students identify the question, its form and its intention.

Variations

1 Give only the basic form of the question, then play the sequence. Students write down the question as actually formulated and suggest why the questioner has used this form.
2 Focus on the answer to the question at the same time, as in **Answers**.

BOX 88 Question types

- **The basic question** simply asks (e.g. *Do you believe in UFOs?*).
- **Leading questions** are questions which expect a particular answer (*Many people have seen UFOs – surely there's some truth in it?*). They seem to appeal to reason and are often provocative (*Are you really going to tell us you believe in UFOs?*).
- **Indirect questions** generally soften the question (*Would you say on balance that you believed in UFOs?*). They can go to

---

extremes (*How do you think you would react if I were to suggest that you do secretly believe in UFOs?*). Or the interviewer presents ideas as if they were not his/her own (*Some would say UFOs must exist – would you agree?*).
- **Open questions** invite the interviewee to talk at length and freely (*What do you now think about UFOs?*). The best-known is *Tell me about ... .* They are used for drawing people out.
- **Follow-up questions** supplement the main question, to get clarification or more detail, or pursue an interesting side track. Good interviewers don't stick rigidly to pre-planned questions.

Questions

Aim: question forms
Level: elementary
Material: drama clips (especially soap operas) rich in natural-sounding questions
Preparation: Use a sequence which has already been well understood.

Procedure

1 View the sequence. Students pick out the questions one by one, write them down and decide what form they are. Use all or part of the table in Box 89.
2 View again to decide if the intonation is rising or falling.

Variation

Ask further questions about whether the question is active/passive, continuous/simple, past/present/future.

BOX 89   Questions

Statement, positive or negative	*He's not coming?*
Statement, positive or negative + tag	*He's coming, is he?*
Question form, positive or negative, with inversion	*Is he coming?*
Question form, positive or negative, without inversion	*Who's coming?*
Short questions	*How come? What about?*
Indirect questions	*I was wondering ...* *Tell me why ...*

Quotes

Aim: identifying utterances which have overall significance; recapping plot

Level: intermediate

Material: drama films; film and book; interviews and talk shows

Procedure

For feature films After viewing the whole film, replay an important scene and get students to pick out three or four 'significant utterances'. Decide which is most significant and why. (What does it do? What does it show? What is its importance in the whole story?) Students can repeat the activity independently on their own self-selected scene. **One-liner**, which focuses on meaning in close context, is an appropriate follow-up.

For interviews and talk shows Students re-view and select three quotations (short, and significant or sensational) that could be used as 'inset quotes' in an interview article. A useful preliminary to **Interview article**.

Variation

For students studying the book, play a single scene before viewing the whole film; students choose significant quotations and call on their knowledge of the book to explain their choice.

Quoting and illustrating

Aim: comprehension; awareness of the importance of illustration in writing

Level: lower-intermediate

Rationale: Non-fiction video programmes 'quote' and 'illustrate' in the same way as writing; this can be used both for comprehension and as a writing model.

Material: sequences from news items and documentaries

Preparation: Find points in the commentary which are supported by visual 'illustrations' (see Box 90 for an example). If you want to review students' writing, make sure they have it to hand.

Procedure

1 Explain that supporting points with illustrations and quotations is like cementing a brick into a wall – it makes the argument stand up.

2 Play the clip with sound only and ask what points are supported by quotations from interviewees.

3 Play again with sound only and ask which points students would expect to be illustrated by images and how (**Picture it**).

4 View to see how the illustrations support the text (this is **Matching** at discourse level).

Follow-up

Ask students to re-read their own writing as if it was a documentary script, identify points which need illustrative support and amplify them with *verbal* quotations or illustrations.

BOX 90   Illustrations

Supporting visual illustrations and quotations from a documentary programme about prisons. 'Points' are underlined and 'illustrations' are in *italics*.

Words	*Pictures*
Commentator: With too few prison staff, <u>about 250 prisoners here have nothing to do</u>. The inspector of prisons recently warned about the <u>problem of inactivity</u> and the resulting lost opportunities for reforming the offender.	*Picture of prison workshop with several machines unused*
Prison officer: <u>We can offer them the opportunity of starting work</u> and developing a degree of self worth as a result.	*Close-up on prisoner working on machine*
Prison governor: Prisoners come from society and go back to society. We must do something to make sure that they go back with a more positive attitude of mind. (Pause) I don't want to see <u>my staff reduced to just being guards</u>.	*Prison warder patrolling with guard dog*

Racing

Aim:	general racing vocabulary; partial comprehension of racing commentary
Level:	elementary
Material:	two or three races of different kinds, with commentary
Preparation:	Check the sequence for useful racing vocabulary (see Box 91) – both in the commentary and illustrated in the action.

Procedure

1 Introduce any racing vocabulary illustrated in the action. Play the clip with or without sound and ask students to call out the words when they see the corresponding action. If possible, use slow motion to focus on significant moments.

2 Write up any further useful racing vocabulary used in the commentary. Play with sound and ask students to note it down in the order it occurs.

3 Introduce the four verb forms: *she's passed him, she's passing him, she passes him, she's about to/going to pass him.* View again for students to notice which are used. If appropriate, discuss the difference between simple and continuous forms.

Follow-up

Role play post-mortem interviews with **Comment**.

BOX 91 Racing vocabulary

Lower levels	Higher levels
Talent and condition	
strong – strength	stamina/staying power
powerful – power	competitive – competitiveness
fast – speed	fit – fitness
Position and performance	
start	set off
in front, ahead, leading	in the lead, take the lead, have the edge, a long way/x lengths ahead, leave someone behind
behind, in third place	fall behind
catch up, alongside, overtake, pass	pull ahead, narrow the gap, make a comeback, neck and neck
speed up, slow down	set the pace, put on a spurt, lose speed
win, lose	come first, come a poor third

Reaction shots

Aim: focusing on significant reactions and feelings; reaction adjectives

Level: elementary

Material: clips showing or expressing very clear attitudes/feelings (see Box 92 for examples)

Procedure

1 Write up a set of reaction adjectives (e.g. *horrified, overjoyed, offended, disappointed*), including some distractors not illustrated in the clips. Discuss the meanings.
2 Play the clips (showing just the reactions and not their causes). Students select the best adjectives to describe the reaction, and speculate on its causes.
3 View the whole sequence.

Variation

Use dramatic sporting moments which show a sweep of reactions to inspire mini-writes, e.g. *When Tiger Woods holed his last ball ...* (describe the reactions of the audience, the commentator, Tiger Woods' opponent and Tiger Woods himself).

Follow-up

Students write about occasions when they experienced such feelings: *I was astonished/horrified when ...* .

Note

This activity can form part of the mini-project *Describing interaction* (see page 52). **Body language** focuses on gesture and movement.

BOX 92   Reactions

- Napoleon's head whips round when he realizes he's lost the battle. (*Waterloo*) (horrified)
- A secretary jumps for joy when she manages to send a vital fax. (*Air Force One*) (overjoyed)
- A soldier describes being left for dead. (news item) (horrified – retrospective)
- A man thumps his fist into his hand in a quiz game. (frustrated)
- A footballer falls to his knees after scoring a goal. (jubilant)
- A man shrugs off an insult. (*Dirty Dancing*) (resigned)

Some reaction adjectives:

surprised, astonished, horrified, shocked, stunned
annoyed, frustrated, upset, offended
happy, pleased, delighted, thrilled, jubilant, overjoyed
indifferent, unmoved, resigned
frightened, alarmed, terrified, panic-stricken, hysterical
concerned, worried, anxious
sad, downcast, disappointed, desolate
appreciative, grateful

Reading aloud

Aim: reading comprehension of dialogue scenes; understanding how books become film and preparing for further activities in the *Make the movie* series

Level: lower-intermediate

Rationale: This time-consuming but enjoyable activity familiarizes students thoroughly with the reading text, using the comprehension strategies of visualization and enactment.

Material: parallel scenes from book and drama film

Preparation: Choose a short scene you would like students to know well, or which you want to use for studying differences between book and film (**Changes**), or for the project *Make the movie* (see page 29). The scene should have very distinct setting, actions, objects and dialogue. If you don't want students writing in their books, photocopy the book scene.

Procedure

1 Explain that you are going to get thoroughly acquainted with the book scene before looking at the parallel film scene.

2 Students read the scene and:
   - underline all the actions (*she <u>yawned</u>, he <u>stretched his legs</u>*), except for speech verbs like *said, asked*
   - box all the elements of setting (e.g. *He was sitting on the ⬚bench in the ⬚waiting room .*)
   - circle all the 'props' (e.g. *He picked up the ⬭phone, then his eye fell on the ⬭letter .*)

   Model the activity by doing the first part together, then students mark up the rest of the text on their own; circulate to check.

3 Students form groups, with one person for each character, plus one narrator.

4 Individuals read the text to themselves in preparation for reading it aloud. Explain that no acting is required but they must prepare not only to speak 'their' words but also to carry out the actions in token form (e.g. walking fingers instead of feet) and have something (pens, books, desks) to represent the props. They must also make sure of the pronunciation and phrasing (especially sentence stress). Circulate to help with comprehension and pronunciation.

5 When students are ready, take one group through the first part as a demonstration, making sure all actions are performed, the words are correctly distributed and the phrasing is appropriate (readers make a

lot of mistakes with all of these). Let the groups finish off the reading among themselves.

6 Go on to **Changes** or **Set the scene.**

Rhetoric

Aim:	recognizing, describing and imitating rhetorical devices (see Box 93)
Level:	intermediate
Material:	speeches; TV commercials; programme trailers; televised parliamentary debate
Preparation:	Choose a sequence with several techniques; for the Variation prepare a script or get students to do so (**Transcript**).

Procedure

1 Ask how people speak when they want to persuade, and go through some or all of the rhetorical techniques in the box.
2 Play the sequence and ask students to identify and describe examples of rhetoric (e.g. *He repeats this three times, louder each time*; *She uses loaded words like 'horror', 'fake'*; *He pauses dramatically*), and discuss if they are effective and convincing.
3 View again and ask students to note what the speaker does with his/her body and voice, and how he/she handles the audience.

Variation

Give out a script. Students underline the stresses, say the words and imitate the sounds and movements they have observed.

Follow-up

Students practise separating the person from the opinion. They make two columns headed *opinion* and *attitude*. In the first, they summarize the opinion objectively, starting *What he's really saying is ...*; in the second, they find an adjective for the attitude of the speaker (e.g. *dogmatic, passionate*; *reasonable, concerned*; *amused, ironic*). Finally, they say how they react to the two *separately,* e.g. *I agree but I don't feel so strongly.*

Note

Related activities are given in **Describing speech style.**

BOX 93   Some rhetorical techniques

Choice of words	Loaded language (see **Purrs and slurs**)
	Figurative language, images, metaphors
	Puns and wordplay
Emphasis	Specially heavy word stress
	Sudden changes in pitch and volume
	Repetition
	Exaggeration (see **Over the top**)
	Balance and contrast in words, phrases and structures
	Pausing for effect
	Climaxes (e.g. three-part lists)
Emotion	Pathos, indignation, anger, sorrow, etc.
Strategies	Insults, congratulations, thanks, etc. (see **Speech acts**)
	Irony and sarcasm
	Quotation (often turning opponents' words against them)
	Rhetorical questions
Illustration	Anecdotes
	Jokes
Persona and style	Presenting oneself in a particular way
	Particularly formal/informal language
Body language	Gesture, expression, movement of eyes, arms, head (see **Body language**)

Rules

Aim: describing how a game is played; practical comprehension by applying rules to action

Level: elementary

Material: clips of sports and games that most students aren't familiar with; game shows (especially with games that can be played in class)

Procedure

1 Give the class a list of the vocabulary necessary for describing the game (select from Box 94); view part of the game and together work out the rules and how to describe them.

2 Play the game (if possible), or test understanding of the rules by asking students to score a new game, frame or round and explain their scoring.

Variation

Give half the class the vocabulary and send them out with dictionaries to work out how to use the terms; keep the other half in the room to view and work out the rules. Bring them back together in groups to exchange vocabulary and information on how to play, then view again together, and play the game.

Follow-up

Students who know the rules can demonstrate their expertise with **Experts**.

BOX 94   Playing games

Actions	*Position*
choose	ahead
come first	behind
compete	catch up
get it right/wrong	in the lead
give a clue	leading by (x points)
guess	out
have a go	
have a try	*Scoring*
lose/lost	penalty
pick	points
score	prize
toss up	score (noun and verb)
win/won	scoreboard
	tie (noun and verb)
People	to be worth
contestants/players	two-all
panels	
questionmaster	*Useful language*
teams	X is played ...
	The aim is ...
Parts	You have to ...
a bout	You do this by ...
a go	You're not allowed to ...
a round	The main strategy is ...
a tie-breaker	
a turn	

Runabout

Aim: prepositions of movement

Level: elementary

Material: runs, walks, chases from drama films – any short sequence where people move from place to place (a high pace makes for more fun)

Procedure

1 Introduce and discuss a selection of prepositions of movement suitable for the sequence (see Box 95 for suggestions). Set them out in a vertical column on the board.

2 View the clip. Students tell you where the parties went, in order; write up the places in a second column.

3 Students join the two columns, e.g. *He went up the stairs, out onto the roof, round the chimney, down the stairs, out into the street, across the street, up the steps and into the hotel.* View again to check.

Note

Repeat the activity several times and give out the complete list of prepositions for independent work. Other activities with chases are **Chases** and **Plan a chase.**

BOX 95	Common prepositions of movement		
across	out of	down ⎫	
along	over	up ⎪	into
down	round	out ⎬	onto
into	through	off ⎭	
off	under		
onto	up		

Scenario

Aim: interactive language; tailor-made simulations of ESP situations

Level: lower-intermediate

Rationale: It comes naturally to many language students to borrow appropriate language from realistic contexts for their own purposes. This activity helps the process along by bringing input and output closer together while leaving the 'noticing' and the choice of language up to the student.

Material: drama clips

Preparation: Find two or three clips of the kind of scenario you want to practise (e.g. restaurant service, meetings, telephoning, shopping, complaining).

Procedure

1 Tell students they are going to create a mini-soap opera, just one or two scenes. Establish the basic situation (restaurant, meeting, etc.).
2 Students invent their own scenario, deciding on the setting, the people (names, personalities, histories), the particular problems and roughly what's going to happen.
3 View the clips and suggest that students search them for ideas and language for their own scenes. They should take whatever they want, but preserve their creative independence!
4 Students role play or write their own scenes.

Note

Such scenarios can be extended ad infinitum – the more the input the richer the output. Video input can be supplemented by short scenes from novels featuring the same target scenarios.

Schema

Aim:	leading in to and recapping the early stages of the plot; predicting the rest of the action
Level:	lower-intermediate
Material:	drama films, especially formula movies

Procedure

1 Identify the genre (Western, sci fi, etc. – see Box 84 on page 215) and ask what students expect to see in this kind of film (i.e. what 'schema' it is built on – see Box 83 on page 214). Map ideas on the board, e.g. lists of the places, things and people you would expect to see; or a flow diagram of the action, with vocabulary around the major elements (see Box 96 for an example).
2 Leave the schema on display while you view the first part of the film; students recap the action by saying which of the elements on the board they saw, giving details (who, what, how many, where, when) and noting any significant gaps. Re-view to complete the activity.
3 Return to the schema from time to time as you view the rest of the film, to anticipate developments or to discuss how original or predictable the plot is.

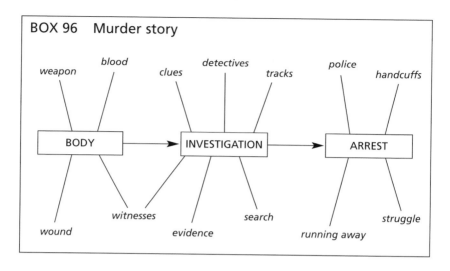

BOX 96   Murder story

Script

Aim:	interactive language for service encounters; comprehension
Level:	elementary
Material:	service encounters (i.e. dialogues with clients/customers) and predictable conversations in drama clips, comedy sketches, telephone conversations (e.g. booking into hotels, buying petrol, enquiring about trains, inviting someone for coffee)

Procedure

1 Before viewing, build up with students a branching diagram which maps out the possible directions of the conversation (see Box 97 for an example).
2 Students role play the most obvious version of the dialogue, or just suggest what is said at each point of this 'standard script'.
3 View the clip(s), trace the conversation on the diagram, then view again and discuss new language.

For comedy sketches Role play the 'standard script', tell students what's different about the scene they are going to see and ask them to envisage the new script. Finally, play the sketch.

For telephone conversations On second view, students record the specific telephone language used and (if in a monolingual group) give the equivalents in their own language. (N.B. Popular action novels often have faithful reproductions of telephone conversations which can be used in the telephone language syllabus.)

Variation

Above elementary level, focus on the differences from the norm (most film scenes are different from the norm!). Ask: *What's different from normal behaviour? What value has been added in emotion, excitement, personality, mystery? What's the effect on the language?*

Follow-up

Students choose a point in the script where it could go in a different direction, then role play the rest of the scene.

Note

This is the dialogue version of **Picture it**. Short encounters like these can be built into a self-created story with **Scenario**.

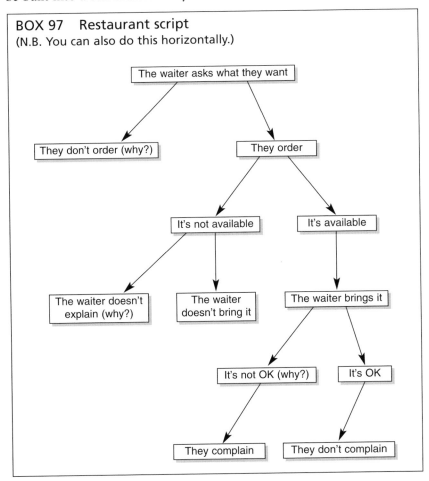

BOX 97   Restaurant script
(N.B. You can also do this horizontally.)

Scriptwriter

Aim: producing script from a book; reading comprehension and word grammar

Level: lower-intermediate

Material: parallel scenes from book and film

Preparation: Select a short parallel scene with simple dialogue and clear actions/reactions. Photocopy the book scene.

Procedure

For lower-level students or those not familiar with dramatic scripts

1 Discuss what a film script must do: give the spoken dialogue; indicate the actions; give an idea of reactions and feelings. Look at an example of a script from a stage play (or use the *Home and Away* script, page 180) and ask:
  - *How can you see which words are spoken and which are stage directions?* (usually the stage directions are in italics)
  - *Where are the names of the speakers?* (always on the far left)
  - *What punctuation follows the speakers' names?* (if anything, a colon)
  - *Are there quotation marks?* (no)
  - *Where are the stage directions?* (between two speakers or in brackets after the speakers)
  - *What grammar/tenses can you find in the stage directions?* (usually adverbs, adjectives, present or past participles, present simple and continuous)

2 Give out the book scene. Together, turn the beginning of it into a script on the board, complete with stage directions. Students complete the conversion on their own.

3 View the film version and spot the differences, as in **Changes**.

For more sophisticated or advanced students

1 Briefly study script conventions as outlined above. Discuss how a film script differs from a novel (everything in a film must be visible or audible). If there is time, discuss the differences with **Book and film**.

2 Tell students they are going to convert a scene into a script before viewing the film version. Give them the book scene and say how long the film scene is to last (e.g. two minutes). Students read and:
  - decide what to cut, e.g. explanations, background information, comment
  - decide how to compensate for important cuts (e.g. feelings *described* will have to be *shown*; essential information may have to be put into someone's mouth)
  - write the script, including stage directions, following the required conventions

- read the script aloud in groups and time it, cut or pad further

3 Students view the video scene and compare it with their own scripts.

Follow-up

This activity can stand alone or form part of the *Make the movie* project (see page 29). **Stage directions** is an easy preliminary and **Set the scene** is an appropriate follow-up.

Note

If students have access to computers, this work is much more easily done on disk.

Seen it before

Aim:	leading in to the film or part of it; preparing for a complicated scene
Level:	lower-intermediate
Material:	drama film (when some students have already seen the film)
Preparation:	Find out who has already seen the film. Select one or two important scenes with visibly interesting interactions, or ask those who have seen it to do this for homework.

Procedure

1 Before starting the whole film, play the selected scenes in class. The 'expert' students explain what's happening and answer questions about characters, events and words.
2 View the whole film. At intervals, experts explain difficulties and give clues.

Variations

1 Make this a guessing game by having the experts only answer *Yes/No* questions.
2 Give a forthcoming scene to a group (expert or not) to watch for homework. They will have to recount it to the class. They adopt one character each and prepare to report on 'their' parts in the scene. They must tell their story to the class individually but collaboratively, making connections with what other group members say, interrupting and handing over as necessary, and answering questions. After this, view the next part of the film in class.

Sequel and prequel

Aim: an overview of the story; recapping the introduction
Level: elementary
Material: any kind of drama

Procedure

Sequel After viewing the story, invite students to say what happens to the characters (one or all) in the next five years. Alternatively, groups divide the characters between them, privately invent a future for each, then come together to talk about 'their' futures.

Prequel After viewing the beginning, get students to go back and invent whatever comes before the story starts. View the introduction again so they can refine their ideas.

Note

Use *Prequel* for soap operas after the first few episodes, but only for one or two plot lines.

Set the scene

Aim: turning a book scene into film: designing the setting; practical reading comprehension
Level: lower-intermediate
Material: parallel scenes from book and film; playscripts

Procedure

1 Working from the book scene or play, students sketch the essential elements of the setting, their size and location, and the entry points of the characters.
2 Students explain their sketches to others, then view the video scene and compare.

Notes

– If students say they can't draw, make a crude sketch with stick figures to demonstrate that artistic ability is unnecessary (see Box 98 for an example).
– This activity can stand alone. As part of the *Make the movie* project (see page 29) it should be done after **Reading aloud** or **Scriptwriter** and before **Walkthrough** or **Effects**.

BOX 98   *Great Expectations*: set

Silly soaps

Aim:	evaluation and discussion
Level:	intermediate
Rationale:	It's valuable to think critically about 'wallpaper' programmes that people normally take for granted.
Material:	soap operas

Procedure

After students have seen a few episodes of a particular soap opera, ask them to recall other soap operas they know. Propose the question *Just how silly is this soap?* and discuss:

- How realistic or unrealistic are the situations? For example?
- What makes them realistic/unrealistic?
- Is there a lot more action and drama than in real life? For example?
- Does the soap deal with real contemporary issues? For example?
- Are the characters one-dimensional or well-rounded? For example?
- Do any of the situations arouse real feelings? For example?
- Do you want to know what happens next? Why/Why not?
- What would you say makes a good soap? What are the essential ingredients?
- Think of other soaps you have seen. How silly is *this* one? Give it a rating 1 to 5.

Insist on examples, challenge them where appropriate and get other students to do so too, e.g. *Do you really care when John is killed in the accident? Do girls really hire detectives to spy on their boyfriends? Who would really believe an obvious liar like Ross?*

Situation report

Aim:	tense study; producing a situation report with the appropriate range of tenses
Level:	lower-intermediate
Material:	video sequences or video-related writing containing 'situation reports' (see Box 99 for examples)
Preparation:	Identify what situation report you want students to produce (e.g. summing up the situation in a soap opera, reporting the state of play in a championship, describing a practical or work problem). Find short video items which demonstrate the range of tenses and can be used as models, or use those in Box 99.

Procedure

1 View/read the item; students take notes under *How are things generally? What's happened? What's happening? What might happen? What's likely to happen?*
2 Re-view or re-read to look at the tenses used.
3 Discuss what the students are to talk/write about and get them to make notes about their own subject (under the same headings as in step 1) before starting.

BOX 99   Situation reports

'Situation reports' describe the present situation and sometimes anticipate the future. They are frequent in topical TV items, e.g. news, weather, ads, documentaries, interviews, discussions, programme notes, summings up of the state of play (e.g. in matches or before a new soap opera episode). They call on an array of tenses: the present perfect sums up the situation up to now, the present continuous describes present trends, and a range of modal and lexical expressions predict the future, e.g. *going to, will probably, should, may, might, is likely to, the outlook is ..., there is ... to come, we are in for ...* . This tense pattern is appropriate for activities which describe the present situation, e.g. **Case study, Commentary/Copywriter, Decisions, Follow the news.**

TV weather report

Today <u>there has been</u> rain in most parts of Wales, especially in the north. Temperatures <u>have been</u> in the range 12–14 degrees Celsius, and winds <u>have been</u> light. Temperatures <u>are rising</u> generally and tomorrow they <u>will be</u> higher, but <u>the forecast is</u> for thunderstorms and heavy rain in many parts, with winds rising to gale force at times.

TV programme note on a big match

2.00, 3.45 Rugby League Challenge Cup Final *St Helens vs Bradford Bulls* Live coverage from Twickenham of the competition's 100th final, kickoff 2.45 p.m. St Helens <u>are</u> in stunning form and, <u>having already secured</u> the grand final and World Club Championship titles, they only <u>need</u> the Challenge Cup to complete an unprecedented treble. Bradford <u>are</u> in their second consecutive final and <u>are looking to</u> defend the cup they won at Murrayfield last year. With players such as Sean Long and Tommy Martyn on show, spectators <u>are in for</u> a classic final.

(*Radio Times*, 28 May 2001)

Soap chronicles

Aim: writing: two projects for soap addicts
Level: intermediate
Material: soap operas

Procedure

Newsletter Once students are familiar with the soap, they individually, or in groups, invent a piece of news about one of the soap characters and write it up as for a newsletter. The news must be *new* (not mentioned in the soap), and *possible* in terms of what they already know. They can make it more realistic by including quotations from the protagonists and finding a picture to represent the event (newspapers and magazines are good sources and also provide inspiration). Bring together all the items into one newsletter and give it a name.

Soap scrapbook Groups plan a scrapbook, with each member making a contribution. The scrapbook can contain characters' personal diaries, information about their background, houses, cats, gardens, relations, etc., descriptions of places and people, psychological analyses, items of imaginary news, imaginary conversations or letters, interviews, quizzes, summaries of plot lines, forecasts of the future, horoscopes, recipes, pictures, etc. Those with access to the Internet can find plenty of ideas on the appropriate website.

241

Note

These activities are only for soap addicts. They can be done as independent projects, as an alternative to studying a full-length drama film.

Soap write-out

Aim: interactive language; creative writing
Level: lower-intermediate
Material: soap operas

Procedure

Tell students that one of the actors in the soap has to leave suddenly and unexpectedly (think of a reason): after one more episode he/she will never be seen again. Students choose the character and write him/her out of the plot (either plausibly or with wild extravagance) in a single scene, making plenty of reference to his/her past life, character, etc.

Speculations

Aim: recapping and predicting the action
Level: lower-intermediate
Rationale: Sets of outstanding questions about the state of play are a standard device of serials and produce a good range of tenses.
Material: drama films; soap episodes; biographical films; TV ads

Procedure

1 After viewing one part of the story and before the next, students formulate the outstanding questions raised by the action so far, e.g. *Why does X lie? Does Y know the truth? Is Z going to live or die?* Keep them specific, e.g.:

> *What does Richard intend to do with the film?*
> *Why did the coffee in the mug vibrate?*
> *Will Kimberley and Jack meet?*
>
> From *The China Syndrome*

2 Re-view to see if students have identified all the major questions, check their grammar, and then play on.
3 At the next break, read out the questions and see if they have been answered. (N.B. It's fun to write the questions dramatically large on a poster, then roll it up and unroll it periodically to answer old questions and add new ones.)

Variations

1 *Crystal ball* In the middle of the story, pause to predict how it will end. Each person or group formulates a prediction, announces it and answers questions about it (those who have seen the film before should be warned to give nothing away, but may smile smugly!). The predictions are reconsidered and rewritten as the film progresses, and compared with the real outcome at the end. For extra drama, students write predictions on slips, correct the English and seal them in an envelope: at the end they are pulled out and discussed. This is good with biographical films, since real life has less predictable outcomes and more dead ends than fiction, and provides a wider range of possibilities (see Box 100 for an example).

2 *Tough spots* In action movies, pause at a moment of maximum peril to gather guesses on how the hero/heroine will get out of it (*With one bound he was free!*). Or get students to collect and describe such predicaments and challenge others to guess.

3 *Who will say it?* Write up three or four important things that people are going to say in the next part of the story. Students speculate on who will say them, to whom and why. If you choose difficult utterances, you can resolve comprehension difficulties before they arise.

4 *For suitable TV ads* Pause just before the end to speculate what the product is.

Follow-up

Wrong predictions are more fruitful than right ones in inspiring written explanations. Pose the question: *Why did we think that this would happen?* and let students write their answers.

Note

Decisions is a related activity focusing on characters' choices.

BOX 100   Predictions

He'll kill his father.
He'll run away from home.
He'll commit suicide.
He'll become rich and famous.
He'll have a nervous breakdown.
He'll become a drug addict.
He'll get married and live happily ever after.
He'll marry the girl he met in the library.

From *Shine*

Speech acts

Aim:	speech-act vocabulary and related structures; close comprehension of important scenes; reviewing longer stretches of action
Level:	elementary
Material:	film drama or drama clips; game shows and talk shows

Procedure

After viewing a scene, make sure students can identify the characters by name or description (*the old man, George*). Write up some statements about the things the participants do with their words (see also speech verbs in Box 101), e.g.:

Someone accuses someone of doing something.
Someone denies something.
Someone laughs scornfully.
Someone sympathizes with someone.

Alternatively, give only the beginnings of the sentences (e.g. *Someone complains ... Some people discuss ...*). Students say who does what to whom, when and why; check that they get the structures right.

Variation

To review longer stretches, give a list of some extended interactions in the film, e.g.:

Someone *chats someone up/comes on to someone.*
Several people have a *briefing.*
Someone does a lot of *grumbling.*
Someone *ticks someone off.*
Someone *blackmails* someone.
There is a long *discussion.*
Two people *have a row.*
Someone *shows some people round.*

Discuss the meanings of the terms (or students look them up). Students then say which scenes in the film represent these events. With more advanced students, include some distractors (e.g. *a row* and *an argument* along with *a discussion*). For lower-level students, give three labels, play three scenes and ask which is which.

Follow-up

Gradually build up a poster with speech language (see Box 101); revive the expressions from time to time by asking who did them, to whom, and in what film.

Note

This activity can form part of the mini-project *Describing interaction* (see page 52).

BOX 101   Speech language

Elementary

Common speech verbs

accept   agree   answer   argue   ask   chat   complain
describe   disagree   discuss   explain   guess   inform
invite   lie/tell a lie   offer   order   promise   refuse
remind   reply   report   say   say hello/goodbye   speak
suggest   talk about   tell

Some speech behaviour

interrupt   pronounce   repeat/say it again   speak up
speak clearly/slowly, etc.

Some extended interactions

give instructions/directions   have a meeting   introduce someone
quarrel (and make up)   question/interview   have a conversation

Intermediate

Common speech verbs

admit   beg   claim   comment   compliment   criticize
demand   deny   discourage   encourage   exclaim   greet
report   request   speak   state   swear   tease   threaten
urge   warn   wonder

Some speech behaviour

hesitate   mispronounce   pause   raise your voice   scream
shout

Some extended interactions

consult/advise/give advice   deceive   do a deal
have a row/argument   make conversation   negotiate/bargain
show someone round   tease

Advanced

Common speech verbs

boast   flatter   grumble   hedge   hint   interrogate   mock
question   remark   slander   sneer

Some speech behaviour

be left speechless   gabble   grope for words   lose the thread
mumble   mutter   not get a word in edgeways   stammer
whisper

Some extended interactions

beat about the bush   boss around   chat up   haggle
have a showdown   lead someone on   make small talk
pull someone's leg   rub someone up the wrong way
sound someone out   stall/beat about the bush
talk at cross purposes   tick off   wind someone up

Sports highlights

Aim: sports vocabulary and sports talk
Level: elementary
Material: edited 'highlights' of big sporting events from the sports news

Procedure

1 If you have class experts, get them to explain the competition background briefly (**Situation report**).
2 Play without sound and collect 'visible' vocabulary (e.g. *stadium, goal, flags, kick, keeper, save, referee, whistle*). Alternatively, first discuss what you will see (**Picture it**), then view.
3 Collect visible emotions and interactions, e.g. *excited, angry, jubilant, distraught, rejoice, dispute, cheer, protest, console*, and the reasons for them (**Reaction shots**).
4 Ask class experts to explain what's happening and why it's important (**Experts**).
5 Play with sound and collect any identifiable spoken sports vocabulary.

Variation

For sports which are unknown to most students, do **Rules**.

Follow-up

On special occasions, expert students can record and report on a big match, selecting video highlights in the same way and imitating the commentator's summary report.

Sports quiz

Aim: talking about sport; asking and answering questions; a series of mini-lessons run by students
Level: lower-intermediate
Material: typical sequences from specific sports
Preparation: Group students into teams according to their sports interests. Make sure the class can tolerate a series of mini-lessons on different sports (one from each team). Find short video clips for each sport represented (the commentary need not be English), or get students to do this. Prepare to talk about a sport yourself, if possible one not very familiar to your class.

Procedure

1 Give out the questions in Box 102, or a selection, to each team, and check that they can read the questions aloud correctly. Explain that they are to run their own lessons by asking the class these questions. They will need to know the answers for their particular sport in English and should prepare themselves for homework.
2 Model the activity: play a clip of the sport (twice), ask the class the questions, elicit the answers, comment, correct, add information and refer to the clip as necessary.
3 Teams run their own mini-lessons in the same way, one per lesson.

Follow-up

Finish the series with a final test/quiz on points of detail.

Note

See also **Experts**.

BOX 102   Sports quiz

- Where is it played/done? (field, pitch, circuit, etc.)
- Are there different versions/categories? (e.g. hard/grass, League/Union, light/heavy)
- How many people are there in a team?
- What clothing and equipment is used? (e.g. bat, helmet, puck, racket, kneepads, oars)
- What qualities are required in the players? (e.g. strength, speed, stamina)
- How is the game financed? (e.g. gate, sponsorship, national investment, TV)
- What organizations regulate the game? (e.g. FA)
- Who is the most famous player ever? Who are the champions now? Why?
- What major tournaments are organized? (e.g. World Cup, Challenge Trophy)
- What's the next big event?

Stage directions

Aim: language for reactions, feelings and physical movement; reading comprehension

Level: intermediate

Material:	drama clips; parallel scenes from stage play and film; a script without stage directions
Preparation:	Choose a short scene with a strong interaction clearly expressed in movement, gesture, tone of voice and facial expression. Make a script with no stage directions (use subtitles, use a stage play extract or piece of Shakespeare).

Procedure

1 Give out the script and explain that students are going to add the stage directions, i.e. full working instructions for the actors (movements, expressions, ways of speaking).
2 Before viewing, students read the dialogue and speculate on what the stage directions might be, using the text for clues. Discuss what is happening physically; what each character is doing; how particular utterances are spoken.
3 View to see how the action has been realized and write in the stage directions.

Variation

Cryptic dialogue A lot of film dialogue doesn't, on its own, reveal much about the action. Give students a piece of pure unexplained dialogue: they have twenty questions to find out what's going on, then view (this can make an absorbing lesson). Students too can transcribe stretches of cryptic dialogue and play questionmaster.

Note

An extended version of **One-liner** and a good preliminary to **Scriptwriter**.

Stand by it

Aim:	writing or speaking a product testimonial
Level:	elementary
Material:	TV commercials with 'client testimonials' as models

Procedure

1 Explain that students are going to find a product they can personally recommend and prepare a testimonial.
2 Prepare by looking at the appropriate tenses (**Situation report**).
3 View the model ads and discuss the length, how the product is shown (in action? close-up? being unwrapped?), what the angle is and what the clients say (What information do they give? Do they say how the product matters to them personally?).

4 Students bring in the object (or a photo or picture of it), 'stand by it' (in both senses), and present the testimonial in speech or writing (maximum 30 seconds).

Structures

Aim: raising grammatical awareness
Level: elementary
Material: any clip featuring a target grammar structure

Procedure

After viewing the clip and working on it for comprehension, students:

- focus on the target structure in some way, e.g. write down the example, count how often it's used, classify the examples
- rehearse the words in some way, e.g. repeat the sentence, act along with the actors, memorize the parts
- explain why this form has been used in this context
- if possible, extend the use by creating a similar dialogue on a different subject.

For examples, see pages 47–50.

Note

Specific areas of grammar are dealt with in **Tenses, Questions, Wordhunt**.

Subtitles 1

Aim: for monolingual classes, a translation activity focusing on interactive language
Level: lower-intermediate
Material: drama clips
Preparation: Select a scene with good subtitles in the learners' language, and a short scene with useful interactive language from an unsubtitled English film. Prepare strips of paper for the final subtitles.

Procedure

1 Explain that students are going to be subtitle writers.
2 View the first scene to see how subtitles are formatted, i.e. the number of words, the number of lines, when the subtitle appears, and how long it stays visible.
3 View the second scene once or twice to understand the interaction, the words and the tone. Students transcribe the utterances and then translate them.

4 Compare different versions and produce a final version with a felt pen on strips of paper.
5 Replay the scene, holding up the subtitles against the screen.

Variation

Advanced students produce English subtitles for a scene from a film in their own language.

Subtitles 2

Aim:	close-focus listening
Level:	elementary
Rationale:	Many subtitles reduce or distort the language spoken. These discrepancies are useful for close-focus listening: a mixture of listening comprehension, dictation and error correction.
Material:	sequences with inaccurate English subtitles, if you can find them

Procedure

View a short sequence. Students write down the words they *see* in the subtitles, then view again and adjust their writing to what they *hear*. This can lead to discussions about the choice of language, e.g. how far *going to* and *will* are interchangeable.

Variation

Good substitutes for inaccurate commercial subtitles are your own students' efforts. Get them to transcribe a short sequence (**Transcript**) and notice their errors. Then prepare a gapfill exercise or error correction activity for other students based on these errors.

Follow-up

Ask students to view a film subtitled in their own language for homework, to spot the mistakes or omissions and to bring them back to share with the class.

Summary

Aim:	comprehension, to recap the action
Level:	lower-intermediate
Material:	all kinds of drama; documentaries; interviews and talk shows

Procedure

To recap the introduction of drama films After viewing the first 15–20 minutes, students produce a summary of the action (using the present tense). They can either do this individually in writing or work in groups and do an oral round-the-table recap with a secretary to write it up. If there is time, they read each other's summaries and suggest improvements. They then re-view and revise their accounts. (N.B. Don't ask students to summarize a whole film – it's a big job.) If you are doing a film in episodes, get individuals or groups to sum up 'the story so far' for others who have missed an episode. For advanced students, give stricter criteria (see Box 103 for an example).

For parts of interviews and talk shows Extract the main questions after viewing and write them up (or get students to do this). Students take on the roles and rerun the sequence in pairs or groups, trying to remember and roughly reproduce what was said. They then re-view to check and run their sequence again. Alternatively, do the rerun with the teacher as host and the students taking turns as the guests – students enjoy prompting the teacher, whose English may be better but whose memory is usually worse!

For soaps After viewing a few episodes, students choose one of the plot lines and summarize it as for drama films, ending with a brief prediction of future developments. Such summaries can contribute to a scrapbook (**Soap chronicles**) and/or be used for future viewers.

For drama series Pause halfway through to summarize the sub-plot if there is one.

BOX 103   Advanced introduction summary

Your summary should:
* be less than 150 words
* contain all the essential information
* contain no unimportant details and no repetition
* indicate where and when the events take place
* introduce the main characters/players by name
* bring out important reasons, causes and connections
* indicate the time sequence clearly
* be clear, correct and coherent

Talk show

Aim: oral practice; management of discussion
Level: lower-intermediate

Material:	a talk show (whole or part) on a general interest topic, to act as a model
Preparation:	Decide how much of the talk show to use as a model.

Procedure

1 After viewing and understanding the talk show, go through the questions in Box 104.
2 Prepare students to do their own show:
   - Decide on a time limit (about 10 minutes).
   - Make up the groups and decide roles.
   - Get each group to choose a topic and three main questions which everyone wants to discuss (there will of course be follow-up questions and interaction as well).
   - If it's possible to record the event (audio or video), arrange for good sound quality.
   - Ask students to prepare individually. The host has to think of how to welcome the audience and present the participants, what the order of the questions will be and how to get everyone to contribute. The other participants should think of interesting opinions, illustrations, personal experience, quotations, books and articles, relevant topical events. They should not memorize a speech in advance but just have something to say, and be prepared to interact spontaneously.
   - Arrange seating and agree ground rules on time (appoint a time-keeper), turn-taking and audience behaviour (e.g. clapping and looking interested).
   - Run the show, either in separate groups or with one group at a time in front of the whole class (the class can be a studio audience and be invited to contribute).
   - Re-view and comment on the recordings, or go through the questions in Box 104.

Note

You may want to distribute the talk shows over a number of lessons.

BOX 104   Studying a talk show

Host
- How did the host welcome the audience and introduce the guests?
- How many main questions did the host ask? Did he/she ask follow-up questions?
- Did the host make sure everyone got to speak? How? Did anyone try to 'hog the floor' (see **Floor**)?
- How did the host sign off at the end?

Guests

- What did each person contribute? e.g. information/opinions/anecdotes/current events/jokes
- How much did each person talk and how did they get the floor? Were some people left out?
- How many main questions were there, i.e. how many aspects were covered?
- How much interaction was there between the guests?
- Did you notice any special expressions for opinion, agreement, disagreement, turn-taking?

Telephone conversations

Aim: a recap activity for plot comprehension; interactive language
Level: lower-intermediate
Material: one-sided telephone conversations from film drama

Procedure

1 After watching the section, go back to the one-sided telephone conversation. Discuss who it's from and what it's about.
2 Students write down the audible side of the conversation (**Transcript**), leaving space for the other side.
3 Students recreate the other side of the conversation.

Note

For work on telephone language, see **Script**.

Tenses

Aim: awareness of verb forms and tenses
Level: intermediate
Material: short sequences

Procedure

1 Once the general meaning of the sequence is understood, students re-view, looking for one or two of the following ('full verbs' only) and writing them down:
  - past verb forms
  - present simple verb forms

253

- continuous forms
- perfect forms

2 Students can then answer the following questions for each verb form:
- Is it negative/affirmative?
- Is it a question/statement?
- Is it active or passive?
- What time does it refer to?

Note

Other 'grammar noticing' activities are **Questions**, **Structures** and **Word-hunt**. They should all be repeated frequently.

Themes

Aim: noun phrases with participles, active or passive (e.g. *a man lying in the street, trees being cut down*); everyday vocabulary; creative writing

Level: elementary

Material: sequences of images establishing a theme – frequent in documentaries, ads, news footage, programme trailers (see Box 105 for examples)

Procedure

1 Establish the noun + participle structure.
2 Show the sequence and ask *What did you see?* Students recall the images and write them down in a numbered list, using the noun + participle structure wherever possible. Supply key vocabulary before or during the task.
3 Students feed back, then view again to revise their lists.

Variation

Students anticipate what they will see on a given theme (as in **Picture it**), then view.

Follow-ups

1 Students use the sequence as a stimulus for voice-over commentary (see **Commentary/Copywriter**).
2 Students use the sequence as a model to create a different image sequence for a programme trailer: select themes to exercise a particular area of vocabulary (e.g. crime, regional cooking) or to generate passives (e.g. wood, fishing).

BOX 105   Examples of thematic sequences

- the elements of a civil disturbance in news footage: police, riot shields, banners, tear gas
- a collage representing World War I on the Russian front: archive footage of soldiers marching, guns firing, propaganda posters, refugees
- a sequence of gardening activities introducing a gardening programme

A sequence on the theme of water

A huge wave breaking slowly on the rocks
Rain falling on the stones of a street
A stream running over stones
Waves dashing against a jetty
Ocean waves in a storm
Calm water reflecting the sky
Water drops splashing down
The sun coming up
A misty lake
Lightning flashing from a cloud

(A BBC World weather report trailer)

Tone up

Aim: practising shifts of register, e.g. distant/intimate; neutral/colloquial

Level: upper-intermediate

Material: short clips with clear speech styles; comedy sketches which play with register and tone

Preparation: Prepare a transcript or get students to do so (**Transcript**).

Procedure

Play the sequence and discuss what makes it formal/informal, collo-quial/neutral, etc. How would the words change if the participants or setting were different? Together, work on the transcript to recreate the script. Lexicons, thesauruses or dictionaries of synonyms can help. (N.B. It's easiest to go from colloquial to neutral, but advanced students can try colloquializing a formal exchange.)

Variations

1 Present one 'marked' utterance from the scene before viewing, ask what tone and setting it suggests, then view.

2 In drama which has formal and less formal characters, get students to pick out expressions which seem characteristic of one group, e.g. older people or younger people.

Note

Related activities are listed in **Describing speech style**.

Transcript

Aim:	focusing on the language
Level:	elementary
Rationale:	Transcripts by students reveal difficulties in hearing sounds and identifying words and can be used as the basis for gapped dictations or error corrections for other students. They can also be used to lead in to language focus activities (**Structures, Questions, Tenses, Wordhunt**) and as input for other activities (**News leads, Telephone conversations**).
Material:	short clear sequences
Preparation:	Choose a short sequence which presents only minor comprehension difficulties. Drama clips should have several characters with roughly equal parts.

Procedure

For dialogue Students view once or twice and write down the names of the speakers in order on the left of their page, leaving space for what the speakers say. They then distribute the characters among themselves and play the sequence again as often as necessary, writing down only what 'their' characters say. Check the transcripts. Students share them and copy up the other parts. Finally, they **Act along** with the actors.

For news, commentary or songs Write up the first words of each natural word group on a separate line (as in the example in Box 106). You can easily do this straight onto the board. Students view several times, extending each group of words each time.

Note

Dictation doesn't come naturally to video, but this approach works quite well.

BOX 106   Transcript: a news quotation

The underlined words are written up by the teacher; students gradually fill in the rest.

<u>The fact that these drugs are going to be cheaper</u>
<u>still means</u> that they'll be very expensive for many African countries.
<u>It doesn't</u> diminish the need for health promotion programmes
<u>to stop</u> people from becoming infected in the first place
<u>and the</u> importance of continuing to invest in a vaccine
<u>because ultimately</u> that will be
<u>the most</u> cost-effective way of stopping AIDS.

(Nick Partridge, Terrence Higgins Trust, in a news item about AIDS)

Trigger

Aim:	discussion; speaking or writing about personal recollections and feelings
Level:	lower-intermediate
Material:	clips which reflect common human experiences (see Box 107 for examples)

Procedure

1 Introduce the clip with a question that will prompt learners to recall their own experience (see the 'Before' questions in Box 107).
2 View the clip and work on comprehension.
3 Ask students to recount their own experiences (see the 'After' questions in Box 107) in groups or to the whole class.

Follow-up

After working on a theme, students put together a collage (e.g. *Earliest memories, Terrible Traffic Tales*) in poster form or on film (see **Voxpop**).

Turning points

Aim:	an overview of the decisive moments in a life or a story; practice in the third conditional
Level:	lower-intermediate
Material:	drama films; biographical films; some biographical interviews

BOX 107 Trigger stories

	Story	Before	Exploitation After
News item	Two blue plaques have been put up in London in the same street – one to Handel and one to Jimi Hendrix.	What is a great man? What are your criteria of greatness?	Who would you put up a blue plaque for? Why? What about other kinds of memorial? Statues?
Drama film	A driver is stopped for speeding by a cop but is let off (*Scent of a Woman*).	Do people here obey the traffic rules?	What is your own parking/driving story?
Documentary	Two children aged eight recall the best moments in their lives so far (programme about African children).	What are the best things about childhood?	Can you remember one great or terrible moment before you were ten?
Animation	A Brazilian lion explains why he would like to live in a hot country (*Aardman Animations*).	Does climate matter in choosing where to live? How?	Compare two places you have lived in from the climate angle.

Procedure

Three possibilities after viewing the film are:

- *Milestones* Explain the idea of a 'milestone' in life (a decisive moment, a turning point) and illustrate by showing the first 'milestone' scene in the film (e.g. Thomas More refuses to employ Richard Rich – *A Man for All Seasons*). Discuss why it is a milestone (because Rich later betrayed him) and (if students can manage the third conditional) what might have happened otherwise. Students identify further milestones in the story, find the scenes, re-view them and explain why they are important.

- *Wheel of fortune* Draw a circle on the board (with hub and spokes) and explain the idea of Fortune's Wheel, which raises people to great heights and then brings them low (the implication being that if you rise you will inevitably fall). Students decide if the wheel figure fits the protagonist's career. If so, they label the spokes of the wheel to show the stages of the rise and fall and ask who/what is turning the wheel: self, society, circumstance or the stars? If not, they decide what other figure would be more suitable, e.g. ups and downs, up-down-up, up and out (early death at height of fame), etc.

- *Nodes* Draw a vertical line to represent the whole plot, discuss the decisive moments and mark them on the line. Students take one 'node' each (see Box 108 for an example) and decide what would have happened if things had been different, then explain to each other.

Follow-up

Students describe or script a milestone scene from their own lives.

BOX 108   Nodes

Nodes	*What would have happened otherwise?*
→They meet again in the airport.	The whole story wouldn't have happened if they hadn't met again.
→Their best friends fall in love with each other.	Otherwise they might have fallen in love with Sally or Harry – which was the intention.
	(When Harry met Sally)

Twin texts

Aim:	a lead-in to viewing
Level:	lower-intermediate
Material:	parallel texts, e.g. book and drama film, TV news item and newspaper story

Procedure

For drama film/book Before viewing the whole film, play two or three short scenes from the film (with or without sound, depending on how easy they are to identify). Students have to find the scenes in their books and say where they come in the story. Include a scene from the film that does *not* appear in the book, but still has an appropriate place in the order of events. Students have to say where in the book it must have happened.

For news items Students read the item in the paper, then view the news item and say what events in the paper are shown in the footage or mentioned in the item. Alternatively, half the students view and half read, then come together in pairs to compare notes.

Viewshare

Aim:	comprehension
Level:	intermediate
Material:	difficult multi-modal sequences, e.g. documentary passages where setting, events and speakers are all of importance; sequences with a mix of information channels (graphics, footage, talking heads, commentary, music and sound effects, etc.); ads with very different visual and aural messages

Procedure

1 After viewing a difficult passage, discuss what message elements are present (use Box 109, first column).
2 Divide students into groups: each member is to concentrate on only one element on second viewing (e.g. only setting, only events/actions, only people, only graphics). View again.
3 Groups come together to recreate the whole message.

BOX 109   Viewshare

	What's the message?
Graphics, stills, special visual effects	....
Footage (setting and events)	....
Talking heads and gestures	....
Commentary	....
Music and sound effects	....
Other	....

Voice 1

Aim: recognizing the contribution of 'voice' to mood, tone, register, etc.

Level: elementary

Rationale: 'Voice' is the style adopted by the speaker, e.g. the sound of an excited salesman; an intimate chatty tone; an ironic or solemn commentary; an exaggerated regional accent. Advertising makes great use of 'voice'.

Material: TV ads; some commentary

Procedure

After viewing, get students to describe the 'voice', using the questions in Box 110.

Variation

Give students the words of the text before they view and ask them to say how they think they will be delivered, or to try them out in various voices and at various speeds.

Note

Related activities are listed in **Describing speech style**.

BOX 110   Voice

- What is its relationship with us?
  intimate/friendly   authoritative/expert/professional
  flattering   mock-aggressive
  formal   informal
  like a father? expert? enthusiast?

- What is its mood? (lower-level words first)
  magical – hypnotic, mesmeric, exotic
  admiring – reverent
  important – portentous
  soft – soothing, reassuring
  excited – urgent, arousing
  joky – humorous

- Where does it come from? (e.g. a country, a kind of TV programme)

Voice 2

Aim: a lead-in; describing physical appearance and character

Level: elementary

Material: sequences (drama films, documentaries, interviews) where the main characters speak clearly, distinctively and characteristically

Procedure

1 Students listen with sound only (it may help if they close their eyes) and imagine what the voice's owner looks like: age, height, build, hairstyle, clothing, face, posture (see Box 38 in **Casting couch 2**). They can also speculate on job, role, character, likeability and identity/ name. They make notes and exchange their ideas in pairs or small groups.

2 View the sequence.

Variation

(Advanced) Students listen for specific words which reveal the accent, and try to identify the origin of the speaker.

Voxpop

Aim: practising expressing opinions

Level: elementary

Material: if possible, a 'voxpop' sequence as a model, i.e. a sequence of short interviews with members of the public; a camcorder if you plan to film; if not, a large cardboard frame to represent the TV screen

Preparation: Do this after discussing a topic that interests students.

Procedure

1 Explain that students are going to create a collage of opinions on the topic, as in a 'voxpop' sequence in a documentary or news programme. Show an example if you have one: note how it is introduced, the number and range of opinions, the length of each 'soundbite' and the physical background.

2 In groups of four or five, students discuss what each plans to say, decide on the order and formulate a lead-in (e.g. *Opinion is divided* ...; *Everyone agrees that* ...). Allow 30 seconds maximum for each opinion, and suggest that students speak spontaneously.

3 Each group runs the sequence. A cardboard frame (for the TV) can be passed from speaker to speaker.

Variations

1 If filming the sequence, advise students to address themselves to someone behind the camera, otherwise they will sound stilted. Make sure they have a pleasant background and good sound-recording conditions (non-echoing rooms, close to the camcorder or with a boom mike). Play each group's production to the class.
2 Students create a voxpop sequence about a product on the lines of a TV commercial.

Walkthrough

Aim: turning a book scene into a film: understanding the action; speaking with acceptable sentence stress and pausing (this forms part of the *Make the movie* project, page 29).

Level: lower-intermediate

Material: parallel scenes from book and film

Procedure

1 After writing a script (**Scriptwriter**) and creating the setting (**Set the scene**), students take the various parts and walk the scene through, saying the appropriate words as they do so. If they are working from a play, they can go straight to the walkthrough. The idea is mainly to get the words, actions and movements right, but appropriate sentence stress and pausing should be emphasized. Do not demand acting talent, but discuss the dynamic of the scene (pauses, pace, high point and how to emphasize it), and rerun the scene once or twice.
2 Students view the scene in the film and compare their version with the film director's.

Follow-up

As an alternative to viewing the scene, go on to establish the lighting and sound effects (**Effects**) and then view (or film the scene).

Weather words

Aim: weather vocabulary

Level: elementary

Material: weather reports

Preparation: Find short weather forecasts covering a small area and a short period, with simple graphics, a clear time frame, slow delivery and standard English. Copy list A from Box 111 for intermediate students, and both lists for advanced students.

Procedure

After going through weather vocabulary, play a short weather report without sound and ask students to name the weather they *see*. View again with sound (or sound only) and ask what weather words they *hear*. Follow with *Where would you (not) like to be and why?*

For intermediate and advanced students Follow the same procedure. Start by going through the vocabulary in the lists, or get students to build up their own list. After viewing, students underline the words they have heard, then view again and give additional information for each word identified (e.g. *sunshine* in the south, less *windy* than today).

Variation

Ask students to note which words go with which gestures of the weather forecaster. View again without sound; students call out the words to go with the gestures.

Follow-up

Adopt the graphic symbols as prompts for students to describe today's weather – large cardboard cut-outs are not only for children! Or get individual students to do a retrospective 'weather report' for your area each day for a week.

Note

Help students listen for salient information with **What weather where.**

BOX 111   Weather words

A Intermediate

Weather		Weather verbs		Areas and directions
sun	sunny	shine	shining	in the north
	fine			south
sunshine				east
rain	rainy	rain	raining	west
	wet			
	dry			on the coast
cloud	cloudy			hills
mist	misty			
fog	foggy			central
wind	windy	blow	blowing	northern
storm	stormy			southern
frost	frosty	freeze	freezing	eastern
snow	snowy	snow	snowing	western
thick	thin			
heavy	light			
strong				

Seasons	Temperature	
summer	temperature	
autumn	degrees	
winter	hot/hotter	
spring	warm/warmer	
	cool/cooler	
late	cold/colder	
early		

B Advanced

Weather	Areas and directions	Temperature
thunder	further	range
thundery	north/south/east/west	
thunderstorm		heat
blizzard	northward	cold
gales	southward	
sleet	eastward	humid
floods/flooding	westward	
falls	northerly	
patches	southerly	
bursts	easterly	
showers	westerly	
dense		

What next?

Aim:	production and comprehension of interactive language
Level:	lower-intermediate
Material:	dramatic interactive scenes where the situation is very clear (or a forthcoming scene in a whole film)

Procedure

1 Play half the scene, then discuss what's going on, the personalities involved and how the scene is likely to develop.
2 Re-view the first half. Students write or role play the end of the scene as they imagine it.
3 View the original second half of the scene.

Variation

Play the scene and pause at a point where the content or feeling of the reply is predictable, but not the form (it helps if there is a pause before the reply). View again up to the same point. Students guess what will be said and write up all their guesses (correct the language as they do so). View on and write up the actual response. Afterwards, ask students to try to remember the exact words which came *before* the reply.

What's going on?

Aim:	describing an extended interaction
Level:	intermediate
Rationale:	This activity involves many important areas of language, including reaction adjectives, reported speech, structures with speech verbs, adverbs of manner and physical behaviour, together with a feeling for the dynamic of the interaction and an ability to express it.
Material	drama scenes and dramatic ads; clips from interviews and talk shows; sports sequences; live interactions

Procedure

1 After viewing, students select a scene where the interaction is important or interesting. The aim is to write a short account bringing out the psychological developments and the dramatic dynamic (see Box 113 for an example).

2 View the scene several times and get students to discuss the questions in Box 112. They should use the present tense to describe the scene and include some direct quotations.

For soap opera scenes The object is to try to explain what's going on to those who don't know the story, and students will need to give all necessary background information.

Note

This activity can stand alone or can be the culmination of the mini-project *Describing interaction* (see page 52). Useful preliminary activities are **Feeling flow, Fly on the wall, Gossip, Reaction shots, Speech acts** and **Writing the book.**

BOX 112   What's going on?
- What feelings are evident?
- What are the characters trying to do?
- What happens in the scene?

- Is there a turning point in the scene? What causes it?
- What is different by the end of the scene?
- Why is the scene important in the whole plot/programme?

BOX 113   Wilma's revenge

Wilma has been feeling oppressed and useless, but she is beginning to take charge of her life. The breakthrough comes when her parking space is suddenly snatched by two girls in a small orange car. Wilma protests but the girls jeer 'Face it, lady, we're younger and faster!' and stroll off. Wilma is cast down and sulks. But gradually her new spirit takes over. She smiles, her hands grip the wheel, her foot goes down and she drives crash into the orange car – again, and again, and again, laughing and whooping. The girls run back horrified. 'Have you gone crazy?' they scream. 'Face it, girls,' drawls Wilma, 'I'm older and I have more insurance!' And she drives off rejoicing.

Fried Green Tomatoes

What weather where

Aim: listening strategies
Level: intermediate
Material: weather reports
Preparation: View the report and list the weather for particular places (see Box 114 for an example).

Procedure

Suggest to students that they can cope with high-speed idiomatic language if they limit their focus. Give out the *What* list and ask them to listen for *Where*, or vice versa.

Follow-up

Students create their own *What* and *Where* lists from other weather reports.

BOX 114   Example of weather report

What	*Where*
thunderstorms	central Africa
a glorious couple of days	Capetown
sandstorms	Timbuktu

From a BBC World weather report

Why and How?

Aim:	recapping all or part; comprehension of cause and effect; question formulation
Level:	intermediate
Material:	any programme involving investigation, explanation, exposé, mystery
Preparation:	Prepare four *Why?* or *How?* questions which are answered by the programme.

Procedure

1 After viewing, write up three columns headed *Topic*, *Why/How?* and *Answer*. Put two topics from the programme in the first column and related *Why?/How?* questions in the second, and elicit the answers.

2 Add two more topics. Students formulate the *Why/How* questions themselves, and answer them (see Box 115 for an example).

3 Replay another part of the programme and get students to find their own topics and questions.

Note

This is the non-fiction equivalent of the cause-and-effect investigation in **Climax**.

BOX 115   The Hope Train

(a documentary about a train which brings medical services to poor rural areas)

Topic	*Why/How questions*	*Answers*
The Hope Train	*Why* is it needed? *Why* did they start it?	Because there aren't enough medical services in the rural areas.
The patients	*How* do the patients get to the train?	They walk, sometimes many miles.
	Why don't the patients go to a normal doctor?	Because there aren't enough doctors in the rural areas.

Wordhunt

Aim:	focusing on language
Level:	elementary
Material:	very short sequences with suitable language

Procedure

1 After understanding a short sequence well, students view it again several times searching for just *one* type of word or sound (e.g. all the -*ed* endings), and writing the words down in order as they hear them. Possible search targets are in Box 116. Students will need to use both their ears and their grammatical sense to do this, especially for unstressed words, which are often difficult to hear or identify.

2 After viewing several times, students compare notes on what they have found. Then they explain what the words mean and how they are used, e.g. whether the -*ed* endings are full past tense verbs (e.g. *He decided to stop*), parts of a verb group (e.g. *They've opened a shop*) or adjectives (e.g. *baked beans*).

Note

Keep it short – don't expect students to hunt for more than ten items at a time. Other 'grammar noticing' activities are **Interactive language**, **Questions** and **Tenses**.

BOX 116   Wordhunt

Students search for *one* of these:

- all the words ending in -*ed*
- all the words ending in -*s*
- all the words ending in -*ing*
- any contracted words
- all the unstressed words (e.g. grammar words like *for, than, the, that, are, of*)
- all the third-person pronouns, possessive adjectives or demonstrative pronouns (*she, he, it, they; his, her, their; that, this, these,* etc.)
- modal and semi-modal auxiliary verbs (e.g. *might, can, could, must, have to, supposed to, likely to*)
- all words with a phoneme or pair of phonemes that give problems, e.g. all the schwas, /ɔː/ and /ɜː/
- all the words with a particular stress pattern
- all the words beginning with or containing a given sound
- all the adjectives or adverbs
- all the proper names
- all the infinitive verbs
- all the prepositions
- all the conjunctions

Writing the book

Aim: writing narrative with dialogue; reporting speech

Level: intermediate

Rationale: Books written from the film (i.e. worked up from the filmscript) are fairly faithful to the film original and offer good models for describing interaction.

Material: parallel scenes from book and drama film

Procedure

Tell the students they are going to write the book of the film for one scene, and give them some accounts to study as models (see Box 40 on page 138 for an example). Look at tenses, speech verbs and related structures, indirect speech, reaction adjectives and the vocabulary of speech events, physical behaviour and speech styles. Students can then select their own film scene to write up in the same way, choosing either a first-person report or an impersonal narrator. Tell them to keep it short!

Note

This activity can stand alone or extend the mini-project *Describing interaction* (see page 52). This is an extension of **What's going on?** into novel form.

Your movie

Aim: describing settings and action (good for the present continuous, active and passive)

Level: elementary

Material: none – this is a film-related activity which does not need any video material

Procedure

1 Review the present simple and continuous verb forms and their use.
2 Ask students to draw a large box on a piece of paper; tell them that this is the big scene from their movie, in which they personally star, and they have to imagine it. Ask: *Where are you? What are you doing? What are you wearing? Who else is there? What is happening?* Demonstrate by drawing and talking through your own scene on the board (see Box 117 for an example). Stress that the only person who has to understand the picture is the creator.
3 Students draw their scenes, in class or for homework, then explain them to a partner.

Follow-up

Students write up the scene, with dialogue, for homework.

Note

For advanced students this activity can lead in to **Plot idea 1**.

BOX 117   Revenge is sweet

3 Glossary

ad-lib	to improvise verbally
anchorman	the news presenter in the studio
angle	a special technique or approach
archive material	old film footage
aside	a remark not intended for the person you're talking to
biopic	a biographical film
blurb	written information about a film/book on the cover
boom mike	a microphone which can be lowered from above
canned drama	an early film with the characteristics of a theatre play
captions	written labels on the screen
cast	all the characters/actors in a drama
cliffhanger	a film or episode with high suspense
clip	a short film sequence
collage	a sequence of clips from different sources relating to a theme
comic turn	a comic performance
commercial	a television advertisement
cover shot	a shot showing the whole scene from a distance
coverage	reporting
cross-cutting	cutting repeatedly and rapidly between one scene/shot and another
docudrama	a fictional story told in documentary style
dubbing	providing voices for a film in another language
DVD	a high-capacity, high-speed CD used for recording films
extempore	spontaneous, unscripted
fade (out)	the slow dissolving of an image
feature film	a full-length film such as you see at the cinema
film/movie buff	film enthusiast/amateur expert
footage	filmed material
freeze frame	the device which allows you to pause the film and freeze the image

272

goodies and baddies	heroes and villains
hype (=hyperbole)	exaggerated language, usually from advertisers or journalists
lead	the first one or two sentences which summarize a news item; the principal role in a film
location report	a news report filmed at the scene of the news
mike	microphone
multi-modal	using a variety of means to convey a message, e.g. pictures, sound, words, graphics
music video	music with video images
off the cuff	spontaneous, unscripted
over the top	wildly exaggerated
panel	a team which answers questions
panning	a medium shot in which the camera swings around the setting
parody	a satirical imitation
prequel	events before the film begins (opposite of *sequel*)
preview	advance publicity for a TV programme
profile	an article or programme about a living person or group
props (= properties)	the movable objects or furniture used in a theatre or cinema production
puff	a short flattering description of a book/programme/film for promotional purposes
punch line	the final surprise line of a joke or ad
quotations	short extracts from face-to-face interviews in news items or documentaries
reaction shot	a shot of a listener reacting to a speaker
recap	repetition/review of content (= recapitulation)
review	a written description and evaluation of a book, film or programme
roundup	a collection, e.g. of opinions or news items
running gag	a joke which is repeated again and again during a show
sales pitch	a technique or strategy for selling something
schema	an established mental picture
sci fi	science fiction
scoop	an exclusive and important news story
screenplay	the script of a film, with basic stage and camera directions
script	the dialogue to be acted (also any standard predictable conversation)
send-up	not very serious satire

set piece	a big spectacular scene (e.g. a battle, a ball, a shipwreck, a speech)
shot list	a list of the shots to be made in a scene, used to prepare for filming
sitcom	situation comedy
sketch	a short dramatized situation
skit	a light-hearted parody
slapstick	purely physical humour, in which the comedians wrestle with each other, throw paint or pies and fall down in elaborate ways
soap box	to do with popular oratory (given from a soap box)
soap (= soap opera)	a continuing TV or radio drama about people's daily lives in a particular setting
sound effects	the sounds in a film, other than the words and music
soundtrack	all the speech, music and other sounds in a film
stage directions	written instructions on a script for the actors on how to move and speak
stills	still pictures taken from a moving film
stunt	a dangerous trick, often done by a stunt man substituting for the actor
take-off	a parody
talking head	a close-up on the person speaking to the viewers
teaser	an opening sequence designed to catch the interest
thriller	a story of action and suspense
tracking	following a moving object/person with the camera
trailer	advance publicity for a programme, usually with excerpts from the programme
'voice'	language suggesting a special character or persona, e.g. fast excited speech with a lot of hyperbole suggests a salesman
voice-over	a commentary by an unseen person on what is happening on the screen
voxpop	a sequence of opinions from ordinary people on one issue
walkthrough	a rehearsal of the movements in a scene
whodunnit (= Who done it?)	a story based on finding out who committed a crime
zoom	a shot where the camera moves in on something quite fast; on DVDs the zoom function allows you to magnify a piece of the screen image

274

Index

Index